THE HONEYMOON'S
OVER

THE HONEYMOON'S
OVER

TRUE STORIES OF LOVE,
MARRIAGE, AND DIVORCE

Edited by

Andrea Chapin and Sally Wofford-Girand

WARNER BOOKS

NEW YORK   BOSTON

Warner Books
Hachette Book Group USA
1271 Avenue of the Americas
New York, NY 10020

Visit our Web site at www.HachetteBookGroupUSA.com.

Printed in the United States of America

First Edition: February 2007
10 9 8 7 6 5 4 3 2 1

Library of Congress Cataloging-in-Publication Data
The honeymoon's over : true stories of love, marriage, and divorce / edited by Andrea Chapin and Sally Wofford-Girand.—1st ed.
    p. cm.
  ·ISBN-13: 978-0-446-58000-7   ISBN-10: 0-446-58000-7
  1. Marriage. 2. Love. 3. Divorce. I. Chapin, Andrea. II. Wofford-Girand, Sally.
  HQ734.H794 2007
  306.81—dc22   2006029974

Book design by Charles Sutherland

With love and thanks to our children, for the joy they bring us, and to our husbands, for endless inspiration.

ACKNOWLEDGMENTS

We wish to thank the wonderful essayists in this book who faced the truth of their marriages with unflinching honesty.

For championing our book, our gratitude to Amy Einhorn, our powerhouse at Warner Books, the indispensable Emily Griffin, and Tanisha Christie, our talented publicist.

We are also grateful to Brick House Literary Agents, particularly Judy Heiblum, Margaret Kopp, and Melissa Sarver, and to The Writer's Room in New York City.

For their candor and wisdom, we'd like to thank Tracy Howell (who is deeply missed and always will be), Patty McCormick and Mark Millhone (writers' group extraordinaire), Riam Sarah Knapp (for asking the right questions), Nancy Kricorian, Steve Murphy, Valerie Pels, Dr. Anna Balas, Dr. Carmela Perri (eternal thanks), and Alice and Allen Wofford (thriving in their forty-seventh year of marriage). And to Kim Barnes, Tasha Blaine, Brettne Bloom (sometimes a dirty dish is just a dirty dish), the Chapin siblings—Lexy, Brady, Winnie, and Doug (who all have stories of their own), Claire Davis, Leigh Feldman, Michael Frank, Elizabeth Gaffney, Cammie and Charles Girand, Joel and May Katz, Johanna Markson, Elaine Markson, Maria Massie, Mimi Miller, Scott O'Neil, Vicky Satlow, Beth Vesel, Mary Telford Williams, Malcolm, Josephine, and Olivia Girand, Brandon and Carden Katz, Torrey and Stephanie Wofford, Bill and Amy Wofford, our illustrious book group cronies and the rest of our friends and family for their support. And especially Annette Evaline Prince for loving child care and home cooking.

Our deepest thanks to Mark Girand and David Katz without whom this book would not have been possible.

And to all those women, in happy and unhappy marriages, who share their stories with us daily—it's comforting and cathartic to know we are not alone.

CONTENTS

Introduction

First, the two of us happily bitched about our husbands as we cleaned up after family dinner parties. What were we doing with those guys sprawled on the sofa? Why didn't we just lose ten pounds and see how well we'd do out there? A fresh start with someone who did all the things our husbands didn't do—was all the things our husbands weren't. We spent more than a few evenings hissing under our breaths, laughing, plotting, drinking wine—we found it all very cathartic. But neither of us were prepared for the day when things went from pretty good to bad and then from bad to worse. When both of us hit rocky patches in our marriages, when it was crisis time and looked like divorce might be the only solution, we wondered how women knew what to do when they reached that fork in the road. And what about the children?

To stay or to leave a marriage can be an agonizing, impossible choice. But people make this decision every day; one of every two marriages ends in divorce. When we pore over the wedding pages of the Sunday newspaper, part of the fascination is: Will these two have a better married life than I've had? Do they hold the key to success? Who in this gallery of smiling faces will stay married and who will not?

In the class directories at our children's schools, the divorce rate rises each year. At dinner parties, at the playground, in our own backyards, we regularly hear bulletins of new breakups. "Till death do us part," it seems, is more appropriate for a Shakespeare sonnet than a wedding vow; many marriages today might not last any longer than they did in the Elizabethan era, but it's usually divorce not death that ends them.

We started questioning our friends to get at the heart of what makes or breaks a marriage. Even the "happily" married women told us: "Oh, I think of divorce *every* day." Indeed, in trying to figure out our own marriages, we noticed a trend: Divorce is no longer a dirty word. From the young divorcée's memoir celebrating her return to single life, to articles trumpeting festive divorce parties, divorce clearly doesn't carry the stigma it did fifty years ago. But does it make the decision to end a marriage any easier? Maybe not easier, but certainly more socially acceptable. Even among retirees divorce is growing more common than ever. In these late-in-life breakups, it's often the women who decide to end a marriage after thirty or forty years, leaving the men stunned and bereft.

When a union is over and when it isn't is very personal territory: What pushes one relationship to the brink might be something the couple down the street has lived with for years, or even decades. At buttoned-up business lunches we hear stories of married couples who don't speak to each other for days on end, those who haven't had "marital relations" in a decade, those who live in different apartments in the same building; we hear even more dramatic stories when gossiping with the gals—infidelities, addictions, compulsive gambling, stealing from one's spouse; the list goes on. Even with less obviously fraught marriages, modern couples continue to struggle with their roles. Who's supposed to make the money, cook the mac and cheese, pick up the kids from school, scrub the tub, shop for last-minute birthday party presents, and play social secretary?

Since what happens in a marriage—how one survives it or doesn't—is a constant topic of conversation, we decided to talk with women writers and see what they had to say.

It was comforting for us to realize just how exhausting marriage can be, for nearly everyone. As one of our writers notes in her essay about her dream second marriage, "Even answered prayers come with work." Marriage, no surprise, is often a very difficult task, an endless workout, where you have to pull your chin to the bar even when you feel all your strength is gone. The strongest and happiest marriages are a lot of work, and even long-lasting couples go through ugly times. As another writer quips, "Divorce? Never. Homicide often."

Divorce is painful, though sometimes it is absolutely necessary and ultimately freeing. Many of the authors who came from divorced homes were willing to work a lot harder on their marriages to avoid inflicting divorce on their own children. Women in their second marriages seemed to choose better mates and by then were better equipped themselves to make a marriage work. (Statistics show that on average men remarry within three years of divorce, while it takes women longer, nine years, to gather the courage to do it again.) As one of our writers notes, there's an old country saying that upon finding oneself lost in the woods, it is a great advantage to have been lost in the woods before: "I know where I can find ripe berries and where the alligators will try to find me."

It may be easier to write about a marriage gone wrong than to divulge the inner workings of one kept afloat. As a novelist friend of ours wrote to us when she declined to be part of the anthology, "It's too personal for me . . . I would love to be able to tell you why I've been able to remain married to my husband, but if I did, he would divorce me."

Luckily, we did find married and divorced women willing to tackle the divisive issues in their relationships with candor and wit. Conflicts in marriages run the gamut—from problems that need constant care and attention to the unexpected events that blindside you. We've culled frank and hopeful stories that explore "sticking it out" as well as "ditching it" when women reach a crisis point in marriage, and we hope that readers will find comfort in the fact that no one's honeymoon lasts forever.

—Andrea Chapin and Sally Wofford-Girand

THE HONEYMOON'S
OVER

Thursday

Daniela Kuper

It's 1971 and Ram Dass has recently come out with *Be Here Now*. You read it in the Chevy to the sound of sweat plopping on plain brown pages in the unbreathable southern Illinois summer. You read the whole thing without stopping, easy because it's mostly pictures and thoughts you've never seen words for.

This is what you take from the book: Underneath this life, which is mostly ego and lies, sits another life that smells like sweet peas—a dormant life that smells like Dad when he was in one of his good moods doing magic tricks for the family. He could take his thumb apart, wiggle both halves, and make cousin Johnny cry till he cemented it back together. He could put the lit part of a cigar inside his mouth and puff. Sometimes he'd make it disappear. He was a traveling chocolate salesman, who once gave his paycheck to an Indian with a sad story. He brought home two gifts you remember: a box of Sputnik bubble gum that turned your tongue aqua, and silk days-of-the-week panties. Your mother takes the panties. She says they'll give you an infection, then bawls out your father in Yiddish. You steal Thursday, though. Thursday will be yours forever.

Dad says when you're good enough, there's a present waiting in the vault of Harris Trust and Savings Bank on La Salle Street in Chi-

1

cago. He says it's a ring of truth, a band with so much light coming from it, they had to put it in a sealed box for dangerous substances.

"When you get it, you won't need electricity and strangers will come to you," he says.

You have no idea what he's talking about, but you want the thing bad.

"Aw, you'll know when you got it. I had it a coupla years. Sold everything I lugged around. Stillicious syrup, Eskimo pie coating, Kayo by the truck. Guy tried to buy my hat off me once. I was a big ball of everything they ever wanted. Get it, kid?"

Sure, Dad.

You're eight. You want to know more. Rubies? Opals? You don't give up on that ring till you're fourteen and tired of his mercurial Ten Commandments. Thou shalt not wear Maybelline. Thou shalt never read dirty books including the poetry of that Russian, Yevtushenko. If God wanted you to sleep over at Judy Cohen's, he wouldn't have given you a decent bed.

You don't go to basement parties with the kids on Friday night, you go to B'nai Zion temple wearing Mom's black coat, her stand-in, waiting for something to happen on that pulpit. But nothing happens, and nothing will happen until college when you're reading that Ram Dass book, a relic now with its clunky drawings of big-hipped women, that fringe-shirted man running down the church aisle yelling, "*Listen to those words you're saying*" to a stupefied congregation. A cult joke, that book, if you can even find it anymore.

You're nineteen and perspiring on words that read like the godmother who never showed up. Yes dear! Yes dear! Here's the life. Smell those sweet peas. Come and get it.

After college, you sell the Smith Corona, winter coat, anything to get to the Bay Area and meet people like in the book. You work as a secretary in the Law Department at Berkeley, go Sufi dancing, meditate, grow out your leg hair.

Sufi dancing is where you meet Jesse. He's tall with a good body and hair thick to his shoulders. A stunning blond man on stage with a stunning blonde woman. It's not clear what they're doing up there looking more like kingdoms than people, but Jesse is holding the room. Right then you want to marry him and become a kingdom. He takes you camping by the ocean in Bolinas, stars falling into waves. You can see his face in the dark. You can see his face when it isn't there. He smells like sandalwood and tells stories with the intensity of a dying man. His voice is Alabama homeboy, and it touches you down there.

Strangers ask him personal questions. He takes as much time as they need; that's how giving he is. He gives and gives. You get pregnant on your third date, but you're still your mother's daughter. You buy day-old bread and would never give your paycheck to anyone.

Things come easily to you and you never question this. As a kid, you read everything. *Archie*. *Rally Round the Flag, Boys*. You read whatever you could sneak from their headboard. *Carpetbaggers*. *Kinsey Report*. You make grades without studying, write plays involving can-can skirts and tropical themes that get performed in bored sixth-grade classrooms. The school visits your parents, tells them to put you in Francis Parker, a fancy Chicago private school for creative kids with money. Your parents take this as a death threat. They don't want you to be different. Different is the evil eye. Different is death. You don't hear about the Francis Parker business till you almost flunk out of high school, having spent four years doodling another planet. You could name every river, battle, and monarch.

They give you a name. Daydreamer. Bed wetter would be preferable. Ass kisser. Daydreamer means you're someplace else, missing in action—and they know you're gone. Daydreamer will be your tar baby until you meet Jesse, who doesn't care. He tells you this world is all illusion anyway. He calls you Mahakali, Radha, the Divine Mother, and all the little Gopis rolled into one. Tells you creation stories as he rubs almond oil on your nipples, which are sore from nursing the baby and, though it's technically impossible, because you're pregnant again.

"But I never got my period."

"This girl is coming from the heavens to us," he says.

You don't question this. What you question is if you have enough calcium to produce more bones. You've been dreaming of losing your teeth and hair.

Jesse puts his big arms around you and the baby, gets in the bathtub, the three of you, and nobody cares that the mat is soaked from the overflow. He rubs your underarms with a French crystal that keeps your sweat from smelling. He lets the boy sleep between you and never crushes him. You can see Jesse's face in the blank bedroom, animated, lit up like he's telling stories when he sleeps.

Life is happening, man.

Everybody comes to stay at your duplex, pulled in by your husband's growing reputation as a spunky spiritual guy teaching at Naropa in Boulder, Colorado. With their special diets, they come. The head of the Sufi Order, Sikhs, dervishes, calligraphers, Buddhists, Hopis, Robert Bly, Paul Reps. You hand Ram Dass a cup of chamomile tea but are too shy to mention his book. You go to parties and get served the first piece of cake.

When the girl baby is nursing, the boy patting your breast, trying to slip in a turn, you ask Jesse to take out the garbage.

"Could you?"

There is a point when a marriage is over, and every woman can tell you precisely that point. Yours is garbage.

One woman tells you she was packing her husband's socks for a business trip, brown to brown, navy to navy—when she notices his socks are wet and digs three times into his drawer before she realizes they are wet with her tears.

Another says her husband was doing the dishes, and she asks him a question. "You want me to talk to you *and* do the dishes?" was her moment.

"Hey, guess what. I've transcended the garbage," Jesse said.

"What?"

"Alhumdulillah! We should talk."

You haven't talked for months, though secretly you've been worrying about the marriage. No money, no laughing, no "You cook and I'll do the dishes." You don't take vacations or go to Scott Carpenter Park or eat together anymore. Little things. Like that.

You think of marriage as a mystery illness they're on the verge of finding a cure for.

"Could we talk after the garbage?"

"I'm a guru." He scratches a spot on his pant leg, smiles with that lit face of his.

The baby pops off the nipple and laughs, milk running sideways out her mouth. Daddy was a man, now he's a guru. Oh that daddy.

You smell old bananas, or maybe the diaper pail or lentils in the Crock-Pot. There are a lot of smells to be dealt with, but Jesse was never a man with a plan. And with the famous lacto-intolerant coming and going, drawing crowds for their evolved lectures, demanding top sheets from you, who needs plans? Boring plans.

Your husband suddenly has ideas typed on paper, compiled into a notebook. He will teach, they will pay. If the lactos can do it, why not him? Somebody gives him a house. Give the teacher a house. It's only four blocks away; the wife is welcome anytime. Get a babysitter. Come on down.

It's remarkable, the size and girth of unseen truths we share our beds with. Like lemon writing that only appears in the sunlight, they were waiting for you the whole time.

You do not give up on family in a day.

You sit in on his classes and want to break the spell, scream things out. Listen you people, he doesn't pick up his underwear. You can't stay with the program and besides, something more worrisome is going on.

He's calling your son Judah Buddha, wants to take him on the road. A road show. He says in Tibet, they know by the time a kid is three or four if he's the next incarnation of Pooh Bear. He doesn't say Pooh Bear, but your ears are mixed up with mothering. You say your son is two and has an ear infection and over your dead body.

It's Thursday. Valentine's Day. You wake and know the boy is gone.

You go through the motions, look in the closet for his clothes, call the disciples. They're disciples now. Everything has a name as if a huge spiritual corporation landed in a day, mission statement intact. Nobody will tell you where your son is.

You say the word *kidnapped*. It's the most negative word you've said in years. The baby pats your chest like you finally got something right.

You saw *West Side Story* thirteen times and still know the songs and most of the lines by heart. There are three or four days in your life you remember like that. This becomes the Thursday you cut your long hair, shave your legs, threaten to choke a disciple named Allah or Eeore if he doesn't tell you where the boy is. You are not coming from your feminine side when you say this. Your hands are squeezing his neck till you get "Alabama" out of him.

You hire a cowboy lawyer who finds another lawyer in Tuscaloosa, where the boy is. This second lawyer hires a private plane to get you there with your best Irish girlfriend who says, "a Jew alone in Alabama?" And she cuts her hair for you.

"Are you married to him?" the cowboy lawyer says. " 'Cause I can't take the case if you're married, it isn't technically a kidnapping."

"Then divorce me," you say.

See? How easy?

You are divorced. The lawyer is making phone calls, writing papers that will take months to finalize, but that doesn't matter. You take off your wedding band; there is no white mark where the ring was. No band of light. Nothing.

The Alabama lawyer has an Alabama vendetta with Jesse's father. He takes the case for free and tracks Jesse down at his brother's health food store. Yes, the boy is with him. Call him now. Tell him you want the boy home and maybe we can make this easy.

With your Irish girlfriend holding the baby girl in the Tuscaloosa Ramada Inn, you call Jesse. But he thinks you're in Boulder. He thinks you're cold cereal, not a woman who will force him to appear in court within two hours, who will ignore his pleas to TALK TO ME and stand in that *To Kill a Mockingbird* courtroom under that slow ceiling fan with bubba judge leaning over you from a high, high place, baby girl in your arms. *Listen to these words I'm saying.*

Bubba gives you temporary custody of the boy, and Jesse has visitation rights. Back in Colorado, you will keep a journal of his caretaking for a year.

1. He brought the girl home sans diaper.
2. He took the children to a mortuary so they could visit death.
3. No naps.

All things are equal in the journal, and your careful handwriting proves you are the sane parent. Something has bent and turned inside you, but emotions cost. Emotions are expensive. You make a living, banish diaper rash, read the kids Maurice Sendak like you were trying out for the role. The children laugh, you win.

In the meantime you meet the man who should have been their father, who to this day *is* their father. A gentle, Ron Howard of a man who will testify at the custody hearing with such nervous sincerity, he will swear to tell the truth by raising his left hand, then his right, then his left.

During a break, Jesse grabs your arm.

"I'll cut you a deal," he says. "You don't ask me for money, I'll give up the parental rights. I won't bother you again."

For the first time, he keeps his word.

He never sees his children until they're old enough to make plane reservations on their own. They come home quiet. Your son puts his arm around you. Your daughter starts a journal. They ask you why.

Why, Mom?

You didn't know then, you don't know now. Not really. A kingdom, a band of light, the determination to live in a world you made up, Daydreamer. Of course, you don't tell the children these things. You look at their faces and have nothing lofty to give them.

Walt, who should have been their father, with his good-smelling skin, says, "Nobody loves you more than me and your mom." He tells the children he will never leave them, and he does not.

You try talking divorce with other divorced women who complain about their husbands' sins. Emotional unavailability. Lack of financial support. Toilet seat up. You don't say much, but even back then, you know where the funny parts are. Garbage. Can you imagine? Ha ha ha. You don't have the heart to unleash an incomprehensible new age sociopathic circus on women with good sweaters, let alone your children.

You become known as a risk taker, an entrepreneur who can make a million-dollar business out of 350 bucks and her kitchen table. You are in a *Forbes* cover story for this feat, which you stop cold to begin writing at forty. Nobody sells a first novel, plus you're old. Novel in the drawer, novel under the bed, they don't know who you are. You are elaborate with reasoning. Unstoppable. The children will never know poor.

The day of garbage is a time you rarely visit. Those were busy days, life arrangements that lasted decades. And you almost made it dry until last year, that car accident in Maine, T-boned by a truck on icy old Route 46.

You don't remember anything but the sound of your daughter crying in a strange room that has nothing to do with time. You don't know what happened. You ask her why she's crying. She tells you she's afraid she can't take care of you the way you've taken care of her.

She's twenty-nine; your son is thirty. Here they are, those children who waited until they were past eighteen to meet their father, still a guru. Those children who stopped asking about their dad and started asking how you pulled together a life they remember as mostly decent.

You're cracked up bad from the inside. Hangman's fracture, they tell you, fastest way to get out of this world.

They tell you so many times that you shouldn't have walked away from this accident—you're ready to offer up apologies. Anyway, you're not looking for a way out of the world anymore.

They rig you up in a somi brace, neck to ribs, for six immobile months. In the end you'll be okay, you'll be fine, but somewhere around the third month, you start weeping and don't stop until you get to that whorl of a marriage, the dreamy girl you were, the shoulder-padded woman you became. You weep until you don't anymore, and you begin to move again.

The Stories We Tell

Joyce Maynard

Seventeen years have passed since my husband and I parted. *Parted.* There's a mild word for you. Describing an event so full of rancor and pain that even a person simply standing on the sidelines, taking in the scene, might have felt the need to shield her gaze—the way we are told to do when viewing a total eclipse of the sun.

But the bitterness gradually subsided, to the point where I could tell the story without the muscles of my face tightening into an ugly mask. My right eye no longer twitches, as it did for one whole season, beginning around October 1989 and continuing all through the long and bitter winter that followed. I seldom feel a need to talk about those days anymore. (And, in fact, when I meet someone still freshly divorcing and inhabiting that terrible place where I once lived, I can spot the signs. When I do, I generally beat a hasty retreat.)

I was once such a person myself—obsessively recounting, to my patient but no doubt weary friends, the injustices, as I perceived them, of the man I'd once loved, the father of my children, the one whose face was going to be the one I looked at as I took my last breath, if mine wasn't that, for him, first.

I have finally gotten on with my life, as they say—preferring to concern myself with the present and the future, rather than dissecting the failures of the past—and things took a dramatic turn for the better when I began doing that. Still, I am well acquainted with the plot of the story, as I told it easily a few hundred times. Title: *My Divorce*. Hero: *me*. Villain: *my ex-husband*. Unfortunate witnesses: our children, aged five, seven, and eleven when the whole thing started. Now in their twenties, they've survived the whole mess, with their love of us both miraculously intact.

I am a storyteller by profession, so of course I got particularly good at telling this one. When someone asked me, "How did your marriage end?" I had my answer down.

We married young, my husband and I, and with no shortage of passion going for us. He was a painter. I was a newspaper reporter. We lived in New York City, but yearned for a life in the country, a home, a family. In an era when young women were more typically focused on career advancement and personal fulfillment, I burned to be a parent and gave birth to our first child (our daughter) at age twenty-four, almost a year to the day from the night of my first date with her father. In the six years that followed, her two brothers joined her.

So we had hardly known what it was to be simply lovers and partners before we became parents. Before making the decision to marry and to have babies, we had never explored the questions of who would take care of them or who would pay the bills, but how it worked out was that I kept writing magazine articles and books, and he made beautiful art works nobody bought. We came up short a lot, and when we did, I took on more work.

I told myself this was okay with me, but it wasn't. I never even kidded myself that the other part was acceptable: I took the martyr role as the main child care provider, while he stepped in on occasion—here's a term no woman is ever likely to use—"to babysit." He played on a softball team, went mountain biking. I stayed home with the children, and hauled them off to his games. He had a six-pack. I had stretch marks.

"When do I get to go out and just have fun on a Saturday morning?" I asked him one time.

"You wouldn't know what to do with a day to yourself if you had one," he told me, and as heartless as his words appeared, he was actually right.

We argued a lot about that, and more. No doubt I felt anger, resentment, bitterness—emotions I expressed with tears, speeches, and sometimes with large and dramatic demonstrations of frustration and rage. One time I held a pair of scissors to one of my long braids, announcing, "I'm going to cut off my hair." Once I upended a bottle of beer and poured it over my head. It was not a particularly successful way to get my point across.

Finding time to do our work was always a problem. Money was always a problem. Child care was a problem. Sex was a problem. We communicated poorly. (I deluged him with words. He gave me silence.)

He gave me a pressure cooker for my birthday, when I wanted a nightgown and flowers. He marked our tenth anniversary by replastering and painting our bedroom, when I wanted to go away someplace, other than our house. I accumulated my list of grievances, and it was a long one.

We went to counseling, without much success. We talked about separating, but were haunted by the prospect of what a split might do to our children. At night, we kept to our own sides of the mattress, and days went by sometimes in which we hardly spoke. I kept a postcard in my desk drawer of that famous photograph by Doisneau, showing a couple kissing in Paris. I wanted to be kissed like that.

In our twelfth year of marriage—when I was thirty-five years old and our youngest son just five—news came that my mother had been diagnosed with an inoperable brain tumor, and I left home to take care of her during what would be the last summer of her life. Before I took off, I hired two babysitters to replace me. One was a married woman with two young children of her own, hired to clean the house and do the shopping; the other (our longtime teenage babysitter) was going to entertain everyone—play games, go on bike rides, take our kids bowling, provide the fun.

Partway through that long and painful summer of caring for my mother, I came home to see my family for a few days. Setting down my bags in the kitchen, I breathed in the smell of chocolate chip cookies fresh from the oven, baked by our teenage babysitter, my replacement for the summer. I looked out the window to the field behind our house and saw my children playing. And a few feet over, my husband and our beautiful young babysitter, looking at each other and laughing in a way he and I had not done in a long time.

That night, when I asked him about her, he didn't say much, but when I asked if he had fallen in love with her, he didn't deny it. I told him I wanted to save our marriage (for no better reason, I think now, than because another loss at that moment seemed intolerable); he said he was done trying to work things out. We'd been unhappy long enough.

∞∞∞

So that fall, two hard things happened, within a week of each other. My mother died. And I moved out of our house.

And though I concealed, from our children, the part about our babysitter, all of this became a part of the story I recounted to sympathetic friends.

"*I was mistreated*" was my message, and of course, my friends (and the series of supportive-seeming men who came into my life over the years) all agreed that this was so. These other men would do better, they suggested, and in many ways, many of them did, for a while anyway. These men kissed me the way that couple on the postcard did, and brought me flowers, and since we had no children together, there could be no arguments about child care or who paid for the orthodontist. But though none of my relationships with any of these other men ended in the manner that my marriage had, neither did any other of those men go on to become my life partner. There are many ways, of course, for a relationship to fail, and infidelity, or neglect, is only one.

Here's something that happens, over the years, in the aftermath of a painful divorce. (There's a redundancy for you. A *divorce*.) Maybe because the actual events were so hard to live through, you stop revisiting them, and instead, you revisit only the story you have come up with to explain what happened. The process is not unlike how the perceptions of our childhood and youth come to be based less on actual memory than on photographs in the family album—memories of memories. In the same way, the story of how a marriage played out, and most of all, how it ended, may be obscured by the story we form to make sense of it.

I got mine down, and I hauled it out many times over the years: the part about my having to earn the money, the part about getting a pressure cooker for my birthday and a plastering job for our anniversary, the part about walking into the house and seeing the plate of chocolate chip cookies on the table.

Among the stories I recounted over the years, there was a little trilogy involving the births of our children, in which, once again, the man I'd been married to took the role of the bad guy. Our second child, our son Charlie, was born at home, and because the birth had come on with extraordinary swiftness, I found myself about to deliver our son with the midwife still a half hour's drive away, and nobody present but my husband. He responded to the situation by telling me he needed to step outside for a minute and have a cigarette.

It was everything a man shouldn't do with a woman in labor, and I had suffered it greatly.

The story didn't even end with my son Charlie's birth, in fact.

Two years later, I would go on to say, I was once again giving birth. This time, my husband had stayed at my side for the birth of our third child, second son. This time, nobody smoked. The trouble came after. The day after our youngest son's birth, the very day of our daughter's sixth birthday party, she took a fall on her new Rollerblades and broke her arm. Two days after that, my husband took off to attend an art show in Georgia for five days, leaving me to care for a six-year-old in a cast and a two-year-old and a newborn.

But it was what happened after that which formed the climactic moment in the story: He'd returned home, just as the rescheduled birthday party was to take place. With twenty children coming to our house the next day, he'd left to go skiing—making the observation, as he departed, that I was always hard to deal with when I was arranging a birthday party.

That afternoon, the call came from the ski slope: He'd fallen badly, and not simply broken his wrist, but shattered it. It was unclear whether my artist/athlete husband would ever have the full use of that hand again.

In the end he did, but only after expensive surgery that nearly bankrupted us, and months of recuperation during which all of his energy had gone to physical therapy and rehabilitation, with little left for our children, and nothing for me.

<hr />

I always say, when talking about the art of storytelling—fiction or nonfiction, either way—that a crucial element is what you choose to tell and what you leave out. The filmmaker establishes point of view simply by placement of the camera: where to zoom in, how to light the actors, what music will play on the soundtrack, even. Even with documentary, we're not getting the whole story, ever. Only the story the director wants us to see. Only the story as he or she sees it.

It took me a long time to admit this, but the same could be said of my own most well-known oeuvre, *The Divorce Saga*. (Most well known to myself, anyway. The one I've been telling for close to two decades now.) The Greeks had their mythology. I had mine. There comes a point when the story takes on a life of its own, and it is hard to know the full truth anymore, if you ever did.

I know now there was another side of the story. When I talked about the divorce, I omitted this part. Not just to keep my listeners from considering certain details, but more destructively, to keep them from my own scrutiny, too.

It is the part my former husband would spin—if he were the type to regale sympathetic listeners with a saga, himself, which he is not likely to do. And in this one, I am a less heroic figure. Not simply a long-suffering victim, but a woman who engaged in her own brand of hurtful behavior, inflicted wounds on the marriage, as damaging perhaps as those of her partner.

Rewind to the spring when I was thirty-one years old, the seventh year of our marriage. Six weeks after my husband smashed his wrist— seven weeks after the birth of our third child—I was on a highway coming back from New York City late one Friday afternoon, with my infant son in the seat beside me.

I'm sure I was feeling neglected and put upon. I was tired from three long days of working in the city, cleaning up manuscripts for a women's magazine. It was a job I'd taken on, with a certain weariness and regret, as the medical bills for the wrist operation piled up. For three days a month, now, I made the round trip to New York City this way, to sit in an airless cubicle and ghost-write articles for a magazine designed to help women take charge of their lives, even as my own spun more and more out of control.

Now the three days were finished; I was heading home with my son (a nursing baby, he came with me everywhere), and I was exhausted. And though I didn't tell myself this, no doubt I was angry, too.

Just as I reached the New Haven exit, I remembered that this was the weekend of my husband's tenth Yale reunion, and that a bunch of his old friends would be there. The thought came to me to pull off the highway, have dinner, show off our baby, before heading back on the road for the last few hours of the drive home. But who knows, maybe I was thinking something else, too. Maybe I was enjoying the picture of getting, from my husband's classmates, a kind of tenderness and support that had been lacking in my life with him, for a while.

One of the people in attendance at this reunion dinner was an old friend of my husband's, whose wife had recently died of non-Hodgkin's lymphoma at the age of thirty-one. He and I barely knew each other. We had met at the funeral, in fact, only a few weeks earlier. He was my husband's friend more than mine.

Now we sat together at dinner, he and I. And in a way I only came to understand years later, we recognized each other: two lonely people, each one grieving a different kind of loss and heartbreak. His was the death of the woman he loved. Mine, the dream of the marriage I didn't have—the kiss in Paris, and the husband who would stay home and help with the birthday party rather than go skiing.

Over dinner and a glass of wine, we talked about our lives, with a kind of naked trust I might not have possessed if he weren't a new widower and I the mother of a newborn son. Over dessert and a second glass of wine, he asked if he could hold my baby, and he did. By the time the meal was over, I knew I was too tired, with too much wine in me, to drive back home that night, so he walked me over to the dormitory where attendees at the reunion were housed, to find me a room.

Then we were sitting on a hard little single student cot, and then we were kissing. Then I pulled out a drawer, from the dormitory bureau, and laid it on the floor, with a folded-up towel in the bottom, and set my baby son inside. Then I lay down beside the young man, still raw with grief from his wife's death, and spent the night with him.

In the morning, I drove home to my family. At her school picnic later that day, I remember my six-year-old daughter commenting on a red mark on my neck. It was where the widower had kissed me the night before.

My husband's widowed classmate paid us a visit that summer, and when my husband suggested that he might like to stay on for a while with us, nobody argued. All that summer—as my husband continued to rebuild his shattered wrist, and I cared for our newborn baby and my other two children—it was the widower who kept me company, coming along with me when I brought the children to the beach or prepared dinner.

On rare occasions, we'd head out by ourselves to the waterfall down the road, or to a brook I knew in the woods behind our house. *Affair* strikes me as an odd word for what took place that summer, but if my husband were telling the story, he could call it that. Though the better terms for what was going on would be *betrayal, abandonment*. The very words I later used, in my head, to describe what he had done to me.

When the summer ended, the young widower returned to New York City and slowly resumed his life. I stayed in my lonely marriage—lonely for us both, I now recognize. The only indication anything unusual had happened that summer lay in how we never talked about it, how his friend's name never came up, until the day—a full two years later—when my husband asked me, in the middle of an argument, if something had been going on between me and his friend that summer, and I told him yes.

We never spoke of it again until a few years after that, when our marriage was breaking down for the last time, and we were in counseling. I brought it up because he hadn't. Otherwise, the fact of my infidelity lay like a piece of rotten food in the crisper drawer of the refrigerator, or a pair of blood-soaked gloves in the back of a murderer's garage.

And when I think back over the many small deaths it took before our marriage was finally, irretrievably over, the events of what happened that long-ago spring and summer, with my husband's newly bereaved friend, are as much a part of the list as the one—much more prominently featured over the years of my storytelling—about the night of Charlie's birth, and the broken wrist on the ski slope, and the babysitter.

Selective editing. It transforms the story, of course, and not just for the listeners. For the teller, too. Because every time, over the years, that I recounted my version of our divorce, I locked it more firmly in place, until it was hard to remember what I had ever loved about this man, what had been good, and what aspects of what had not been good were my fault, as much or more than they were his.

Anger and bitterness breeds more of the same. I look back with huge regret now, on the years from age thirty-five to forty-eight or so, as having been filled with a foolish and wasteful measure of self-righteousness and blame. The fact was, the man to whom I was once married, and I, both did a poor job of treating each other with love, a poor job of being partners to each other. We knew nothing of stepping outside of our own stories with sufficient imagination and compassion to recognize what the other person's story might have been.

Somewhere around age fifty—having lived longer divorced from him than I did married—with our children in their twenties, and the son who was born the night of that costly cigarette approaching the age his father was the night he said, "Let's get married and have babies"—something changed, finally.

I was immersed, that year, in writing the story of a woman my age who had murdered her husband after a thirty-year marriage. (With a hatchet, yet.) And so I was thinking a lot about rage and bitterness and the stories we tell ourselves about what is going on in our lives, that may be easier to stomach than the truth.

The story of this particular woman, the murderer, was that her husband had been abusing her for years—a claim only one of the couple's two adult sons supported, while the other laid out a very different version of what had gone on in their family all those years. And though I had entered into my exploration of the tragedy with a certain predisposition to sympathize with the wife, I ended up viewing her as a liar. Though I knew, too, she probably believed her own story, she'd been spinning it so long.

—————⚭—————

It was around this time that I found myself having a conversation with a young woman going through a divorce—and practically dripping with bile, she was so angry at her children's father. The thought came to me that I must have been a woman like her once, and I was ashamed.

I looked at my children—at how they loved their father, and at the kind of adults they'd become, many aspects of which were easily attributable to him—and because I loved them so much, I had to love those parts of the man who'd produced them. So many things about them—the way they tackled demanding physical endeavor, the unconventional eye they brought to the making of art or music or the formation of ideas—were things I had once loved about him. Even the part of our life that had caused me so much grief in the past—the shakiness of our finances, over the years, and my husband's role in that—had, in some ways, contributed to a set of values in my children that I felt proud of now: their refusal to view material success and comfort as the measure of a person's worth, or to let that determine their happiness.

I looked around at all the trouble people I loved were struggling with: health problems and money problems, career disappointments, depression, ailing parents, sadness over what was happening in so many parts of the planet—and the idea that I would still be sitting in a coffee shop somewhere, recounting the story of some injury inflicted over two decades back, seemed petty and foolish and wasteful.

I was sick of my story. And if I were truly to hold on to the habit of talking about it, I knew I would have to add the other part to my telling: the part that I had played in the whole mess, the betrayal that was mine.

My children had evidently forgiven me for the many years they'd lived through of witnessing my anger at their father. It seemed fair to forgive him, then. It had never occurred to me before, but I needed his forgiveness back.

This wasn't a totally new concept, I should add. Many times, over the years, I'd imagined a scene in which some large and dramatic truce occurred between my children's father and me—something along the lines of the Japanese surrender aboard the USS *Missouri*.

More than once, I delivered some dramatic pronouncement: *I won't talk about it anymore.* One time, I concocted the plan that we might all of us get into a raft, in class-five rapids, and barrel down the American River together (or cross the San Francisco Bay in a kayak, to Angel Island). If we could traverse some large and chilly and even dangerous body of water and reach dry land, maybe then it would be over, I thought, though each of my plans was rejected, ultimately, and wisely too, I suspect.

But when the sense of forgiveness finally overtook me, I felt no need for large dramatic gestures. I didn't call anyone up and talk about it. I did not notify my ex-husband that a change of attitude had occurred. It was enough to know this was so.

There was a time, when people asked why my marriage ended, when I used to say, "My husband fell in love with our babysitter." But this was not the answer, anymore than it would have been the answer to tell them, "I had an affair with his friend." It was never about the babysitter, or about the young widower, or about the cigarette, or about his playing softball and my folding laundry, or my earning the money and his not doing that, or my failure to recognize—as I do now, so many years later—that plastering the bedroom, slowly, and carefully, by the traditional method, to mark your tenth anniversary, was in fact a beautiful gift. And one I rejected.

Though in another way, that was it precisely. What he offered I didn't value. What I offered back he also missed. We were two people who loved each other, I think, but we had such different ideas about how to express it. The other people we sought out (both of them long gone from our lives now) were really just a way of making the connection, somewhere, that we couldn't make with each other.

I was in Michigan recently, researching the book about the woman who murdered her husband, and talking with a young man, age nineteen, who had loved and admired the murdered man. This young man was debating whether or not to trust me enough to participate in my book. So he had agreed to meet me at a restaurant, for the purpose of putting a series of questions to me, he said.

I had supposed he'd be asking about my career, my previous books, my credentials as a journalist. So it took me by surprise when this not particularly savvy or worldly young man had begun his interview of me by asking, "Why did your marriage end?"

It was a question I'd considered a thousand times, of course, and one for which I'd supplied abundant data, over the years, in coffee shops like this one, on a few hundred blind dates and visits with friends. Now he was asking, I suppose, as a way of assessing where my loyalties might lie in the story of this particular disastrous marriage I was writing about. Maybe he wanted to know if I'd been a battered wife and was therefore inclined to sympathize with a woman who claimed to be one herself.

But the fact was, his question left me without words. I sat there in the coffee shop, unable to form a single sentence. Something about the openness and guilelessness of this young man's face, and the simplicity of what he was asking, made it unthinkable to haul out my old stories.

"We both screwed up," I finally told him. Nothing particularly profound there, but it was true.

All right, he said. Then, evidently believing my story, he told me his. And we moved on from there.

Here Is a Boy

Nicole Lea Helget

Here is a boy. Look at him. He's almost three, has the face of a fresco cherub. He has an enormous blond head, curly yellow hair. He's the youngest of three, the baby, the beloved one, the child who sometimes climbs into the same bed as his mother in nights black as pitch. No bother about the feet in her face or the drool on her pillow. He's one of three children from the marriage of a father and a mother that lasted almost eight years. He's a child who is now "shared" by his divorced parents, meaning that each week, he, along with his brother and sister, travels back and forth between both homes. He puts his shoes in two different places. He drinks from different sippy cups. He watches different TV shows, adjusts to different rules, wears different clothes. He doesn't use the same shampoo or toothpaste or toothbrush. When he sleepwalks, he uses different walls to guide him. He's a child you want to bury in your womb to protect from the nonsense of his parents, of divorce, of the world of courts and lawyers and affidavits.

He's also the boy plagued by a patch of psoriasis on his scalp and a nose rubbed raw from wiping. Here is the child who pulls his sister Isabella's hair out by the handful, who eats his brother Mitchell's crayons and crumples up drawings because they're *ugwy*, who bites his cousin on the back and, once, on the cheek; the child who hit the neighbor girl with a stick and told her she was *dumb* and a *cwybaby*. Here is the child who once ran away in Home Depot and hid in a cupboard and wouldn't respond for twenty minutes while his mother, sister, brother, and most of the staff of said establishment looked high and low for a boy in a Bob the Builder shirt. Here is the child who set his mother's chair on fire. This boy, standing here with his hand down his pants (he's newly potty-trained and now wears Scooby-Doo underwear rather than diapers—he likes to feel down there, make sure everything is in its place), can be naughty, very naughty. This boy is Phillip Raymond. Pip for short.

It's all my fault. I am this boy's mother. I am the one who was called from my shower by my screaming daughter. *Phillip set the chair on fire! Phillip set the chair on fire!* I twisted a towel around myself and dashed downstairs to find, lo and behold, my chair on fire, flames spiking up the wall, smoke filling my living room.

I interrogated Pip with my video camera shortly after I put out the flames, cleaned up the water damage, painted over the scorch stains on the wall, and hauled the charred mess out to the porch. Why did I want the interrogation on tape? I'm not sure. Mostly, I think, because this child is gorgeous. Honestly, I can't get over him. I want to capture every nook and cranny of his face at every age and memorialize him forever on film. Even when he's naughtiest, he's gorgeous. I did the same with the other two. I have tapes of them with Cheerios stuffed in their diapers, tapes of them with spaghetti in their hair, a tape of Isabella with popcorn kernels stuck in her nose, of Mitchell's atomic poop on the wall. I keep the video camera handy always. Always charged. Always set at the right place on the tape. Just in case. Just for moments like this.

In the video, Pip looks cherubic. His bright blue eyes are deceptively innocent. He inherited the color from my mother. She looks deceptively innocent, too.

Video Interrogation, December 19, 2004

Me: Pip, why did you set the chair on fire?
Pip: Da Wockababy got on fy-oo. (The Rock-a-Baby got on fire.)
Me: I know. How did it get on fire?
            (Pip looks off camera, out the window.)
Pip: Hey. Dawoo's snow. (Hey. There's snow.)
Me: Pip. How did the chair get on fire?
Pip: It got on fy-oo.
Isabella *(off camera)*: Put him in time-out, Mom.
Mitchell *(off camera)*: Yeah, Mom, put him in time-out.
            He's naughty.
            (Pip snaps his face toward his brother and sister off camera.)
Pip: No. I not nonny. You go in time-out, Bewa-Mitchoo.
            (No. I'm not naughty. You go in time-out, Isabella and
                Mitchell.)
            (Pip runs off camera, arms swinging. Video goes black.)
            *(Five minutes later, video back on. Pip stands in same position
                as before, only poutier and with more snot smeared across
                his cheek.)*
Me: Pip. What happened to the Rock-a-Baby?
Pip: It's on da pooch.
Me: Why's it on the porch?
Pip: It got on fy-oo.
Me: How did it get on fire?
Pip: A pencow.
Me: A pencil started the chair on fire?
Pip: Da chai-oo got on fy-oo.
Me: Did you use a pencil to start the chair on fire?
Pip: Yeah.

Me: How did you get the chair on fire?

Pip: *(indistinguishable)*

Me: What?

Pip: I got up dawoo. *(He points to the bookcase behind him.)*

Me: Did you climb up the bookcase?

Pip: I got up dawoo with a pencow.

Me: Did you put the pencil in the candle?

Pip: Yeah.

Me: Then what did you do?

Pip: Da Wockababy got on fy-oo.

Me: Who got the Rock-a-Baby on fire?

Pip: I do it.

The chair waited patiently for weeks on the snowy porch for the insurance adjuster to determine its replacement worth ($550). The chair was one of the very few things I took from my old house, the house I left behind when my husband and I separated a year and a half ago. The chair came to me shortly after I discovered I was pregnant with Isabella, my oldest, almost nine years ago. I was a twenty-year-old, pregnant, stay-at-home newlywed then. I didn't know anything about anything in the world except how to be pregnant and how to cook a hot dish or two. Her due date came and went. For seven days, I sat in that chair waiting for any sign of labor. I stared out the window and remained completely silent. Something seems biblical about that now, though it didn't then. Then, the staring and the rocking seemed to indicate that I might be crazy. After seven days, the doctor, who'd been at his family's lake cabin for the week, induced me.

I rocked her in that chair while my next child, Mitchell, grew long and fat in my womb. He grew even longer and fatter once he arrived, and still all three of us rocked in that chair. It was crowded. I went into labor with my third child, Phillip, on that chair. I was rocking myself after I put Isabella and Mitchell to bed. The pain started low in my back, I remember, and moved to my center where a great pressure settled. The rocking helped ease the heaviness of the contractions until the babysitter arrived. After Phillip's delivery and homecoming, I rocked him there, too. Isabella and Mitchell hung on to the chair's armrests.

In the depths of postpartum depression, I sat silent again, for hours and sometimes days, in that chair. I spoke to no one but my children. I only read, rocked, and looked out the window. My husband threatened to throw the chair and my books away. I just stared at him, sat in the chair, and piled the kids on top of me. *Just try it*, I was probably saying.

When my kids got older, could go to school or day care, I went back to college, something I had abandoned when I got pregnant with Isabella. God, how I had missed the university world, how it seemed to solve every iota of loneliness and boredom and lack of intellectual stimulation.

I had an affair. But it wasn't just a regular old affair where you cover it up and keep it as this sweet little secret you have with yourself. Maybe look in the mirror and smile at yourself once in a while. This was the kind of affair that begins a new relationship and that ends a marriage. This was the kind of affair that makes you give your own reflection a dirty look, but where the reflection looks back at you with such hope and desperation that it won't be denied. That's the kind of affair I had.

My co-affair-haver, Nate, once sat in that chair while my husband was away on business and while my kids were sleeping. We talked about what we were going to do with our situation. We wondered if a happy life for my kids and me was possible with him. I took him to the doorway of each of the kids' rooms, and we peeked in on them. How could we even consider changing the lives of each of these children? Look how peacefully they sleep. Look how comfortable they look, all wrapped up tight in familiar blankets in a familiar place. Back in the chair, Nate asked why my connotation with change was negative. I had to think. I didn't know. Was change always bad? It couldn't be. Hard in the present doesn't always mean bad in the future.

We decided yes. A happy life for my kids and me with Nate was possible, even probable. So we flew headfirst into that happy life with the kids on our backs. I packed that chair into my Suburban and hauled it away to a two-bedroom apartment when I left my husband standing and staring at me from the garage. I rocked all three of my crying children in that chair then. Isabella and Mitchell asked me really hard questions. I tried to answer them. Pip just plugged the ear of his stuffed animal into his mouth and looked around at the new walls. And, sometimes, we'd all cry together and wipe our noses and eyes on the chair's green fabric. It's about this time I decided that I was the world's most selfish woman, the worst mother, the meanest, ugliest, awfulest creature alive. I had to *make it up to them*. I decided I would. My first act of penance was out with discipline, in with bribing. Out with consequences for bad behavior and in with rewards for good, or for mediocre, or for just being alive.

The nightly rockings helped my children rebound from the divorce. So have the new bikes, clothes, and cat that I'm allergic to. Helping with dishes? No longer necessary. Picking your clothes off the floor? What for? Cleaning the cat litter? Yuck. Clean room club? Who cares. I remember the first tentative looks from Isabella and Mitchell. *Hmmm. I haven't fixed my bed. Let's just see if I can make it to the door before she notices. Yes! I made it.*

Nate and I and the kids bought a new house last year. The chair was one of the first things to find a home, a nice spot under a dull lamp and next to a case full of books. I've read and sung to and rocked a child in that chair almost every night for nine years. Lately,

Pip's been the one who settles on my lap most nights. He wears Pooh Bear pajamas. And his head is bigger than any other part of him. I always sing a little jingle to him until his lids cover his eyes and his breaths come even and full. *Rock-a-baby, rock-a-baby, rock the little baby. Rock-a-baby, rock-a-baby, Mom's a nice lady.* It's silly, I know. But Pip loves the song, loves the swaying motion, loves to fall asleep there—Phillip, who's three, who we call Pip, and who started the fire that ruined the chair.

❧

We're raising a terrorist, says Nate of Pip.

He's only a terrorist sometimes, I say. Mostly he's too charming and cute to stand. Honestly, I can't stand it. Can you stand how cute he is? Look at him. Doesn't it drive you nuts?

Nuts? says Nate. No. His cuteness doesn't drive anybody nuts but you. He's cute, sure, but he's got major behavior issues. He can be a tyrant. He rules this house. It's ridiculous.

Put him in time-out, Mom, says Isabella.

Yeah, Mom, put him in time-out, says Mitchell.

Mitchell takes the brunt of Phillip's bad behavior. Phillip takes Mitchell's rescue heroes, his trading cards, his Popsicles, his place on my lap. *My mommy. Get off.* Oh, there's room enough for both. Here, Mitchell, scoot over. See Pip? Here's a nice spot for you. *My mommy. Not you mommy.* Don't pay any attention to him, Mitchell. He's just a little boy. He doesn't know any better.

Put him in time-out, says Mitchell. He hops down, goes to play video games with Isabella and Nate.

Do you wike me, Mommy?

I love you, Phillip. I love you like crazy.

I wuv you, too. Mitchoo's nonny.

When I called Nate at work to tell him that Pip lit the chair on fire, he listed off a catalog of Pip's recent, unpunished offenses:

- Locked himself in the bathroom, on purpose, wouldn't open the door
- Wrote with a pen on the new couch
- Markered my white dining room chairs
- Destroyed Isabella's snowman
- Colored on the wall
- Stuck an army man down the tub drain
- Told a complete stranger (an adult) at McDonald's to *get out a da playgwound*
- Kicked our friend, Hans, in the leg
- Whacked Nate's French relative (she's eighty) in the arm, told her she's *nonny*
- Peed in Nate's shirt closet
- Pulled down the curtains in his room
- Sat on our friend Dan's cat
- Hid my cell phone
- Ran away in the mall, hid in the center of a jeans rack, wouldn't respond when I called him

I told Nate how I'd interviewed Pip on videotape. I told Nate how cute he looked all snotty-faced and messy-haired.

Nicole, you've got to stop indulging him. Rather than videotape him, give him a swat on the behind.

No, I can't. I don't spank.

The boy needs some guidance. You're letting him down if you let him get away with this.

I think it was an accident.

He climbed up to the top of the bookshelf with a pencil, lit the pencil on fire, and set the chair on fire by accident?

(yelling from the other room) Mom, put him in time-out, says Isabella.
(yelling from the other room) Yeah, Mom, put him in time-out.
(a swatting noise from the other room)
Ouch, says Mitchell. Mom, Phillip hit me.

Isabella and Mitchell are well behaved. Seriously. Their report cards read, *What polite children you have. They're so kind. They're good friends to other students. Say please and thank you all the time. Offer to help clean up. Volunteer to aid other students.* So how has Pip avoided the benefits of my obvious great parenting skills? you might wonder. I don't know. Maybe it's just his genes. Maybe he's just different from Isabella and Mitchell. Maybe he has more testosterone, less patience, less fear, more physicality. Maybe he's so smart that he's bored by the childish games and rhymes that once entertained Isabella and Mitchell for hours. So maybe he has to find other ways to stimulate himself. With fire and toilet paper bombs, for instance. Or maybe, it's really because I indulge him. Maybe there aren't enough consequences, or any, for naughty behavior.

I share the kids with my ex-husband. It's a situation that has brought me to my knees in tears before; it's a situation that brought on my worst stretch of depression ever last winter. There were times, when the kids were with their dad, that I'd go back to that chair and just sit and rock and cry the day away. I didn't teach my writing classes, didn't go to my own classes, didn't see anybody, and wouldn't answer the phone. I'd think about the mess I made of everything, of everybody's lives, how my kids would be scarred for life, how I might make Nate go crazy. And I hoped that my ex-husband would commit suicide so that the kids would be where they belonged. Every day. But he didn't. Those bad times were the reality of the choice I made to leave my husband. The reality of divorce in this day and age is that moms don't automatically get the kids anymore. If the dad wants them, he gets to spend time with them, too. I didn't really think that it would work that way. I told the judge, I've raised them. He's been working the entire time. I changed their diapers, got up to feed them in the middle of the night, rocked them to sleep, not him. They've been with me every single day of their lives.

He gets the chance to be a good dad, the court said. He wants to be.

And he really has been a good dad since our divorce. That comforts me some. I know the kids are well taken care of and, more important, loved when they're with him.

But that doesn't stop me from feeling guilty, from feeling like I don't want to spend any of my mothering time bothering about consequences and punishments. While I was married, I was the enforcer. I was the person home all day who had to reprimand the back talk and sibling fighting. I've never spanked the kids, but time-outs or missed privileges were common. When my husband was home, he was the fun one. The one who could make a mess with the kids and tear around the house and throw balls in the living room and eat snacks all day and stay up late with the kids. But then he'd be gone again on another business trip. And the kids and I would be back to the same old routines. Memories of their cool dad hung around their little heads like pesky mosquitoes. *Mom, you're no fun*, they'd say. After I rocked, read to them, and got them to bed (by curfew, of course), I'd settle into that rocking chair and stare out the window and be bitter about my husband's life—his great career, his large paychecks, his multitude of friends, his education, his merry, only merry, times with the kids.

Since I left him, I'm getting some of that for myself. But it comes with a huge price: Three days a week, I don't have my kids. Mondays, Tuesdays, and Wednesdays the kids spend with their dad. At first, I used to do nothing on these days. I didn't know who I was without my kids. Finally, Nate told me to get off my ass, stop indulging my despair, and do something. I started reading, then I started writing, and before I knew it, I wrote an entire book, and then sold another one. And I started taking my classes seriously, and I started planning my Composition class more carefully. I started making some friends. I started picking up the telephone sometimes. I tried to work on my relationship with Nate. Now we try to make sure we never put my kids through another separation like the one they've already suffered. Now I'm refreshed, not desperate, when my kids come back to me on Thursday morning. Around the time I decided to get off my ass and do something with my life, I also stopped punishing my kids for misbehavior. I figured I'd let my ex handle that. It's the least he can do.

After I put the video camera away, I gather all three kids into the chairless living room. Okay, I say. Time to practice Stop, Drop, and Roll. We stop, drop, and roll for a long while. Nobody gets a time-out. Nobody bothers about the burned chair. Nobody's thinking Pip might grow up to be a terrorist. Nobody calls for a time-out. Soon, we get blankets and pretend to put out each other's flames by smothering and wrapping. There's giggling all around.

When Nate gets home, he plants Pip on his lap. His face is serious. Pip, he says, what happened to the chair?

I bwoke it, he says.

What should you say to your mother?

Pip looks at me. I'm folding blankets.

I's sowwy, Mommy.

Oh baby, I say. I know you are.

Nate pops Pip off his lap, tells him, Off you go. Go play with Mitch and Isabella.

See, says Nate to me. You've got to hold him accountable. He needs it.

Yep, I say. I see.

The Electric Husband

Patricia McCormick

When my husband and I weren't feeling especially close, I would often spend long, contented afternoons on the chaise in the sunroom reading a novel or napping with the cat on my lap. Once in a while, the cat would open his eyes, gaze dreamily at me, then nuzzle me, pressing the flat of his head to the underside of my chin, then stretch out on my chest and go back to sleep. Sometimes he'd stand on his hind legs, put his paws on my shoulders, and regard me with those golden, soulful eyes of his. My heart melted at the touch of his wet nose against mine. And sometimes he'd curl up in my arms like a baby, blink blissfully, and fall asleep.

Sometimes I would wish that he were my husband. I even made jokes, calling the cat my "fur husband." I was kidding, of course, but there was something so instinctively affectionate, so uncomplicated about our relationship, that I often thought how simple and delightful it would be to be married to the cat.

Meanwhile, after years of a low-grade marital malaise, my husband and I had gotten entrenched in a cycle of ever-more-hurtful arguments that seemed to erupt over issues both large and small—some we had been battling about for years; others were brand new. During a particularly sour family vacation, when I'd stormed off to take my frustrations out on a treadmill overlooking a wide-open prairie, I pictured myself running and running, and never coming back. Back at home I pored over the apartment listings; when my husband, Paul, saw what I was doing, I told him what I hadn't fully admitted to myself: I wanted to move out. For the next week or so, we talked about our relationship—more freely than we ever had before. We agreed that after nearly twenty years we didn't want to end our marriage. We wanted to work on it. But we both knew it would take a radical step to force us out of the unkind and ugly patterns we'd gotten into. And so, with surprisingly little drama we agreed to see a marriage counselor and to separate.

When I moved to a small apartment a few blocks away, my one consolation was fantasizing about the cozy, fireside nights the cat and I would spend alone together. I would have "custody" of him one weeknight and every other weekend, a schedule similar to the one I would keep with my thirteen-year-old son. I bought him (the cat, that is) a new litter box, toys, his favorite canned food, and counted the days until our first date.

Weeknights and alternating weekends with my son turned out to be delightful. I cooked the meals he liked, we watched WWII movies, and read the sports section together over breakfast. The one and only weekend when I had feline custody, however, the cat spent every minute cowering behind the dish drainer crying. When I tried to pull him out of his hiding spot, he peed all over the counter. No amount of sweet talk—or canned chicken giblets—could coax him back into my arms. The fur husband, it turned out, was a wimp.

I sulked, considered taking up with a kitten, then accepted the idea that I had separated from both my husbands.

One of the terms of the trial separation was that Paul and I each agreed not to see other people; we had separated to work on the marriage, not to dismantle it. But after a few months of single living, my needs for affection and companionship had gone beyond what the cat used to offer.

It was at this point that I met the electric husband.

We found each other at a store called Toys in Babeland, a feminist-owned sex toy shop on New York's rough-edged Lower East Side. I arrived looking every bit the former Catholic schoolgirl I am—that is, guilt-ridden and nicely dressed—only to be confronted with a Star Wars–like assortment of vibrators, dildos, whips, and harnesses. I instantly headed for the corner of the store where the books were shelved—my comfort zone—and pretended to read a tract called *Good Vibrations*, a kind of textbook for Vibrators 101, until I worked up the nerve to ask for help. The only clerk on duty was a very, very large woman—picture a Sub Zero refrigerator with a shaved head and more studs on her face than on Dolly Parton's jean jacket—seated behind a desk on an elevated platform where she kept an eye out for shoplifters. The word *intimidating* doesn't come close to describing her.

"I need help," I said in the tiniest voice.

She grunted, then came down from her perch and in a very loud voice asked what I wanted help with. "Nipple clips?" she practically yelled. "A Big G?" She pointed to an industrial-strength tool that looked like it would require a license to operate. She went on—"Maybe a butt plug?"—until I laid a manicured hand on her tattooed arm and whispered, "I've never done this before."

At this point she morphed into a kind, gentle big sister of sorts—albeit a gigantic one in a flannel shirt and work boots—leading me around the store, explaining, still at a high-decibel level, the basics of vibrators (latex vs. plastic, G-spot vs. clitoral). It was the sort of conversation I've never had with my actual sisters, let alone with a large, studded stranger who seemed to have a hearing problem.

After I'd made my selections—a cute pink teddy bear–shaped clitoral vibrator and a less-menacing-looking version of the Big G (a whimsical, tie-dyed purple banana-shaped thing mounted on something resembling a hand mixer)—she informed me (and everyone else in a twelve-block radius) that, "You're gonna need some lube with that!"

I paid, thanked her, snuck out of the store.

"I threw in some batteries for free," she yelled after me. "Typical first timers' mistake: get in the mood and realize you don't have any batteries."

I offered a silent prayer of thanks for this loud but thoughtful stranger and went home to try out my new purchases.

It was the purple Big G that I fell for. After an awkward first time, we spent some lovely evenings together. And some lovely afternoons. If we had a quickie in the morning, my friends would ask about the glow in my cheeks. Had I had a facial, they'd ask. I'd stammer something incoherent, then change the subject. One day, I even played hooky from work so Big G and I could spend a whole day together.

It was about this time I started thinking of my vibrator as the electric husband. This was not a thought I shared with my friends. They were having a hard enough time trying to understand how moving out was supposed to help my marriage. One well-intentioned girlfriend—determined to keep me from becoming a shut-in during my separation—called and invited me to the movies. No thanks, I said, I don't feel like it. Next time she called to invite me out I said I had plans. I did.

I'd fix a nice meal, have a glass of wine, put on some romantic music, light a candle, then retire to the bedroom with the purple Big G.

One night after I'd had a glass of wine (okay, maybe two) at the candlelit table I'd set for a romantic dinner, I got a *New Yorker*–style cartoon image of the two of us sitting there together: me and the electric husband. I pictured the purple banana-shaped part propped up at the table across from me, a little napkin tied in a neat triangle an inch or so from the tip, while we engaged in witty banter. I pictured this same scene at a fine restaurant, an attentive waiter showing us the wine list. I imagined the two of us at the movies, at a posh hotel, taking a drive in the country (in this scenario, I was in the driver's seat, the electric husband seat-belted in next to me). I imagined all kinds of romantic fantasies. Walking down the beach hand in hand was the only one that I couldn't quite make work.

Meanwhile, I was learning to live alone. I'd met my human husband when I was a senior in college. I remember thinking, even then, "Right guy. Wrong time." I hadn't ever really had my own apartment, let alone had a *Sex and the City*–style love life. But those things seemed increasingly unimportant as we fell headlong in love. Before we knew it, we'd moved in together and settled in a surprisingly traditional division of labor. Paul handled the home repairs, the auto mechanics, and the grilling. I took care of the cooking, the laundry, and most of the child care when our children came along.

Now that I was on my own, though, it was up to me to assemble the entertainment center, change the oil, and grill the steaks that my son and I consumed along with our WWII movies. To my great surprise, I found I wasn't bad at the kinds of household chores I'd automatically entrusted to Paul. And I discovered that jobs like hanging a coat rack or installing a window fan were supremely satisfying. I even developed an affection for tools—so much so that I bought a tool belt to wear during my home improvement efforts, along with a baseball cap and work pants. (Anybody inspecting my closet might have reasonably guessed that I was dating the large, pierced woman from Toys in Babeland, instead of one of the items for sale there.)

Despite these I-Am-Woman-Hear-Me-Roar triumphs, I cried. A lot. Especially in the beginning of our separation. I think I was feeling a lot of unexpressed sadness that I finally had room to notice and crying a lot of pent-up tears that I finally had the privacy to shed.

The marriage counseling also took an unexpected course. At times it seemed we were well on our way to working things out; at others, we left sessions steaming with rage and ready to dial our attorneys.

And as my apartment went from a stop-gap way station to a potential home, I began to have moments of contentment—even a newfound happiness. I rediscovered the pleasure of listening to music. I got into exuberant Irish fiddle music in a way I would have been too self-conscious to do within earshot of anyone else. I fell back into the habit of reading late into the night. And I reveled in keeping my tiny apartment absolutely spotless, knowing no one else was going to come along and mess it up.

I did things Paul used to do: I refinished a set of garage sale chairs, changed the windshield wiper blades. I did things that I'd always wanted to do: I decorated my bedroom in lavender and green, strung paper lanterns across the living room mantel, and had chocolate fondue for breakfast. And I did things I assumed Paul wouldn't have wanted me to do: I visited a psychic, wore my hair long, and ate tofu dogs. (Turns out I didn't like the tofu dogs either.) Meanwhile, I bought batteries and scented candles by the dozen for my dates with the electric husband. I did, to paraphrase Napoleon Dynamite, whatever I wanted.

All the while, my real husband and I were meeting twice a week with a gifted marriage counselor. The process was alternately daunting and promising, infuriating and humbling, tedious and unpredictable, brutal and inexplicable. As we excavated the issues that had ground away at our marriage—mutual and lingering resentments from the bad old days when Paul was drinking, old betrayals, and ancient grudges over money, in-laws, and child rearing—we realized that if we were really going to fix what was wrong with our marriage, we'd have to dig deep. We started the process thinking we just needed a little distance and a few months of counseling to patch up the cracks in our marriage; we ended up doing a gut renovation.

Eventually, reconciliation began to look like a quaint but impossible notion. We still trudged dutifully off to couples' counseling, but sometimes it was as if we were going to a funeral. Without either of us realizing it, we had begun to talk in tones full of resignation and sadness; we both hired lawyers and we were using terms like *amicable*—which is nearly always followed by the word *divorce*.

Nearly a year and a half after I'd moved out, we seemed to have exhausted the marriage counseling process. All the old grudges and disagreements had been aired—we had each apologized, in profound and meaningful ways and, as best as we were able, had made amends. But we were at a loss as to what to do next. I trudged home after one particularly downbeat session unable to stop crying. I looked so miserable, that a complete stranger—a twenty-something kid who I now suspect was a cult recruiter—came up to me in Union Square and gave me a hug.

Later that day, I called Paul. I asked if he could come over to my apartment. I was finished with marriage counseling, I told him. He nodded wearily. He was, too. My heart nearly broke. I hadn't had a chance to finish; I'd called him over to tell him that I wanted to get back together. I'd felt we'd done all we could to look at what went wrong, that the only thing left now was to make things right. I was about to propose a step that felt even scarier than moving out—moving back in—but he didn't seem interested. He said it was a shame, but he didn't really think we could get back together after all.

Maybe I was just being contrary—a trait that had helped land us in marriage counseling in the first place—but I disagreed. I said I thought we could. He looked at me expectantly. I went a step further. I said I thought we should.

"Really?" he said.

"Really," I said. "That's why I invited you over today."

"Really?" he said.

"Really," I said.

Then Paul confessed that he'd only said he was finished with counseling because I said *I* was, that he really wanted to reconcile but was afraid, after all we'd been through, I'd say no if he proposed it.

"Really?" I said.

"Really."

So much for the honest communications skills we'd worked so hard on all these months in therapy. But the truth is we had walked through fire together. We had had to put our marriage completely at risk to save it. And by some miracle, we had actually done it.

Getting back together was, after all that, surprisingly easy and totally right. We decided not to go for a trial reunion, a cautious "you take one step closer I'll take one step closer" arrangement where either party could call it quits over the smallest slight. We wanted to get back together, totally, completely, immediately.

Our kids were thrilled, our friends delighted. The only hitch: giving up the love nest where the electric husband and I had had such happy times. (Okay, there was one other hitch—explaining the electric husband to the real one.)

Paul wasn't particularly surprised. Or even jealous. He confessed that he had developed a relationship with a video involving some nurses. I wasn't exactly jealous, either (maybe a little grossed out, but not especially threatened). He had also, it turned out, gotten into some exuberant music of his own—including a new age vocalist whose music made me run screaming from the room. He'd gone back to smoking cigars and eating meatloaf with mayonnaise and ketchup. And he'd added some flourishes to the décor of our old home that would charitably be described as Early Frat House.

We had conquered the thorniest of marital issues. But we had—literally—grown apart. By that I mean that we had grown while we were apart. Long-buried parts of our personalities were able to thrive, and new qualities were able to emerge, once we got out of each other's way.

THE ELECTRIC HUSBAND 43

That, after all, had been the point of separating; we were too close to see how we'd been hurting—and cramping—each other. Absence, as well as couples' counseling, really had made our hearts grow fonder.

We were thrilled to be reunited. Thanks to all that work with our therapist, most of the old tensions were gone. Our kids looked on in disgust as we held hands and beamed at each other; our friends looked on in awe.

We rarely fought now, which felt odd since that had been one of our main ways of interacting before, not even when the big issues that led to our separation came back in new disguises. But we were, to our great confusion, having a hard time with some of the little things—especially in areas where each of us had developed a certain independence or competence without the other. I was a bossy, back-seat driver when Paul grilled; he kept switching off my bedside light at 9:30. He turned the volume on my exuberant Irish fiddle down so low it sounded like a cricket chirping; I hid his exuberant new age vocalist CD under a sofa cushion.

After everything we'd shared in the therapist's office, there was one confession left, one that turned out to be somewhat trickier than all the others: we each had to admit there were aspects of living alone that we had really *loved*.

And so when a tiny fifth-floor walk-up apartment across the street from our house became available, I took it. Paul was all for it. Just as he had helped me move into my apartment when we separated, he helped me get the lavender and green bedding and the paper lanterns out of storage and haul them up the steps to this one.

Owning an apartment when I have a perfectly good house across the street is beyond extravagant. It is excessive. It is ridiculous. And it is the best money I've ever spent. I don't live there; I live with Paul. Happily. Ninety percent of the time.

But when we are at odds—even after all that counseling, we still have our moments—I tell him I'm thinking of spending the night at my apartment. He doesn't look surprised. Or even especially disappointed.

At first, I was a little hurt when he didn't beg me to stay. He got the hint, made a halfhearted attempt at pretending he wanted me to stay. And I got the hint, too. He actually wanted me to leave just as much as I wanted to go. And so I went. And loved it.

Now we don't have to get on each other's nerves for me to sleep across the street. Sometimes I just go over to listen to my music, to read, to write, or to just be alone. I love being so close that I can be there in less than a minute; I also love that my apartment is situated far enough up the block that I can't see Paul at our house across the street and he can't see me. It's not as comfortable as our house; I would never want to live there. I'm always ready to return to my real life the next day. And I always come home happier, saner, and nicer.

Once in a while, I'll confess, I also come home with that telltale glow from a fling with the electric husband. Not often, though, because now that I have my real husband back—in new and improved condition—I'm not all that interested in the electric one. We had some good times together, sure, but sometimes I wonder what I ever saw in him.

Occasionally, when I've spent the night at my apartment, my real husband brings me my morning coffee and the newspaper. And once in a while the two of us go across the street for some romantic time alone. But mainly my apartment is a place to simply savor my independence—as well as the knowledge that we have a secure, battle-tested marriage that has room, literally and figuratively, for two kinds of exuberant music. It was a hard-won victory—something I can view with more appreciation from across the street.

And I don't even *consider* inviting the cat.

By This We Know Love

Debra Magpie Earling

In the late evening, in the summer of 1984, the telephone rang. I had been reading a poem that had been sent to me by a friend. It was a disturbing poem about life in New Orleans, about businessmen being blown away on hurricane cocktails, young boys dancing stick in the dim frail light of dusk. The hot summer shimmered at the edge of the field in the cooling Montana evening. My parents were visiting me at my cabin. They had just pulled out the bed in the living room and had retired for the night. The telephone call was from my former husband's grandfather; his voice was pipe-pitched and nervous, his sentences riding the high lift of his voice. I didn't recognize his voice at first.

"I'm afraid," he said, "I have some bad news for you."

I held my breath.

My mother called to me from the living room, astute to the sudden slump in my posture. "What's the matter?" she was saying, but I couldn't grasp her question. Grandpa Holt's voice had taken on the eerie, serious tone of ill news. I waved off my mother's insistent questioning trying to hear.

"Barry is dead," he said.

I dropped the poem I had been reading, letting the pages splatter the kitchen floor. There was a low sound shifting in the room, my own voice, pale now, quavering.

"How," I managed to say, "how did he die?" There was a long pause, but I already knew the answer. In the absence of explanation, Barry's image rose up before me.

My mother kept calling. "Someone died?" she said. "Who died? Who are you speaking to?"

I saw Barry with a rifle lifted to his mouth. I saw his beautiful hands on the black barrel, then I saw the trigger pulled.

"He killed himself," Grandpa Holt finally said. "I am so sorry."

"How did it happen?" I said, not willing to say the true words, to ask him how he had killed himself.

"I'd rather not say," he said. "But you'll find out soon enough. I just didn't want to be the one to tell you." He paused again.

This time the room shifted focus for me. I saw my own reflection in the darkening window. My hair seemed garishly long to me. I stared at myself. I was twenty-seven years old, too young I thought to receive such news. My father was calling to me now, too, but neither my father nor my mother got out of bed.

"Who died?" my dad asked, his voice almost timid.

"Barry," I managed to say. I heard the sound of mourning, a low guttural moan in my dad's throat.

"He jumped off a bridge," Grandpa Holt said. "He's still in the river."

I couldn't comprehend this statement. "In the river," I kept saying. "I don't understand."

"The current swept him under. We haven't found him yet."

That evening I threw on my jacket, and as I was heading to the door, my mother told me not to go to the old haunts. "Don't punish yourself," she said.

I went to see my sister. My sister and her husband owned a local bar where they performed music nightly. I had no sooner broken the bad news to my sister when my brother-in-law called her up to play the next set. Cheryl sat me down with a double scotch, even though I didn't drink at the time. Unbelievably, the first song they sang was "Ode to Billy Joe," an old song about a boy who jumps off a bridge to his death. My sister mouthed silent apologies to me. I couldn't stop myself from laughing. Well, I thought, Barry always did have a sense of humor.

My sister jumped down off the bandstand after the song. "I am so sorry," she said. "It's crazy." She tried to prevent herself from laughing, but couldn't. It wasn't funny, but we couldn't help ourselves. It was the giddy laughter of grief. "We just learned that song last week. I don't know why we had to play it tonight. This was the first time we ever played that song."

When I returned to the cabin that night, my mother was waiting up for me. She had gathered up my friend's poem and had placed it on the kitchen table. I took the poem with me to bed and finished reading it. The last stanza leapt out at me. *You knew it wasn't going to work . . . And here my memory is haunted . . . when you jumped from the bridge, and felt the hard back of the water shatter your teeth.*

Seven days after Barry jumped from the bridge, his body was found snagged by the low-hanging branches of red river bramble. When I returned to Spokane for his funeral, the funeral director kept his voice even, his hands out directing me to sit. Remember him as he was, he kept saying. His body has been too long in water, too long in the warm river. I would have done well to remember him as he was, but remembrance, I learned, is a tricking thing when the process of grief lay before me.

I had one more year to complete at the University of Washington. I thought I would return to the comfort of routine, writing workshops and lectures on literature, a blessing of distractions that could block the image of my ex-husband tossing twenty-five cents into a toll basket, stopping his car on the bridge at seven o'clock in the evening when the reflection of birds rushing over the evening-dulled river would hold the image of him in the empty blue sky for a lightning moment before his body shattered the unforgiving water. As I walked to my classes, an angry light surrounded me, a strange electrified light that illuminated the trees, the candlelit veins of leaves. The Seattle rain was neon, the days a searing sheet of metallic light. The edges of the buildings glinted, cutting the dull sky. When the sun split the swath of clouds, the sidewalks almost hissed. Everything seemed hard.

I took a creative writing class that fall. There was nothing remarkable about the writing in the class or the students, myself included, who sat vacant-eyed and staring. This was the first writing class that didn't enthrall me. It wasn't the teacher. She tried to ignite the class with remarkable ideas for our writing, even told us stories, the North Dakota blizzards that had threatened her life, the frostbite circles that had scarred her cheeks. Still, the third week into the quarter the class lacked that indefinable magic that could make it interesting, make it bearable even. The professor leaned on the podium and took a deep breath through her nose and exhaled what sounded like steam.

"I'm going to ask you to share a story," she said. "You know, like what I did on my summer vacation."

We all looked at each other. One woman seated in the front row leaned forward on her elbow and looked back at all of us, her hair, whacked off at the collar, swept the desk. She looked lazy and out of place, like maybe she was still enjoying her summer vacation. She reminded me of Carson McCullers, in looks anyway. Most of us had shifted back in our chairs, glancing down, crossing our arms, attempting to avoid the professor's eyes.

I was hoping that the strange man who hulked in the corner in impeccable clothes, his long coat and black turtleneck, would volunteer his story. There was something sinister about him, maybe it was his hair gel, the gleam of his treacherous spiked hair. He was the only other minority in the class. He was Japanese, cool eyed, and distant. I had noticed on the first day of class that his nails were polished, and I thought that his grooming alone was interesting. He often smirked at me like we held a common secret. I liked that most of the time he looked at the lot of us with disdain, his upper lip curling to reveal remarkably white teeth. But it was the Carson McCullers lookalike who spoke first. I loved a good story but thought she might tell a travel story, something I hated. I had heard many travel stories from students at the university, and the tales were usually endless and boring and pointless, the gist behind the stories was always the same: I have money, a lot of money.

She took a deep breath and squinted at us as if to gauge our interest. I remember that her eyes opened wide like she was ready to tell a good ghost story, and then she began talking, a rapid-fire spewing, a machine-gun blaze of a story. And though this could never be verbatim, this is what I remember her saying.

"I was a volunteer fireman this summer," she began. "I saw things I thought I would never see. The death accidents were the worst. I always thought people knew when they were going to die, but I saw faces of men and women who had been caught in the thick of life, and a lot of times their eyes were open as if they had been caught completely unaware. It was their eyes, their open mouths, that revealed their surprise. Sometimes, especially in the young accident victims, there would be this look on their faces like astonished disappointment.

"We were called in to revive a man who had fallen from a ladder from the second story of his house while he was cleaning the eaves. His wife thought a bee had stung him, or that maybe a crow had startled him with sudden flapping. He was a young man. His wife stayed behind the screen door of the house while we worked on him, unable to face her husband still and startle-eyed in the garish green grass of their front yard. He was already dead."

And the next thing the Carson lookalike said carried the weight of her emphasis, because she lowered her voice to a spooky growl. "The sound of the wife's wailing seemed at times not to be coming from her at all, but from the husband. I got the distinct feeling that his spirit was strutting back and forth between his wife and his still body, and he was angry and sorrowful to find himself on that beautiful summer morning, with a gorgeous wife and years to left to live, dead as a doornail in the summer grass.

"My first suicide run I felt sick to my stomach. A woman had hung herself in the basement of her home. I dreaded seeing her hanging from the rafters, her tongue black and swollen and her big eyes bulging, but as I walked down the basement stairs, I experienced a tremendous sense of calm and peace. The woman's face clearly showed evidence of struggle, but there was something about her, a release. Her spirit had left her body. There were no ill feelings there. Unlike the accident deaths, this woman seemed at peace."

The curious thing about that class was two-thirds of the students had experienced a significant death that summer that had changed their lives. The spiky-haired man revealed a story about the murder of a prostitute in his apartment building. His story was disturbing. He described the open door to her bedroom, a purple brassiere hanging from the dresser mirror, the yellow police tape barring entrance. I avoided him then. He knew a little bit too much. If he was making up the story, it was creepy. If he wasn't, it was even creepier. I wasn't sure what to make of these revelations. I felt they were some puzzle piece that would help me understand Barry's death.

I had a recurring dream. In the dream, it is summer, so hot my back prickles with sweat and I long for cool water. I walk across a bridge in the shimmering light of a hot July day. I come to a bridge, not a high bridge, not "the" bridge. And Barry is calling to me. I see him standing in a blindingly brilliant shallow stream, bare chested, splashing water with the cup of his palms, his arms open. "Come in," he says to me, "the water's just right." He is laughing and playful. "Just jump in," he tells me. His voice is gentle but insistent. "If you just jump in we can be together." I look down to him and he lifts his hands to me. "Don't worry. I'm here to catch you." I hesitate. And then I climb the rail and let go. I feel the fall in my stomach, a long and torturous fall. I see the sky passing over me and realize too late that I have given up everything. He is not here to catch me, I think, when I feel his hand on my forearm, a grip so tight my arm aches and I gasp awake, my fingers gripping the mattress.

⊰⊱

That winter I applied to graduate school at Cornell University. I had grand visions of changing my life, shedding my troubles, and creating a new me. I would move back East as they say, become sophisticated and worldly. But I know now I just wanted to get far away from my past. I was looking for a geographic cure. I never really believed I would be accepted into an Ivy League university. It was a fantasy. Even though I had done well in college, I still saw myself as a high school dropout with a GED. Unworthy. Stupid. I didn't even apply to another school. When I got the acceptance call from Cornell, I was intimidated, meek. "Of course, yes, I accept. Thank you. Thank you, thank you," I said into the receiver, my hands trembling.

My first walk onto the Cornell campus, I passed over the main bridge and attempted to peer over the retaining wall. I didn't see a bottom to the steep-sided rock walls even when I looked in the distance. I had to pull myself up a way on the wide stone railing to capture the view. The sight caught me off guard, as if someone had come up behind me and had clapped his hands to my temples. Musty cliff walls clattered down to dark, green water. I gripped the rough retainer wall and tried to breathe slowly, let myself back down easy. The rushing height made me want to drop to a crawl. I was stunned that I had found myself at Cornell for many reasons, but I was shocked to learn a little later that I had been drawn to a place famous for the very thing I was attempting to escape. I did not know I had accepted an offer to attend a university that was notorious for students killing themselves by hurling off bridges.

That afternoon I mentioned my surprise at the towering gorges to a fellow student; she looked at me quizzically.

"You didn't know about Cornell's reputation," she stated, half-questioning, her eyebrows suspicious. Then she sneered at me. "Suicide?"

My memories of Barry collected like small droplets of water on the walls of the gorges surrounding me, small perfect cages of light evaporating, brilliant and brief, and frightening. Even though she posed suicide as a question, the word was solid, a grotesque confirmation. Had I known or heard from somewhere, and concealed the truth from myself, that this was the place where students leapt from bridges? I came here to study, to redefine myself, to forget, to live, to move on. Suddenly, here was the stark reality of his death again, hard and unforgiving, more substantive than a photograph. The ghost of my ex-husband had followed me.

And that first year in graduate school, Barry became a beatific apparition, his soul flickering at the edge of my new life. I'd look up from my coffee cup to see him take a back exit. I would spot a glimpse of him strolling across campus. Other times, I would catch his distinct scent, sweet and woodsy, lingering in the foyer of the library, rising from the dark halls in the stacks, always teasing, just ahead, just behind me. His illusiveness made him more and more memorable to me. I recalled the exact color of his hair, his Baltic blue eyes.

I was convinced he was in upstate New York, of all places. He had to be because I had to believe I had been given another chance to save him. In my hopeful heart, I believed that the Lord would grant me this mercy. If the dead could return, surely, he would return to me at Christmastime, I reasoned. I waited for him, even believed he might tap at my windows, sweetly whisper to me that he was all right, that he was safe now. And I could settle his death once and for all, tell him that I had loved him, that I would have been there for him. But my vivid hopes of his Christmas visitation faded to days of endless snows, a fury of white sky, sudden blizzards that hid the roads I recklessly drove.

Barry's suicide had erased the truth of his life and the heartache of our marriage. I could see only the spirit of my desires, one-dimensional, without depth or humanness. A falsehood is never kind, never generous. I was ignoring the import of his life and the suffering and hardships he had endured. If I was to forgive myself and ultimately forgive him, I had to face down his foibles, his violence. I had committed the sin of omission. And for a long while, self-deception stalled my life. I behaved like a mad woman.

My behavior was so destructive that by the end of the first year after Barry's death, I was diagnosed manic-depressive. I wasn't crazy, I told myself, I was sorrowful. I took risks with my life, stayed up for days on end, and drove back roads and highways searching for some kind of answer to love. I was fooling myself. My life with Barry had been neither glamorous nor dramatic. Something had changed for me. Suddenly, I was looking for his love to rescue me. But he wasn't the elusive angel who could save me. I was sick, lonely, and alone.

When I finished graduate school, I thought I was through with grief and believed I had settled my life. I returned to Montana, and for that first year, I immersed myself in my writing and became obsessed with the curious idea that I wanted to live my life as a cowboy. I bought a lasso and books on roping. I even traveled to Idaho to take lessons in Western riding from a woman who was touted to be the best. I told myself I didn't need anybody. I would be independent and cool as a ranch hand. I had met Indian cowboys in Montana, and it seemed they were living the life of the old-time Indians. They weren't trapped in HUD housing or working in offices.

I believed there was a life for me out there in the great beyond, herding cattle, roping, and riding. The thought makes me laugh now. The truth was (and still is) I'm afraid of horses, their big teeth and quivering nostrils. I didn't know the first thing about cattle or cowboys, didn't know a naval knot from a noose, but I wanted to live what I imagined was an unencumbered life, live out on the wide-open prairie under the stars. I was clearly deluded.

I had grown up in the Spokane Valley in eastern Washington when there were still remnants of farms, chicken coops, and barns in open fields, but the paper mill smell would descend upon our neighborhood in late afternoons and small planes would circle our street to land in the little airport we lived near. When I was twelve, my best friend had a horse. She didn't know I shut my eyes tight when we would ride double, praying the horse wouldn't slip as he galloped beside the railroad tracks at wind-breaking speeds.

There were two other Indians besides me at the Catholic school I attended, and one was my older brother. I grew up in a mostly white neighborhood, a mostly white town. The only cowboys and Indians we saw (besides my family) were on television. I have friends who have assumed my ex-husband was Indian, I suppose, because he was an alcoholic and because he killed himself, but he wasn't. It is the type of misconception I'm familiar with from years of growing up in an all-white community that had little tolerance for difference, little understanding of my life or culture, a community that steadfastly held to the belief that Indians were doomed to live a stereotype.

I was fifteen years old when I dropped out of public high school after a school counselor told me I didn't have to worry about getting an education.

"Indians," she said, leaning close to me, her voice oddly reassuring, "aren't smart."

I was inclined to believe she was telling me the truth. I was bussing tables at a greasy spoon, going out on weekends. I hated school and my grades were abysmal.

"Just try to fit in," my brother told me.

"Just get married," the counselor said with clear-eyed conviction. "It's probably your only chance."

I took the counselor's advice.

Barry had grown up in my neighborhood, but we didn't meet until I was fourteen, and then we met at the Idaho state line where my cousin and I would go to dance after hours. I wasn't a drinker or a wild kid. My mother was a housekeeper, my father a surveyor, and though they were loving parents, I didn't get much supervision. I don't think they knew what to do with a high school dropout, a daughter with no prospects. They wanted my life to be better than the life they were living. Maybe a husband would save me from a life of menial jobs and certain poverty.

Barry was five years older than I and he had lived in an orphanage-like institution just across the river from where I grew up. His parents had placed him, and his brothers, in a home when they divorced. He was seven years old. He lived at the Hutton Settlement until he was eighteen. When he left that sad place, he had dreams of becoming an artist. And though he cultivated his talent, he was enslaved to construction jobs. He never had the chance to live out his dream of becoming an artist, moving to New York or San Francisco. Like almost all of my childhood friends, he also lived his days in our hometown, only leaving for a brief time when he joined the navy.

When I got hired at the University of Montana, I'd drive the 140-mile round-trip from home to work and see cowboys riding horses in the hazy fields and dream of a better life or maybe a life I thought held no responsibilities. But I was thirty-four years old, an assistant professor, teaching a full course load with large lecture classes, and no time to learn another way of life. My mother would sigh with my endless musings, listen to my long-winded telephone calls, and ask me if I was taking my medication. She knew too well my big dreams and my daily sorrows.

One day my mother told me she had been praying for me. She was praying for a man for me, a very specific man. I remember rolling my eyes, and yet, as she continued talking, I held the receiver tightly to my ear.

"You've been lonely for too long," she said.

And though I didn't feel all that lonely, I felt the sting of loneliness suddenly well at the back of my throat. I didn't want my mother to know I wanted to blubber at the thought of her praying for me to find a man. I sounded pathetic. She told me she was praying for a man who would share my interests, a man kind as an angel, faithful and true. She was praying for a man who would be loving to me, a man who would never brutalize me.

"I am praying that you find a writer," she told me. "I am praying for a cowboy but not a womanizer."

"You're praying for a cowboy?"

"A cowboy and a writer," she said. "I'm not praying for a handsome man," she said. "I mean, he can be handsome, but the important thing is he will be good to you."

"You're crazy," I said. "It'll never happen, but I appreciate the thought."

"You watch and see," my mother said.

But all I could see were the years laid out before me, years of guilt and loneliness. I didn't even see an ugly man in my future, let alone a cowboy and a writer. My mother knew my doubts.

"No," she insisted. "You just wait. It will happen."

I was quiet, hoping I would get the chance to change the subject.

"It's going to happen," my mother insisted. "You have to pray very specifically for these things, otherwise, you won't get exactly what you want. The Blessed Virgin has heard my prayers," she told me. "And she has never let me down."

I didn't believe my mother. Who would? My mother is a devout Catholic. And even though I believed in my mother's prayers, she was asking too much to pray for the perfect man for me. A man who was all good and loving was one thing, but a man who was a cowboy and a writer was another thing entirely. But she was so steadfast in her belief, I found myself wondering if such a man did exist. I entertained the idea that long summer, felt giddy with hopefulness. I listened to sappy songs on the radio. *Somewhere out there*, I sang along, *somewhere out there where dreams can come true*. The brilliant summer shimmered into fall. And in the fall of that year I did meet a man, a writer who lived in a small town in eastern Oregon.

When my mother and father first met him, my mother's first comment was, "That's not his real hair, you know. No one could have hair that color. He's obviously dyed it."

I didn't know how to respond to my mother. It was a lame observation. She wasn't very eager to believe he was the man she had prayed for. I'm not sure why she was dubious about Robert at first. My father eagerly embraced him, enjoyed his company, and immediately started regaling Robert with old fight stories, my dad's glory days as a boxer. Maybe my mother didn't truly believe in the power of her own prayers. Okay, I told myself, he wasn't a cowboy. And to my mother he was a man who dyed his hair. First impressions are all-important to my family. I knew Robert hadn't dyed his hair, but I could understand why she believed he might have. Robert's hair is the color of palest wheat, so light in the summer it's almost white, but he doesn't have the thin hair of a white blond. His hair is thick and beautiful. He's a striking man.

I met him when he had come to study writing at the University of Montana. Robert was older than the other students, almost four years younger than I. He was mature, an adult. We became quick friends. He was easy to talk to, funny and kind. He reminded me of a good friend from my early college days. I felt comfortable and comforted by him. We laughed a lot. But by the end of his first year, I was afraid my feelings were deepening for him.

I dreamt one night that Robert and I had kissed; the kiss was so passionate and real I awoke believing at first it had really happened. I checked the clock. It was 3:30 in the morning. The dream seemed flatteringly silly but bothersome. I didn't want to fall in love with a graduate student who had taken a class from me. And though I thought he was attractive, wonderful, and kind, he had never indicated anything beyond friendship in his behavior toward me. I had felt a charge of electricity when I first met him that I had immediately dismissed. I didn't think the feeling was reciprocal, nor did I want it to be.

I was to meet him for breakfast that morning, and I felt embarrassed by my dream. I had that peculiar feeling that somehow when we met he would be able to read my thoughts, but I was relieved when I saw him. The dream quickly dissolved as we chatted over breakfast, talked about literature, books, and his home in Oregon. He told a lot of stories that morning. We laughed a lot. As we stood outside saying good-bye, he turned to me and his face was suddenly serious. The day was turning cold, cloudy. He looked me in the eyes, a gaze held long. And then he said something that I will never forget.

"Last night," he began, and then he stopped short.

"Yes," I said.

"I dreamt about you," he said.

"You're kidding," I said. "Me too. I dreamt I kissed you last night."
I laughed, suddenly embarrassed, too girly.

His face flushed. "Really?" he asked, but I couldn't measure his
response, whether the dream had bothered or pleased him.

The wind rushed upon us, and my coat flared, then flapped behind me. I felt exposed. He didn't speak for what seemed like a very
long time. Then he turned to me, his eyes expressive.

"I dreamt I kissed you, too," he said. "I woke up at 3:30 in the
morning," he said.

I couldn't believe he was telling me this. I felt my heart soaring.
And this thought, the thought of our imagined kiss, hung between
us as we parted.

※

I was anxious when Robert invited me to come visit him in Oregon. After our shared dream, we had spent a lot of time together.
But I still kept him at a distance. I wasn't comfortable with the
growing feelings I had for him. I was afraid I would be hurt again.
I believed Robert's invitation revealed he was ready to take a step
toward a more serious relationship, a big step. He had talked about
the mint farm his parents had once operated. I'd seen photographs
of him standing beside an old tractor in a John Deere cap, his pants
dusty, his face tan. In Missoula, he wore sport coats and ties, sweater
vests and white, white shirts. He was lean and muscular, a former
high school basketball star. Sometimes when he wore sunglasses, I
thought he looked like a movie star, too. I wanted to see his life on
the farm. I wanted to know everything about him. I packed quickly
and drove to Pendleton, where I stayed the night. I awoke early the

next morning, had breakfast, and drove the long and winding miles to his home place.

I arrived in the late afternoon. Sun lit the yellow fields near his home. A country bathed in pure light. Lonesome desert country, surrounded by red cliffs. The river scattered light to the bluffs, the dry fields. This was cattle country. Near his house, close by the river, a herd of cattle grazed. I could smell the sweet breeze washed clean with the scent of mint and juniper, and I realized the scent was Robert's scent. I rumbled over a cattle guard and drove on. I was anxious to see him again, afraid to be hopeful. Two big dogs ran out to sniff my tires and bark at my car, and I could see his home place in the distance. Robert always referred to the place where he grew up as "the home place." I thought it was a quaint phrase, a mere colloquialism, but as I drove toward his home I understood that this was where he came from, his family history, a claim to the land, not just his home but a home place. A great-uncle had built the house a hundred years before. He told me generations of his family had lived in the house: his great-grandfather first, then his grandmother and grandfather, his mother and father. The house had always been filled with family.

The country road followed the river line, and I heard the dense tick of grasshoppers along the fence. I saw the grand vista of the country, his country, wild and spare in its immensity, bigger it seemed than Montana. I felt overwhelmed and giddy. Robert stepped out on the porch to greet me and called off his overly friendly dogs. I felt awkward and shy when he pulled me close and kissed me in front of his parents' home. The boards were rough hewn and solid. In the warm autumnal sun, an olive tree blessed the house with shade.

His mother called to me from the kitchen as I entered the house and smiled at me as she dried the dishes. His father was seated in a large easy chair beside a tobacco table. The house smelled like good tobacco, and years of a family cooking good meals. The windows opened to the broad fields, a large dramatic bluff that lifted up over the riverside. Bright crocheted pillows adorned the couch.

His father nodded to me, his voice easy and kind. "Have a seat," he said.

We all sat in silence for a while, but it didn't feel strange or uncomfortable. I could feel the nearness of Robert, and I was surprised to remember how natural it felt to be in his company again. I wasn't sure I loved him yet, but knew that love was supposed to feel like this, not jangly and loud, but quiet and sweet. I had the realization that his life, his home here, held a contentedness that proclaimed a certain end to longing. It was perhaps the first true and romantic idea I have ever had. Robert's mother offered me coffee, asked me about my drive. Supper rattled the cooking lids on the stove.

"I hope you'll like what we're having," she said. "Venison and red beans, squash from our garden."

Robert's father turned to him. Sunlight shifted, entered the windows with the sleepy last rays of early evening. "Well, Robert," he said, his voice held an accent, mid-south, old-timey and comforting. "I think it's about time you fed the cattle."

"Okay," Robert said, and before I had time to register my surprise at the request, Robert was returning from the back porch tying on a pair of leather chaps. He sat down in front of me and pulled on a pair of cowboy boots.

"You didn't tell me you were a cowboy," I said.

He grinned at me and rolled his eyes. "I'm not a cowboy," he said.

I didn't know that being called a cowboy was a disdainful comment then, reserved for dudes, not ranchers, but right then he was a gorgeous sight. When he pulled on his cowboy hat and reached for his denim jacket, I swooned a little, but hid my pleasure. Could this be the man my mother had prayed for? Can't be, I thought. But as I stepped from the porch and followed Robert out into the golden fields, as the cattle were running up from the river, and the evening wind rushed toward us, and Robert placed his hand on top of his cowboy hat and walked with purpose toward his chores, unbelievably handsome and smiling back at me, I wanted to believe it was true. A miracle. I was in love. Hopelessly romantic. I didn't know then that even answered prayers come with work.

When spring came, I moved down to Monument, Oregon, to be with Robert. There was no wedding ceremony. He didn't carry me over the threshold. There was no wedding cake, no flowers, but he told me every day that he loved me. And for the first time in my life, everything seemed perfect. We lived five miles outside of town on a ranch that had once been owned by trick rodeo riders. Robert owned the house now. There was a long hitching post at the end of the long driveway where I imagined the old cowboys who came to visit would tie up their horses. There were outback houses and a garage haunted by pack rats. We lived hidden in the juniper trees at the mouth of a canyon. Behind us was twenty miles of reclaimed wilderness, sagebrush, a few pines. We could see only one light in the far distance, a neighbor's lithium light, the only sign that we were not alone, that and the sound of the animals moving around us. At night the stars closed in, glittering so close in the dark sky they seemed only a hand's reach away.

It seemed I had entered the dream of the life I had wanted for so long. Although I wasn't a cowboy myself, I was living in the life of a cowboy. For the first time in my life maybe, I wasn't struggling to survive, but I was still struggling. Love came with the price of knowing myself. I had kept myself so busy with work and distractions, I had not considered my life. I didn't know that I had not grieved for my past life and the marriage I had failed. I hadn't given much thought to the events that had culminated in my divorce. I had reinvented my ex-husband for years. Now I found I had a lot of time to think with no distractions.

———— ⚬⚬⚬ ————

Robert rose early and disappeared to endless chores before the day had even arrived. I awoke to sun lifting over the steaming fields, nothing but myself. I cleaned the house and took long walks in the canyon, where I would be suddenly scared, the back of my head tight to my skull, sure I was being stalked. It was a strange time. The house had been left uninhabited for so long that the wild had reclaimed it. Rattlers ticked in the woodpile where I went to chop wood. At night a cougar screamed like a woman attacked, the long trail of her cry echoing ghostlike in the canyon. Pack rats walked like heavy-booted men in the attic. Birds fluttered down the chimney flue and screeched, then chirped pitifully, then died, the stench of them unbearable in the growing summer heat. Starlings scratched and flapped in the dryer tube until finally the dryer stopped. When we went to clean it out we found robin's eggs, shattered and whole.

"They must rob the nests," Robert said.

Flickers throbbed at all sides of our house, pecking holes the size of fists clean through the doors and eves. I caught a badger outside our house one morning. I saw the three-inch curl of his black claws, his moody squint.

"Be careful of that thing," my mother warned me when I called her on the phone to tell her about the badger's visit. "They aren't supposed to be out in the day."

Deer trails riddled the hillsides, so many deer you could see a thousand lit paths at night. I would look up from my writing to see deer traveling across the yard in large numbers, bold in their claim.

Unmistakably this was their territory. We were obstacles in the path of a wilderness corridor. Some nights we would wake to the sound of snorting animals, and we would lift our heads to peer out the window. On a moonlit night we could see the pale steam of breath lifting like clouds as a herd of giant elk passed by our windows, their massive heads silhouetted in the darkness. Cottontails shot out from beneath our porch, some tiny, some large, hundreds everywhere. Then the bunny population would thin. Coyotes howled day and night, their voices like stick game callers, like a powwow gathering beyond the back of the house. I was certain all the Indians who had passed here were haunting me.

Coyotes threw their human voices to us from all directions. Sometimes Robert or I would follow their calls, convinced there was a gathering of people near the house. We would find ourselves alone, called far into the hills by humanlike voices that turned to coyote yips. There were rattlers beneath our porch, rattlers everywhere. In the pump house they had crawled the walls three feet high to find the nests of mice. When Robert had to fix the stalled pump, he found the scraped-peel of their shed skins lining the pee-stained insulation. When I sat outside to catch a cool breeze in the late afternoon, I swatted the ground with a willow stick to chase away any hidden snakes.

I felt like I was losing my mind. Memories of Barry returned. The man I married at the age of seventeen and had divorced at twenty-one was no longer the loving spirit I longed to resurrect. I punished myself with memories of nights he had threatened to kill me. I kept seeing over and over again the image of myself standing before him, trembling and pleading for his life, then my own.

I had come home from work early one night to find him seated in the living room, the barrel of his deer rifle shoved in his mouth. It was Christmastime, and the Christmas tree glittered behind me. I could see tinsel from the corner of my eye, the homemade ornaments I had bought at the church bazaar for a handful of quarters, the pitiful presents I had wrapped the night before. We were living in a small apartment close to downtown Spokane. At the end of the month, we didn't have enough money to buy food. Often Barry would spend his whole paycheck on booze. Had I really been so hopeful to decorate a Christmas tree when every working night for the past year I had beat a path to every bar within a mile of our apartment to search for my husband before I headed to work? And those were the lucky nights.

Sometimes, after a late-night shift of waiting tables, I would come home at one or two in the morning to find a stranger in my home, a wild-eyed man Barry had met at the bar. And I would lock myself in the bedroom, waiting for the sound of the door to open then close, praying until dawn that I would be safe, falling in and out of a sleep that wasn't sleep, but Barry's continuous alcoholic nightmare. Our small apartment began to smell like the lung-sour breath of a thousand binges.

Barry wouldn't remove the barrel from his mouth for seven hours. I stood fixed at attention not wanting to move for fear I would cause him to set the trigger off. I stood still for so long my rubber knees shook. I had been up since five in the morning that day to get my schoolwork done, had put in a full school day, waited tables without a break hoping I'd get to go home early. My tight muscles rebelled. I shook like a dog.

"Please don't," I begged him. Please, please, please. I tried to describe the beautiful life we could live. I remember my shirt was wet with the unending stream of my tears. And he must have been tired, too, when he finally turned the gun on me, my stories useless.

"There's nothing worth living for," he told me. "Your life is worthless, too."

"Oh God, Barry, maybe so, maybe so," I stuttered. "But I want to live."

As much as I had remembered Barry as all loving and kind, I had turned to see him only as my tormentor. When he finally pulled the gun from his mouth, my muscles became a thousand elastic bands exploding, ticking beneath my skin.

I hadn't lived with another man other than Barry for over ten years, and I found myself growing distrustful of Robert, blaming him, even punishing him for the events of my past. I would drink too much and the evening would turn sour. I began to endlessly recollect and recount the bad events of my marriage. Robert would listen to me for hours on end. If he went to bed, my mania would only escalate. I would pace the floor, bemoaning my past. Robert was ever patient, arising from bed to keep company with my complaints. He held me when I cried.

"I know what happened to you was terrible, but I will not treat you badly. I will never knowingly be unkind or cruel to you," he told me. "Don't blame me for what happened in your past. I love you."

"I'm sick," I would tell him. "I just want you to know what you have gotten into. I'm manic-depressive. I'm a complete mess."

He would nod his head, his eyes heavy, sometimes sorrowful, sometimes just sleepy. I became convinced he was tiring of me like I had grown tired of Barry's illness. I was afraid I had become a burden to him.

After one long night of my sad complaints, Robert held me firmly and made me look him in the eye. I was afraid he was going to tell me it was over—he couldn't put up with me any longer. He had every right to tell me to scram. He made certain that I held still and listened. He was quiet for a long while. I waited for his sigh, but his breath was steady and sure.

"You've never been loved like I love you," he said. "My love will heal you."

That did it for me. I blew up. "Don't ever say that to me," I yelled at him. "It's my life, my very life. You have to take my illness seriously."

He tried to reassure me again. "My love will heal you," he said quietly. "Trust me."

And after that, even though I continued to be dramatic, making him chase after me, making him prove he loved me again and again, he remained calm and true in his expressions of love. "I just need a little time to heal up from these arguments," he would tell me after each of my long night flare-ups. His love was constant and unfailing. Often he would tell me I would be okay if I would just let him love me.

And there came the day when I did heal. It was Christmastime again. Robert had driven me to Spokane to visit my folks for the holidays and surprised me with a week's stay at an elegant hotel downtown. He had planned the event for a long time, had saved for it. After a romantic Christmas dinner, I found myself crying, rattling on about all the bad Christmases I had endured throughout my life. He was resting in a resplendent bed lovingly listening to me as he always did, but he looked weary and sad. And I felt suddenly ashamed of myself. I abruptly realized the stories I was crying about really didn't affect me anymore. I was weeping for nothing. And what astonished me, even more, was that I was boring myself. I don't know how he stood me all those years, my sadness, my tears, my anger—well—yes, I do. He loves me.

———————⚬⚬⚬———————

This fall marks twelve years that Robert and I have been together. Six years ago, I told my psychiatrist I was quitting my medication. "I don't need it anymore," I said. And I haven't. Robert's love has healed me.

The summer he died, Barry called me on the phone. He wanted to see me. But I waited too long to return to Spokane. I never saw him again. In the last letter Barry ever wrote, he told the world that I was the person he had loved most in this world. I pray that he knows I hold his memory still, that I remember the good times we had, and have forgiven the bad. I hope he also knows that I loved him.

Robert is the blessing my mother prayed for; I know he is. And my mother knows it, too. When I tell him he is the answer to my mother's prayers, he gets annoyed sometimes, probably because our relationship has not been easy. And certainly, my mother did not make him materialize, though I bless her every day for her fervent prayer for love. Someday soon, I want to marry Robert in front of our family and close friends, even though in the state of Montana we are already married by common law. But I don't need a marriage ceremony to be bound to him. We are bound together in the small activities of our daily lives, in the love we have for each other, in the eyes of our community and our family and friends, in our writing, in our coffee breaks and dreaming. We chatter like birds at each other every morning. And he has to tell me to settle down at night when I come to bed because I am so happy. He possesses all the good things my mother prayed for and one more thing, a love for humanity that makes me believe in miracles, and marriage.

A Love Story

Lee Montgomery

On the morning of Pearl Harbor Day, my husband, Thomas, sneaks about in the morning darkness. The tendons in his feet make hollow popping sounds as he tiptoes around the bed, kisses me, and whispers, "Happy anniversary." And then he's off to fetch coffee, his moon-white ass disappearing in shadow, the floorboards of our century-old Victorian creaking as he goes.

Tom loves to wander in the twilight of dawn. He discourages anything loud or light within an hour of rising. "Shhh," he insists. "My subconscious is wide open."

It is a difference we have, the way we take on the world each day. I like to launch myself into the day like a rocket, but over the years, I've learned to cherish the dark and quiet of morning, too.

This year marks twenty years of being married, but today, we are celebrating twenty-five years of sleeping together. We can't remember the actual date, so we marked Pearl Harbor Day as *the* day. An evening concert moved into a night of spectacular lovemaking, another morning, an afternoon hot tub with cognac, and another night at his house. Three days later, snowed in by a record-breaking blizzard, I was shipwrecked in a water bed and in love. We were in our early twenties, at the end of other relationships that had soured, which made our weekend escape even more lovely because it was unexpected. And because Tom knew my boyfriend Jack and I knew Tom's girlfriend Susan from our college days, our pairing was controversial enough to be otherworldly.

There are many qualities Tom and I share that keep us together: a flair for drama, a sense of humor, a desire for wild adventures, and a propensity for declaring holidays to celebrate us! We were married on Independence Day! We got together on the Day That Will Live in Infamy! And not long, we announced to friends and associates that we were also celebrating Twenty-Five Years of Fidelity! We even talked about throwing a party to celebrate! Pearl Harbor Day 2005! All Bets Are Off! Free At Last! Done! Over and Out!

We were too busy to arrange a party, and weeks later, I actually sat down and thought about it.

"Tom, I think it's actually twenty-four."

"Details!" he said. "I'll spot you a year or two for good behavior."

So we celebrated twenty-five anyway. Even though it was probably twenty-four, and more likely twenty-three, because we weren't exactly together as of that night. We broke up countless times in that first year or two. God knows I wasn't faithful. And Tom was having difficulty letting go of his psychotic girlfriend. I would wait while he listened to her whine on the telephone about God knows what. Our dates occasionally included emergency pit stops at her apartment, for example, when she lost her menstrual sponge. (*Guess where?*)

Jack, the boyfriend I had left, was swift and resolute in breaking it off. Even after five years of torturing one another. Even after he befriended my dearest friends, and slept with many of them, including prep school friends and childhood friends, he announced that he was devastated and refused to talk to me. A year or so later, we began talking again, which meant a series of stilted conversations every few years on his birthday, usually initiated by me calling his office because he asked that I not call his house because his wife was bummed out that I never talked to her. This was our course until about five years ago when late one hot summer night the phone rang. I lay in bed and listened for the answering machine. I was hoping it was Tom, who was away at a trade show, but when I heard Jack's voice, I picked it up.

"Is everything okay?" I asked. "You never call me."

"Sure," he said.

"Where are you?" I asked.

"In the backyard," he said. "Is it too late? Have I called too late? You used to go to bed so early."

"It's okay. Tom is out of town."

"I'm sitting in my backyard with a nice glass of Pinot," he said.

He then inhaled sharply, and I knew he was smoking. I had just quit and instantly missed the sensation, the awful smell, and the dull ache of smoke moving in and out of my lungs.

We ended up talking for hours. He had settled near where we had briefly lived when we were twenty. Now, that's where I saw him: sitting in an old-fashioned backyard chair made of woven nylon ribbon, surrounded by tall cement walls like the California I knew so well from decades before. The reason for the call, he finally admitted, was his marriage was over. His wife—the one who had forbidden me from calling the house, the one who periodically erased my name from his electronic organizer—had asked Jack for a divorce, and then left him home to stew alone for a few weeks while she took the kids to some exotic locale.

"That's terrible news," I said. "Are you sure?"

"I had an affair a while back," he said. "We never really recovered."

I went silent, mentally calculating the time of the affair. Was that, for example, the year I called to wish him a happy birthday and after his brief hello, he yelled, "How's *your* marriage?"

"You got caught," I said.

"I did," he said softly.

"Bummer," I said. "Can you beg?"

"It's too late. I even bought her a twelve-thousand-dollar diamond ring and proposed again. I actually bent to my fucking knees and asked her to marry me."

"She said no?"

"She said yes. Then, a few weeks later, changed her mind."

"Changed her mind?"

"And kept the ring . . ."

"Get out."

"She did." He laughed, but his voice was so hollow and sad, I imagined it rolling around the floor, darkly, like a marble.

"Shit. I hope the sex was good with whoever you had the affair with; I hope it was good enough for all this."

"No."

"No? No? Jesus! This is horrible."

"You don't understand," he said. "She is the type of woman who was born with a silver spoon in her mouth."

"Who?"

"Maryanne." The wife.

"How did you get caught?"

"Oh God."

"C'mon. That must have been some barnburner of a day."

"She wanted to get caught. Her husband sent a detective."

"In San Jose? Who is she?"

Jack told me a woman's name that I instantly forgot, a silly, puffy name like Sheila or Shirley.

I knew this scenario would never be my problem. No matter how I longed to have affairs, to be a wife who lived with a silver spoon in her mouth, a someone who might inspire others to hire private eyes, it wouldn't happen. It would never happen, because I am the type of woman who fails self-esteem tests posted on America Online, and had just recently bombed the "Are You Afraid of Success?" test posted on psychology.net.

"Can I call you again?" he asked.

"Surely?!"

"Not funny."

"It is too funny. It is very funny."

"It just has meant the world to me to be able to talk to you, to talk to anyone. Are you sure it's okay?"

"Yes, it's fine."

"But I don't want to cause any problems with Tom."

"Tom who?" I laughed. "No worries. He's cool. He is very cool. Besides," I added, "he's never home."

If Jack were to tell how we met thirty years ago, he might spin this romantic tale about demanding to be introduced at a party where there was a pool table. I was eighteen; he was twenty. I have absolutely no memory of this, but it's something he brings up in the e-mails he writes to me after our late-night conversations.

"You are the only woman I have ever *had* to meet," he writes. "You are my first true love."

I had loved Jack, but he was not my first true love. I began falling in love early in life. By the age of eighteen I had already had several boyfriends, some serious. So, Jack was a man I loved, but the one man I was never faithful to, a man I dumped three years into it with the utmost bitchiness because I was having an affair with my supervisor at work—a blond honey from Idaho ten years my senior. But a year or so after I dumped Jack, after he had slept with almost every best friend I had, and after the supervisor fling was over, we ended up living around the corner from one another in Boston. Being around him again, I convinced myself that I had made a mistake. Of course, he was not convinced. So we switched from the Torturer to the Tortured, and for a short time, I confused the game of longing for love.

There's not a lot I can remember from these days except what I wrote in my journals—mostly stories and bad poems, chronicling a wide range of embarrassingly bad behavior: screwing other boys, snorting drugs, having the time of my life, though I didn't quite know it then. Jack comprised a two-year obsession, and his torment provided great inspiration. Every time I tried to slip away with another fellow, Jack would profess his true love and I would come back. He then would sleep with his roommate, another good friend, or whomever. And we'd be off again.

During one of my side adventures, I had gotten pregnant. An ectopic pregnancy that nearly killed me. When I was in the hospital, Jack slipped into bed with me and according to my journal said, "Can you tell I've been thinking about nothing but you, and can't you see that I'm so very afraid to fall in love with you again because I am afraid you will leave?"

We got into therapy and slowly began to put it back together until Tom began sniffing around. Tom and Jack were friends, and I had suffered a long-distance crush on Tom for years. So when he called and innocently asked me to join him to see Ornette Coleman, I thought nothing of saying yes. Jack had been growing distant again. He had blown me off for dinner. He was going away for the weekend. He was probably sleeping with someone new, I told myself.

———— ✇ ————

I fell in love with Tom Byrnes so hard it took my breath away. I had never loved, nor will I ever love anyone as much. At the age of twenty-three, he was wildly exotic. He had worked his way through college as an ironworker. He climbed rocks, studied philosophy, and spoke Spanish. He had spent a year during college hitchhiking around the world. He wore knickers and 1940s ski pants. He was also drop-dead handsome with a smile that would make any girl swoon. But most of all, he was a kind, hysterically funny man, who bent his head down to talk to me. After decades, I look at him and cry. I cry because he is my best friend. I cry because no one has loved me as much, and I cry because this love is embedded in the smallest and simplest of things. I love to hear him sing. I love the way he dissects the Sunday *New York Times* the same way every week. I love to watch him do stupid things with our stupid dogs or accost strangers with their dogs on the sidewalk. "Hi, Killer," he yells. I love to watch him play with kids, flirt with my mother, or hold his own mother's hand. I love that he is a clothes horse, no apologies offered, and the fact that he studies catalogs full of English handmade shoes. I have had the best sex, the best love, with my husband, and friends often comment on how we are made for each other. They tell us that they don't know any other couple as dedicated or so in love. It's true, I think, but it doesn't mean it's true every minute of every day.

My second wife will not be a writer, he says.

My first wedding was my best, I say.

When people ask if we've ever considered divorce, we laugh, and quote some wise soul.

Divorce? Never. Homicide often.

We've had some dark days, but the light ones outnumber the dark.

The days that Jack returned to my life comprised some of the darkest.

The thing I noticed the morning after Jack's late-night call was a feeling of being disconnected. It was as though life suddenly slipped under water, where it slithered along the bottom of something, dreamily out of focus. I pulled out all my journals, and within an hour found this poem that beamed me back into the cloud of longing from that time, and it amazed me to touch it again, to be so completely transported by the girlish, fluish feeling of impossible love.

> *When I pack*
> *To go to the Laundromat.*
> *In the pouring down rain*
> *What I bring is carefully chosen*
> *(To stop time)*
> *Streetlights glow luminescent in a flat dark*
> *I sift through my change pile*
> *Lift the lint from the corners of the room*
> *The light of you*
> *Still.*
> In me
> > *(I don't know what love is)*

A few days later, I received an e-mail note thanking me for talking and reiterating again that the last thing he wanted was "to be the guy that after twenty years gets between you and Tom." Liar. He went on to tell me that he thought of me when a certain Joni Mitchell song played no matter who he was with or where he was. It was a welcome diversion. I had just entered the strange land of the forties. My father had just died. Tom and my efforts to have babies were bombing badly, and we were running out of options. We had just moved to Oregon from Topanga Canyon outside of Los Angeles, and Tom was traveling nonstop. If he made it home, which was rare, he was tired and crabby, and for months I had been dying of loneliness while Tom was consumed with himself and his airline miles. We were in the thralls of the bitter side of Eros. I hated him. And then? Poof! Here comes Jack, not as an illusion, but in full human sex-on-wheels form, still insisting I was the love of his life, still craving the attention of women he couldn't have, still obsessed with a particular piece of anatomy, a term that I could barely utter with a straight face.

"You call it a schnauzer?" I said one night over the phone. "I have a schnauzer, a real schnauzer, the dog."

He told me a joke about shaving the other schnauzer, and it all sounded so peculiar the whole thing flew out of my mind except the shaving part.

"I shave both," I lied, "on the same day of the month. It's like taking out the yard debris. I run around the house and say time to take out the trash! Time to shave the schnauzer!"

"You shave it?" he asked, whimpering, and then I felt the air between us grow heavy with wanting, and this was what I was beginning to again mistake as a positive and possibly transformative thing.

So, the slippery slope of phone calls and e-mails begin. We review the ins and outs, the ups and downs: the impossibility of us. The game is tantalizing: *Come here. Go away.* After we had reviewed everything ad nauseam, including the danger of reconnecting and the affair, we decided to be friends. Why not? If it were meant to be, it would have been. We're adults, right?

In service to this notion of friendship, I asked Jack to join Tom, me, and another college friend, Hannah, and her nine-year-old daughter Izzy for a long weekend skiing and boarding in Bend, Oregon. Hannah had lived in the same dormitory as Jack and I in 1976, and has been a close friend for just as long.

At first, Jack said no. He then said yes, then no, then yes. I rented the house and everything was all set until two days before we're to leave we received a telephone call from Tom's mother in Florida. Tom's father had suffered a mild stroke, and because of this, in a last-minute decision, Tom decided to go to Florida instead. He had recently dislocated his shoulder and was recovering from shoulder surgery, so he wouldn't have been able to board anyway.

"But, Tom, your father is okay," I say. "You sure you don't want to come and then pop down to Florida?"

"No time," he said.

"You should probably come," I said. "I would really like you to be there."

"I trust you," he said, smiling. "Why wouldn't I? You already made your decision."

The morning Jack, Hannah, Izzy, and I set out for our big ski adventure, I stood in front of a glass case of baked goods at Marsee's Baking Company, loading up for our drive from Portland to Bend. Jack came up beside me, smiled, and began surveying the pastries.

"Tom has been very nice to me," Jack said. Tom had picked up Jack at the airport, and they decided to hang out without me. By the time I arrived home, they were into their second bottle of expensive red and it was Lee who?

"I guess everything worked out for the best," he said.

"What is that supposed to mean?" I asked.

"What I said. It seems everything turned out for the best."

"I guess so," I said. "But I also guess we'll never really know."

I looked at him, still handsome with a big shit-eating grin, and found myself wanting to cry, which I finally did, over the three hours driving up to the mountain and for the rest of the afternoon skiing, and at lunch, into my clam chowder as Jack cried, too. It was late, so we sat alone in the restaurant at the top of the mountain. Outside, clouds of white air floated by in clumps.

"The thing is," Jack said. "Do me a favor. At least love the man for who he is."

Tears began to drip down his face. "That's all you have to do."

I know he was crying about his marriage, about not being accepted for who he is, and I, too, was crying about my marriage, but I was also crying about the enormity of life. I was at a turning point: absent husband, dead father, no children, and the path not taken. I could feel my face, cold and chapped; my nose was all stuffed . . . and for that teary instant I felt as if, peering down a long hallway, I could locate myself on the other side, elsewhere in time, at the beginning, where I saw all the doors wide open spilling splashes of light, and now, one step forward, one step backward, one step who knew where, I was on the other side, maybe in the middle, but not there: I was no longer at the beginning.

"The thing is I don't think I could have done anything differently. I wasn't capable of doing anything differently," I said. "As much as I loved you, I could have never married you and lived your life."

"That's what I mean," he said. "Everything turned out for the best."

Outside, the night was crisp and black and cold. I watched it descend through the windows as Jack moved in and out of the doors to the barbecue.

"Jesus, Jack, I'd marry you," Hannah said, looking at me. "We both would. Does that make a difference? Doesn't that make you feel better?"

"What?" he asked. He looked at us spread out on the couch, his wet hands suspended before him.

"We would both marry you," Hannah said.

"Great," he laughed. "Just what I need—two wives. You're kidding? I just got rid of one."

Hannah and I drank the good bottle of wine while watching Jack cook dinner. We watched him wash the lettuce and lay each long Romaine leaf lovingly on the counter and pat it with a clean dish towel. We watched him chop a colorful array of vegetables to grill. And we watched him prepare a marinade for the chicken out of chopped ginger and garlic and soy and sherry.

"I didn't know you could cook," I said.

"After twenty-five years, there's a lot you don't know."

"Like what else?" I asked.

"A lot," he said.

"Are you a homosexual? Did you kill your brother? What?"

He laughed.

"Well, that's a lot."

Hannah smiled, proud that I was flirting. We'd been having a long-running argument about fidelity after she had suggested, a few years earlier, that I should have an affair.

"It's not as if I don't agree with you," I had told her. "And it's not like I hadn't thought of it before, but having an affair just seems . . . well, complicated and unfair. It is just too complicated."

Seeing as Hannah had lived in Nicaragua for twenty years, been arrested at a post-shooting protest at Kent State, and was once married to a real Sandinista, politics had always been one of her favorite subjects. Over the last few years, however, since her divorce, her old arguments about communist principles, the militaristic/industrial complex, and imperialism had jumped to spirited discussions about free sex and monogamy; how it doesn't work, couldn't work.

"People are just not made to have the same sexual partners for life," she had said. "Name one monogamous relationship that works."

I couldn't think of one, except my own marriage, which didn't seem to be working so well anymore, since I'd been fairly miserable since moving to Oregon.

"Well, name an open marriage that works?" I countered.

Hannah was not only persuasive, beautiful, and fluent in Spanish, but also, as I had to remind myself, had new obsessions: She loved to sleep with other people's husbands. And other women, too.

"You're having a midlife crisis. Ever since you saw Frida Kahlo."

"My hero," Hannah swooned and then raised her hand in the air, smiling a big smile, both index fingers mindlessly picking the cuticles in her thumbs.

This kind of talk made me really uncomfortable, partly because my politics or philosophy had not yet led me on anything but a confused walk around the block.

"Don't be jealous," Hannah added.

Maybe that was the problem, I thought. *Maybe I was jealous.* Maybe all I really wanted was to sleep with women, speak Spanish, and go on wild sex tours of foreign dangerous lands—maybe even war zones—with handsome, middle-aged, married European cinematographers.

Later that night after dinner, after the hot tub, and Hannah and Izzy having gone to bed, Jack and I sat on leather couches on opposite corners of the room, talking in the darkness. Jack's long, slender body folded into the couch like a teenager's. He had little hair left and brown eyes that pooled into dark puddles. What was most surprising was that he had grown up to be surprisingly well dressed. Before this moment, I didn't know if I had ever seen him in anything but sneakers and an L.L.Bean 60/40 jacket.

"Would you give me a kiss?" he asked. "Just a little one?"

"A little one," I agreed.

We stood and moved together into the center of the room, and kissed until he pulled himself away.

"Not so fast," he said.

"Not so fast?" I repeated, confused. Here I had resisted, resisted, resisted, and when I couldn't resist anymore, this. "You look remarkably like the man who has been flicking his tongue at me for the last hour."

I pushed him away, and returned to my couch, circumventing any further possibility of infidelity, as if I had calmly taken all of it, the kiss, the history, the imaginary magnetic force, and placed it outside in the snow and left it there for the night and possibly forever. A moment later, I stood up quickly and left the room.

The next morning, I awoke to the muted reflective light of snow falling filling the room. After I pulled myself out of bed and put on the coffee, I walked around the perimeter of the great room looking out all the windows, one by one, stopping momentarily, opening and closing my eyes very quickly as if taking snapshots of the black spindly branches against a white sky. I wanted to call Tom, but my cell phone was not in range.

"Lee," Jack called.

"What?"

I stood at a window and continued to look out, amazed again at the deep color of winter, deliciously moody.

"Come visit."

A moment later, I stood in the doorway to his bedroom and then walked to the edge of the bed. He reached up to rub his eyes, and I instantly recognized that gesture from long ago. I knew other things about him. The way he crossed his feet under chairs and wiggled. The look he had when he was thinking about sex, his eyes always turning away, upward inside his head as if he was watching his own private movie.

I patted the blankets and pulled them up around his face, indicating that he should stay put as I climbed across the bed over the covers.

We lay facing each other, he on the inside of the covers, me on the outside.

"You stay there," I said.

The morning light scattered through the curtained window, fighting its way through an overcast winter sky. A little later, Hannah stood at the doorway eating a piece of toast, already dressed for the slopes.

"We didn't do a thing," I said, not moving. "Nothing."

"Just a little kiss," he said.

"That was your idea."

"I don't like to think about whose idea . . ." he said.

"That's 'cause it was your idea," I laughed. "You asked! You took it back. Now, if it were mine . . ."

Disgusted, Hannah turned and walked away.

I watched her go, looked around again, taking in the small condoish room, decorated as if, like me, the house was also stuck in a time warp: shag rug, perplexing print of a bedspread in happy colors.

I was glad we had stopped, but now as we lay talking, I wondered at what point lay dishonesty: wanting or doing.

By noon, it was snowing again. Jack and I left Hannah and Izzy in the base lodge and headed for the top of the mountain with the idea of skiing the backside looking for steep vertical and virgin snow. I have been a big skier since I was young, but Jack skied like an old man, bent over in the shape of a question mark. The snow fell softly, spreading silence like a blanket as we made our way down the back of the mountain, I following as he disappeared around corners and under hills. Sometime later that afternoon, he told me that he might have considered exploring a relationship with me again, if I wasn't married, but that he wasn't sure. We were covered in ski gear behind scarves and goggles, so everything seemed muffled and far away. I pulled up my goggles and turned to him.

"Not sure?" I said. "You called me."

"I needed a friend," he said.

"You have made our relationship impossible from the beginning. You did that, not me."

"What are you talking about?" he said. "You left me."

"But I came back."

"But you left me."

"I was like twenty-one, and I came back."

"You ran off with Tom when I asked you to marry me."

"After I waited around Boston for two fucking years while you slept with all my best friends."

"If you hadn't left me the first time," he said, "we wouldn't be in this predicament."

"That was over twenty years ago."

I grabbed and let go of his hands in one motion and stared at him.

"I'm not here to rekindle a romantic relationship," he said.

"Me neither," I said, waving my hands around. "But what do we do with all this?"

"With all what?" he asked.

"All this?" I spread my hands out into the air, and from the top of the chairlift on top of the mountain, I pointed to all that was hidden around us, behind the falling snow, all of it, the sky, the mountain, and everything that lay below.

"We let it rest," he said.

———— ❧ ————

A day or so later, after we returned home, me to the north in Oregon and he to the south in Northern California, he e-mailed pictures of his wife and family. I studied the photographs of his wife carefully to make sure it was as I suspected, that I was more beautiful in every way, but what I found was the opposite. She was beautiful and she stood on a mountaintop in the middle of what appeared to be a very happy family. I called Jack. "Wow, you look happy," I said. "She's beautiful. Can't you get her back?"

"I don't want to," he said. "I'm not attracted to her." Plus, he now had a new relationship with a woman who worked for him; she liked to mountain-bike, fly-fish, and even knew how to tie her own flies.

"Sounds perfect," I said. "I bet she screws like a rabbit, mends your shirts, makes breakfast, and mountain-bikes in a bikini, too!"

"What is that supposed to mean?" he asked.

"And the best part is you're the boss," I said. "Sounds great."

"Yes," he said. "It's very peaceful."

After we hung up, time passed quickly again, and our contact grew less and less frequent. Tom has always been characteristically quiet about my time away. He asked a few questions about snow conditions, but never indicated that he suspected any funny business. When I teased him about not caring, he always responded with, "Why should I? I trust you."

The weeks turned to months. One afternoon out of the blue, Jack called to say that he and Maryanne had reconciled. I didn't bring up all the stuff Jack had said about not loving her anymore. Instead, I listened to the long stories about Maryanne begging him back and falling in love again, his long stories about the broken-hearted fly-fishing fly-tying girlfriend, and a few little storylets about another woman who was hitting on him at his kids' soccer.

"She's only thirty-two!" he said, laughing. He then paused a moment, and whispered, "The thing is I could actually handle all of you."

"Fine by me," I said. "Why not?"

I listened to the air grow into just breath and saw the snow falling, and felt the silence of our time together, but didn't know yet what this was all about besides the frozen part, picking up parts of that girl I had left behind and moving forward. I once loved Jack deeply, but he is now just an old friend. Anything else has always been a game to distract me from doing the hard work of life and love.

"It seems like I'm always taking from you," he finally said. "What can I give you?"

I laughed. He was baiting me again, I knew, and I rolled the sentence around for a few minutes and thought about saying blow job–snow job ten times really fast, but said nothing. I couldn't think of a good answer, and whatever I said, I wanted it to be just right. I asked myself, what if this was the end of a movie? Then what? If we were in a movie, and this was the end, I might laugh a beautiful laugh and say something smart and cheerful. *But what exactly?*

"Just as long as you don't forget," I said. "I still have seniority."

"Aha!" he laughed. "How could I?"

But he did forget, and months later I complained to Tom. "Just because he returns to his wife doesn't mean he should stop calling me." A few weeks later, he finally called to check in. Tom picked up the phone.

"Hey, man! How are you?" Tom said excitedly. "Now, what's this I hear about you neglecting my wife?"

That was five years ago. Jack reconciled with his wife and then finally divorced. He's recently met a really wonderful lady and admits he might have fallen in love again.

"I would really like to find something like you have with Tom," he said.

———— ∞ ————

Tom and I met his new friend when we ventured down to San Francisco to help Jack celebrate his fiftieth birthday, and she is lovely. She may be The One. And still Jack and I continue to talk a few times a year, and every once in a while we play let's have an affair, allowing our conversations to swirl around the pros and cons. We never act on any of it nor do I imagine we ever will. We just like to talk about it. Our ideas for our rendezvous range from Let's go to Australia. Let's meet in Boston. Los Angeles?

"How about dinner?" I suggested once. "I'll be in San Francisco. Can we have dinner?"

Apparently not.

I am committed to full disclosure, so when I announce to Tom that I am still thinking about having an affair, he looks up from his paper and laughs.

"Whoof, whoof," he says. "You're all bark."

When I tell Jack about what Tom says about the bark part, he agrees. "Tom is probably right," he says.

Other old friends and flirtations wave their hands dismissively. "Right," they say.

Apparently affairs are for other people. Screw you all, I think. I could.

———— ∞ ————

Not too long ago, Tom and I received a call from our college asking us to share our love story for the college alumni bulletin. Alumni Relations had been contacting couples who came together at college and had stayed together. We never sent anything in, but we found the concept endlessly amusing. It provided fodder for a several-month-long live narration we called "The Love Narrative."

"This would be great for the love narrative," we would say.

"Put that in the love narrative," we cried.

"How do I write this into the love narrative?" I queried.

Tom is remarkably good natured about my trespasses, so much so I have often wondered the extent of his. He claims he's loyal, but he flirts mercilessly, and when I call him on it he refuses to admit it. I make it a point of telling him all my crushes, but he shares little. Every once in a while I'll catch him in a turn of the head, or overhear him mumble a simple declaration to a friend: *she's a hottie*. I haven't believed he was capable of having an affair, because he has claimed it is too damn complicated and that he can hardly deal with one woman in his life.

"That's right, honey," he says, using his tried-and-true strategy of aggressive agreement. "I only have eyes for you."

I make a note: *spouse is often disingenuous, prone to wild exaggeration*.

Truth is, knowing that I am writing this essay, Tom has been on excellent behavior, cooking dinner *and* delivering flowers to the office. But to his credit, Pearl Harbor Day's anniversary of twenty-five /twenty-four/twenty-three years happened months before any news of the essay. That morning, he arrives bare-assed with the coffee, the newspaper, and a little box. I'm immediately pissed because these celebrations have always been a ha-ha holiday, a holiday in spirit: We roll our eyes. We have dinner. But not today. Today Tom delivers a beautiful emerald ring. When I open the box, I begin to cry, and he takes my hand. "Dolly, when you look at this ring, I want you to think about how much I love you. I love you more and more each day. You are the best thing that ever happened to me. I couldn't live without you. I want you to know that. I love you, Lee."

And then he squishes his face all up like he is going to lose it.

100 Questions I Meant to Ask Him

Terry McMillan

1. I watched you on the *Oprah Winfrey Show*, and you said something I'd never heard you say before: that you were having sex with men during the last two years of our marriage. If I wanted to, I could hate you all over again for this, but my feeling is that you were the coward, and everything that has happened to you is a result of you being a liar and a cheater. It still breaks my heart to think that you were living two different lives for at least eight hundred days of our marriage. Do you think admitting this on nationwide TV made you look sympathetic?
2. Who was your first? Do you remember? How old were you?
3. Did you ever feel guilty or weird or ashamed about these feelings?
4. Did you ever tell anyone you had these feelings? If not, why not?
5. Do you feel the same kissing a man as you do a woman, or I should just say it—kissing me?
6. How different is it when a man gives you head versus when I gave it to you?
7. Have you ever swallowed? Do you like doing this? Why is it a turn-on?
8. I want to know how different it is penetrating a man's anus

versus a woman's vagina? Did you actually ever get any real pleasure having sex with me?

9. Why was it easier for you to give a man oral sex versus giving it to me, your wife?

10. Have you ever had an anal orgasm? What did it feel like?

11. Was it more fun having sex with men while we were married and you were sneaking, or is it better now that you are free to have it whenever you want?

12. How did you meet Vince? At the gym?

13. I know Vince has been in my Porsche. I want to know if he has been in my house. In my bed? Did you have sex with Vince at your shop? In the Navigator I bought you with the backseats that let down all the way?

14. Were you in love with him? All the times you "worked late" or called to tell me you were "going to the gym" were you meeting him (or the guy in Oakland, Steven)? And what about when you were just "checking" in with me to make sure I was at home? Was it so you didn't have to worry about any surprise "sandwiches for lunch"?

15. How could you have an affair with a man who was already in a long-term relationship? Didn't you ever feel cheap? Used? Like a sideshow?

16. Did you feel you finally outsmarted me the longer you were able to get away with juggling and living your double life?

17. Did Vince help you to despise me? Was he just jealous of me because I was your wife and I was a woman and I was pretty and black and rich and famous? Does he hate all women because he's jealous he isn't one?

18. Do you not see how good Vince probably felt in being able to pull you from me? Not just a woman, but your *wife*, and a famous one at that? You didn't see the underlying lure of this attraction? Or did you just think it was *all* you? Do you

remember what Reggie said in Chicago about how many married guys gay men can get? Were you surprised by this? Or did you not take the whole "married" thing seriously because in your heart you were only really married on paper and not really in your heart? Were you always really gay and the marriage to me just the longest detour ever?

19. Why do men like Vince try so hard to act like women, and why do men like you like them so much?

20. Did you think you could use your charm and good looks to woo Vince from his boyfriend? Were you pissed when it didn't work? *What* were you talking to Vince about on the phone thirty times a day, and how could you not see how desperate you were by calling him so much? Have you ever gone back and looked over your cell phone bills to see the real story they tell? A story about you and your neediness? You should. You really should. I hope you don't ever do this again with anybody. It was downright scary, Jonathan. I don't care what you talked about, there is no one in the world you should have to phone this many times a day unless they're dying. This is what you might want to share with a therapist. That neediness. This is why it freaked me out. If you still don't see this, you are still lying to yourself about a lot of important issues. You never showed that neediness to me and you supposedly *loved* me. Did you confuse neediness with charm? With love?

21. After we split up and Vince didn't leave his lover for you, didn't you feel like a fool? Were you hoping to move in with him after we split up? Or did my subpoena scare him? Make him feel that your relationship with him wasn't worth losing his job over? I bet. I hope so. Love isn't completely blind then is it?

22. What does loving someone mean to you?

23. Do you remember the slip of the tongue in the garage in

December 2004 when asked whether you'd seen Vince's AIDS tests and you said no, and I was so fucking pissed off by either your stupidity or your arrogance when I asked if you weren't worried, and you slipped and said, "Well, maybe just a li'l bit?"

24. Do you know that I have *not* forgotten you said this, as much as you continue to try to make me seem like I'm a little crazy when it comes to my memory?

25. I *know* you have had some unprotected sexual activity with Vince. Have there been others?

26. Have you had sex with more than one man at a time yet?

27. Did you have oral sex without a condom?

28. Have you had any sexually transmitted diseases?

29. I have had two Pap smears come back indicating some kind of sexual infection, like chlamydia. Can you explain this?

30. Do you know all of the men you've had sex with? Can you count them?

31. I remember all the times you got painstakingly dressed to kill for what you claimed were "dog shows" and the nights out clubbing with the guys where they played music you *knew* I didn't like. Did you not realize that I was "testing" you to see how far you were going to go? Did you not realize that every single time you came in from "the club" I was *always* awake?

32. Didn't it ever occur to you that what you were doing was *just wrong*? Gay or not—that you were cheating on your wife? And for two whole years (so you claim, but we now both know it was much longer than this)?

33. Did you ever worry about getting caught? Did you ever wonder what would happen if I caught you? Either finding evidence of your cheating or even catching you in the act. Is this part of the thrill and excitement that comes with sneaking? You had no shame. No remorse whatsoever for what you were doing

and when you were doing it. Was it more thrilling because it was like a game?

34. If only I had known, when your attitude toward me began to change, to sour, what you were doing, I could've saved myself a lot of unnecessary grief. You went off on me and called me a bitch after I gave away that amp and stereo stuff to Aaron and got irate when I asked you to put the top on my Porsche and said "fuck you" all up in my face in the bathroom. Do you realize if only you had been honest enough to accept who you were instead of using me to do all of this, you would not be in the position you're in today either? Hindsight is twenty-twenty vision for some of us, but not if you don't get it or learn from past mistakes.

35. Of course, now I know why you were always so understanding whenever I went to Tahoe or had all those professional obligations that took me away from home/you—because when my son wasn't here, you were free to be *your true self* and play and party as hard as you wanted, right? This made me an ideal wife, making it convenient and stress-free for you to cheat without the fear of being caught, wouldn't you say?

36. Why wouldn't the thought alone of hurting me be enough to stop you from cheating?

37. What if I had cheated on you, would you have been so quick to forgive me? And what if it was with a woman? A man?

38. Do you think cheating was okay just because *you* wanted to "test the sexual waters"? What made you feel so entitled?

39. Do you feel any guilt whatsoever for your promiscuous behavior, and for having used my life and our marriage as a playground for you to explore your sexual curiosity?

40. What will you do when you fall for a guy and he also decides to "test the waters" with someone else? Is living an open lifestyle

an acceptable part of an honest and caring relationship? Will sharing be okay then?

41. One day this will happen to you, Jonathan. It's almost guaranteed because God won't let you dish out this kind of behavior without seeing to it that you experience it firsthand. Will you realize then how deeply it hurts to be betrayed by someone you loved and treated so well?

42. Do you have any idea how important trust is in a relationship? Do you know that once a person realizes you are a liar that it is difficult, if not impossible, to ever regain their trust? Do you know how ugly a person is when they are known to be untrustworthy? Do you realize that millions of people may know that you were my husband and that you are handsome and now gay, but do you realize that these same millions also know that you are dishonest?

43. Is this how you want people you meet to perceive you?

44. Why does lying come so easily for you? And do you always think only about Jonathan whenever you do things that are immoral, unethical, or illegal? Do you see where your poor judgment has landed you? Do you not see it? Do you care?

45. Can you imagine what would have happened had the tables been *completely* reversed: that it was me who did *every single* thing you did (and have done), from the time you stole money from me, during each and every time you cheated, up to and including every single lie you told in your court documents and on TV about me? Do you have any idea how you might have felt upon discovering that your wife had managed to carry out this level and extent of ongoing betrayal and deception? Not just a weekend or two here and there, but *years of deceit*? Have you bothered to take the time to imagine this? If not, you should one night or one morning, just rewind the

"film" and stroll down memory lane. How warm and fuzzy do you think you'd feel toward me then?

46. I have been suspicious of your mannerism and your ease around gay men as well as the number of gay friends you've had for years, but it just never occurred to me that you were a practicing closet-homosexual, because it never really clicked that you could possibly do both: purportedly love and have sex with me, a woman, while simultaneously and secretly having sex with men. Do you remember in Tahoe when we watched the movie from the fifties with the married gay man, I watched your face when the wife opened that door and saw the two of them kissing. I think I knew then. How long were you planning to live a double life?

47. Do you remember in July of 2004, when we were broke, but you said you had such a deal on a hotel room in Las Vegas when I told you I wanted to go you almost jumped on me? You loudly expressed how you didn't want me to go because it was going to be your first trade show, and you wanted to experience it alone. I knew then that something was wrong, but it never occurred to me that you were cheating on me. I gave you more credit than you were due. I realize that after discovering you had stolen from me, I should never have trusted you in any capacity, none.

48. In the months of solo traveling, when you called me from Vegas with yet another "I'm broke" sob story, and then your South Beach thirtieth birthday, and Halloween with Jason in San Francisco, I now realize you were readying for your debut into the Gay Life, but it did not occur to me that you could possibly have already been active. This broke my heart, Jonathan, and I am still hoping that one day you experience this kind of betrayal and deception because don't you think you deserve to feel it, too?

49. Why are most gay men so gorgeous? There also seems to be a kind of narcissism inherent in your behavior because there is clearly an obsession with your looks, your bodies, and body parts? What is this about?

50. Have you been surprised by the promiscuous behavior of a lot of gay men? Are you going to be like this or are you already? Are orgasms and sex really *that* important? What about when it seems to overshadow genuine intimacy and committed long-term trust and love?

51. Why do so many gay magazines and books focus on cruising, bondage, sex: any-way-you-can-get-it, S&M, looks, beautiful bodies, etc., etc., with very little or no attention given to how to achieve or maintain healthy relationships? I'm not trying to stereotype or to be accusatory, but it seems like so much of gay life is physical—is it sex for sex's sake? How do you ever expect to have a "normal" (no pun intended) relationship if this is the focus?

52. Do you ever feel like a piece of meat in gay clubs?

53. How many times have you used E prior to having sex with a man?

54. What about crystal meth?

55. How do you expect me to believe that you're so "shy" when it comes to having sex with men? Don't you drop your guard when you're out cruising? How do you expect me to believe that you're still "finding your way"?

56. I know you had sex with Nigel, and I know you did it in this house. I know that Nigel may have been your first "queenie," and I want to know how many of your so-called straight friends are actually gay? Like Frank and Ricky?

57. Oh, and please tell Vince that if I ever meet him I want to see what an Italian dick looks like. Would he show it to me?

58. If you married a man could you be faithful to him? He to you?

59. Do you know that even though I've forgiven you for what you've done, that it breaks my heart and actually makes me nauseous thinking of you even kissing a man?

60. What was it about me that you liked?

61. What was it about me that made you feel like you loved me?

62. Why did you have such disdain (hatred) for me?

63. How did you expect me to react when you told me you were gay?

64. You didn't really think of me as a homophobe because I called you all of the "F" words I could, did you? Don't you understand that this was the only weapon I had?

65. You used your sexuality as a weapon to hurt me after I asked you to look for another place to live, do you not see this?

66. Once you knew I was serious about pursuing divorce proceedings do you realize that you resented me even more because you knew your power (fooling and misleading and manipulating and lying and taking advantage of) over me was about to come to an abrupt end? Is this what really pissed you off and is it why you decided to "out" yourself to me, and not because I was badgering you for answers?

67. If I had been badgering you so much, why did you spend the last two years (as you claim) cheating when you could have left, especially if you were so miserable? I know you stuck it out until your citizenship was in the bag, I don't care what bullshit excuses you keep trying to come up with, when it's soooo obvious . . . but what's done is done.

68. Despite the "last two years" claim of being with men, I now know it was throughout our marriage. I know when you made trips to Miami and when you came to NYC to visit me and whenever you went back to Jamaica and to England and whenever you saw Nigel. I even know now when you were cruising when you were with me: at concerts, standing tall so

you could "eye" them right over my shoulders—which is why and how I started noticing gay men checking you out. Little did I know that it was a two-way street. I wonder when you're ever going to tell the truth about any of this carefully orchestrated, hidden pack of lies you've been telling yourself, and me, for years.

69. Have you always known you were gay?

70. Do you really expect me to believe that you lied to me in order to keep the peace? That's lame.

71. You lied to the IRS and the INS; what kind of peace were you trying to keep with them?

72. Now that this is all over, can you see how your lies have backfired on you? You have pretty much what you came here with: nothing. No credit. In fact, your credit is tarnished forever in this country, and for the next seven years, it's ruined. You can't even get your mother a green card. You are renting a room from someone who was initially a stranger. You have lost a perfectly profitable business. You have intentionally hurt me by the manner in which you dismantled the business. And after all the lies you and your lawyer told about me, she ended up with $27,000 and you ended up with not much more. Do you not see this as karma?

73. Do you not realize that most of this could have been avoided had you had some foresight and handled this with some compassion and dignity?

74. Do you realize how much trouble you've gotten yourself into, not just because of your "dick" but because of what I'd call bad character traits?

75. Even though I haven't exactly forgiven you for what you've done, I won't hold on to the anger and hurt you caused me forever. Do you realize that I am not getting any satisfaction from knowing how bad off you are financially and otherwise?

76. Do you know that I do not believe anything you've told me about your so-called sexual activity and your relationship with Vince? That it's over. That it was mutual. If you are still seeing him, off and on, I feel sorry for you. Are you more stupid than I ever dreamed you capable?

77. Do you not see that both of you were cheaters? Were you proud of that?

78. I would not go out with someone who was cheating on his wife, under any circumstances; does this make me prudish in your eyes?

79. Most women in general, and just about all of the women I know, have never cheated on their boyfriends and/or husbands. What is it about men and their dicks that makes it so easy for you guys to do it (straight or gay, it's all the same, obviously) and to actually "justify" it and, in many cases, to even talk your way back into our lives?

80. Do you think you'd ever go out with another woman?

81. Do you think you could be bisexual?

82. Do you miss me?

83. What is it that you miss most? Me or our "lifestyle"?

84. Do you envy me?

85. Are you aware that I am not unhappy? Do you wish I was miserable without you?

86. You can see that I'm moving on with my life; do you think I'm trying to "throw it in your face" or that I just want you to know that this is what is happening with me? (Both may actually be true, but I'm not sure yet—too soon to tell.)

87. Do you believe that I truly hope you find happiness?

88. I'll answer that for you: the answer is yes, but it's a conditional "yes"—because I would like you to discover what inner happiness feels like without fucking anything or anybody to the point where you feel good about being Jonathan Plum-

mer, because you have expunged yourself and exorcised all the horrible traits you've managed to use to get what you want. It should be clear, fame and attention will not get you to happiness, and if you don't stop long enough to grow up and to accept responsibility for what you do, and think about your future in concrete terms, and make smart and well-thought-out plans and goals that don't include using people, then you will never be happy for any length of time. Chances are you will one day experience pain and heartache and disappointment and misery to a far greater degree than what you're experiencing right now. Do you not see this?

89. What have you learned as a result of all that has happened in the past year?

90. What have you learned from me in the ten years we were together?

91. What did I ever do to disappoint you? Hurt you?

92. Did you appreciate the way I loved you?

93. And I don't hate you. Are you glad?

94. Did you ever once consider the impact all of this would have on Solomon? He is not a toddler, and he has had to face a lot of unnecessary things because of you. Since this is pretty much a done deal now, have you thought about apologizing to him personally? If not, it would be a major step in the right direction. And for the record, he doesn't hate you either, but like me, he hated what you tried to do to me. He sees that he has "his mother back" and that I'm moving forward with my life. So is he. He graduates in June.

95. What do you want me to do for you now?

96. What do you want from me now that we're divorced?

97. Can you imagine your life without me in it?

98. If you could do any of the past ten years over—up to this very minute—what would you do differently?

99. You thought if I gained a bit of weight or looked worse for the wear, that it would mean that I missed you. It has not happened. You on the other hand have gained weight, and your six-pack is gone. You actually have a little paunch. Do you think this makes me feel good? Unfortunately, the answer to this question is a yes, but not for the reasons you think.

100. Does the fact that I don't want to have sex with you make you think that I no longer love or desire you? And if the answer is yes, then you are wrong. Sometimes we love the wrong people. Sometimes what we see in a person is what we want to see, not necessarily what's there. At this point, having sex with you would not add anything to our romantic repertoire; it would not prove anything except that you still feel like magic, but that the magic is gone and so is the magician. These are ten years of my life that will forever be inscribed in the social history books when all I had hoped for was to be able to express and experience love so intensely and so fiercely and honestly that the rawness and beauty of our lives meeting and merging would make us feel so free inside that our joy, our happiness, the calmness of our euphoria would help us to evolve as better, more caring, more civil, more compassionate human beings, and as a result, the thick clouds of all of this goodness would permeate out into the world and maybe others might one day be so lucky as to feel it, too. We hit some of the right notes, and almost made the symphony rock. Maybe next time we might both be even more fortunate and achieve the *emotional* orgasms we both crave. I'm still a believer. How about that? How about you?

A Real Catch

Isabel Rose

July 4, 2002—Bridgehampton

I'm sitting on the deck an hour after everyone has left, realizing that my marriage needs to end. I don't understand what ending the marriage actually means, but I know we can no longer go on this way. It's been too hard for too long. I'm drained. I'm sad. I'm lonely, and my husband is just on the other side of the screen door, sleeping on the sofa we bought together with mad excitement at Ikea right after we bought the house. On his chest, our eleven-month-old daughter drools in her half-sleep.

The day passed me by, and I never located a feeling of happiness despite our thirty guests and the success of the summer corn salad that we made using fresh corn instead of canned; despite the fact that I apologized for buying toilet paper my husband felt was too expensive because I got it at the pricey Country Market instead of at the Kmart farther from the house; despite the fact that we finally got the grill to work—it was way too late by the time the grill started to work. By then the tension had corroded the sentiment with which I gave the grill to him for his first Father's Day. The guests were due in less than an hour, and he had already cut himself off from me in an impregnable fortress of smoldering silence.

Red Flag #1, April 1995—Manhattan

One of my girlfriends leaves a message on my machine Saturday evening at six. "A bunch of us are meeting at that new bar in SoHo at nine-thirty. It's gonna be a great group. See you then." I've already planned a night of order-in Chinese food and *Middlemarch*, which I have to read for graduate school. I roll my eyes at the message and go ahead with my original plan, but at 9:45 I overcome my innate inertia and force myself out. It's a Saturday night. I remind myself that most people who are twenty-seven and single are going out tonight, too. I remind myself that the girlfriend who left the message works on Wall Street and parties with a pretty sharp crowd. I guzzle down a cup of instant coffee and head out into a chilly, late April night wearing just enough makeup to look good but not enough to look like I care.

My future ex-husband is sitting at a long, candlelit table, chatting with a few other guys. He looks familiar. Really. Over the din of the hip bar, I say, "You look familiar. Really. Have we met before?" and then I realize that actually he just looks like someone who works in my sister's office. I'm about to tell him this, but he says, "You're right. We *have* met. It was last summer in the Hamptons," and he recalls a Friday night in August when I stopped into a restaurant in Bridgehampton to say hello to some guy I was interested in. It turns out, that guy was in a share house with my future ex-husband who was also at the table that night with a date—a woman I chatted with for a few minutes since we had both gone to the same summer camp as girls.

We're both elated by the truth of my allegation and by his phenomenal memory and launch into a giddy conversation in which we try to discover every person we know in common.

"It would be Jewish geography if you were Jewish," I say, sure he's not Jewish because of his hard-cut features, steely blue eyes, and sandy hair that I imagine was platinum in his class picture from nursery school.

"Who says I'm not Jewish?" he challenges in a playfully arrogant tone I will become all too familiar with years later when the playfulness is long gone. "Swedish mom, Jewish dad," he smiles, and he launches into the *shehechianu*, a Hebrew prayer said to thank God for bringing us to the present moment.

We laugh in the way two single people in their late twenties do when they have met someone they might sleep with soon. It's an intimate laugh, a laugh that says we're part of the same club; we can trust each other; we speak the same slang. His whole face lights up when he smiles, and his eyes sparkle intelligently beneath his round, tortoise-shell-rimmed glasses.

At midnight the group moves on to another bar. We go, too, talking the entire time. We talk while everyone else dances. We talk while everyone else does tequila shots. We talk while others smoke cigarettes or slip outside to share a joint. Neither of us drinks more than beer. I alternate between beer and seltzer, and there is a clear admiration for each other's discipline.

We talk about everything that isn't too personal: politics, sports, our favorite music from the '80s. He seems to be an expert on every topic, which I find sexy. He isn't what I think of as my type, but he's definitely cute with his impossibly straight Nordic nose and orthodontically perfected smile. I decide it's time to explore a new type.

I'm on the treadmill the next morning listening to Gloria Estefan sing "Everlasting Love" and sweatily fantasizing about my future ex-husband, when the girl who got us together the previous night gets on the treadmill next to mine.

"I really like your friend," I gush.

She looks shocked and says, "You two? *Ew*. You're completely wrong for each other. I seriously do not recommend anything. Please. Trust me. You two are the most wrong for each other people I can think of."

I laugh, mostly at her clear ignorance of his true character, and ask why she thinks we're so mismatched.

"Trust me," she says gravely. "He's not for you." Then she shrugs and adds, "Hey. It's your life, babe, but I don't think you'll be happy."

Red Flag #2, July 1995

One of my friends has a rule: If you don't kiss by the third date, there's no real chemistry. My future ex-husband and I don't kiss until the third month.

Red Flag #3, August 1995

We're walking down the street on our way to dinner and I ask him a question that he ignores. I repeat the question and he still ignores me. I say, "Can you hear me?" and he says, "Huh?" I decide he must be preoccupied and drop it.

After dinner we go to the movies. While waiting for it to start I ask him if he thinks Jennifer Lopez is attractive. He ignores me. I repeat the question and he still ignores me.

I ask him, "Are you going deaf, or are you just ignoring me?"

"I don't like to answer dumb questions," he says. Then he adds, "There's nothing wrong with silence. Sometimes I think you say things just to hear the sound of your own voice. I'm sure you don't really care what I think of Jennifer Lopez. It's just not relevant. It's all right for two people to be together without talking."

"Actually, it's boring," I want to say. Actually, silence frightens me. Actually, *his* silence, in particular, frightens me because it makes me feel isolated and depressed. Actually, I'd rather sit in shit than sit in silence with him unless we're in temple, out in nature, holding hands, reading together, or sleeping. When he goes silent, I stop feeling him; it's as if he becomes a sudden stranger.

I wish I knew how to communicate this. Instead I tell him I actually *do* want to know what he thinks of Jennifer Lopez, but before he can either respond or continue to ignore me, the lights dim and the previews start. I decide to break up with him well before the main feature begins, but by the time it ends, I decide to let the whole thing go because it's a complex thriller and I need him to explain it to me. Besides, we just came home from a lovely hiking trip in Germany, and I don't want to spoil things now that I've told all my friends what a great time we had.

Red Flag #4, May 1996—Paris

We have a lovely day and a lovely evening that concludes at a lovely restaurant, which he pays for, and then we get back to our lovely hotel room and get in bed.

With the lights out I whisper, "Did you forget something?"

He says, "What do you mean?"

Against my better judgment, I say, "A card? A present? I don't know. Something. It's my birthday."

After a pause he says, "*I'm* your present."

I begin to sulk. I know it's childish, this desire to receive a gift, but it's who I am and who he isn't, and he knew long in advance that today is my birthday. I think about saying to him, "*You're* my present and *I'm* your ex-girlfriend," but instead I kiss him good night and tell him I'm too tired to make love, and I lie there feeling bitter because my sister's husband lavishes her with gifts, and in comparison I feel like I come out in second place. I beg myself in silent self-recrimination not to compare myself to my sister, but I can't control it. Like some insidious germ, it worms its way into my mind and heart, releasing a poisonous cocktail of hurt, anger, and disappointment. *He paid for dinner*, I repeat to myself like a silent mantra, but it doesn't assuage my resentment. *I'm spoiled*, I tell myself as sleep evades me. *I'm just lucky to have someone to go to Paris with; I'm lucky to have landed such a brilliant boyfriend; I'm just . . .*

I'm just miserable for some reason; a reason that I begin to doubt even has to do with the issue of a gift. I try to crack open the egg of my dismay to examine its yolk, but the shell is too hard or perhaps my efforts are too weak. Either way, the reason for my sadness is as elusive as the sleep for which I now yearn. After tossing and turning for a cranky hour, I take a Tylenol Nighttime and let *it* put me out of my misery instead of finding a more natural solution.

Red Flag #5, July 1996—the Hamptons

We're in the car on our way to a cocktail party discussing our goals for the relationship.

"I just want to get to a place with someone where I can coast," he says.

I say, "Coast? What do you mean, 'coast'?"

He says, "You know, not go from crisis to crisis. Just kind of exist together."

I say, "But you can never coast. You have to always evolve, always work on it. You have to struggle through tough moments and hold tight during the good ones. *Sometimes* you can coast, but you can't *get to a place and then coast.*"

I think about what it means to coast—no pedaling, no work. It sounds appealing but profoundly boring. I shudder, although I do think it would be nice not to clash as often as we do.

He says, "You've misunderstood me. Of course I think you need to evolve. I just mean not everything has to be such a struggle."

I say, "I agree," but for the rest of our relationship I will remember that word, *coast,* and every time he avoids an argument or refuses to discuss something with me, it will pinch me in the side or jab me in the ribs and I will think, Why didn't I coast out while I could?

Red Flag #6, August 1996—Bavaria

We're on another hiking trip in the Alps. We wake up early because we've planned a big trek, but it's raining out and cold so I get back in bed, relieved. In my heart of hearts I'm not a true mountaineer, I'm a Jewish girl from the Upper East Side who went on a few hiking trips at camp. I'm trying hard to please my man; still, there are limits, and hiking in the rain is one of them.

"It's clearing up," my boyfriend says, standing eagerly by the window. "Look." He points to a piece of sky in the distance that resembles every other piece of sky on the horizon: gray and menacing.

We head onto the trail, and for the first hour, there's just a light drizzle that nevertheless turns my skin to gooseflesh. Then the rain picks up.

"We should be getting close to Grindelwald," my boyfriend says.

But we aren't close at all. Another torrential hour goes by, and now I'm not only wet and increasingly freezing, but I also really need to pee. I try to undo my shorts, but my fingers are frozen. He undoes them for me like a nanny, and I squat down on the trail, too cold to look for better shelter. A wild waterfall of rain slides off my back and ass and soaks my shorts and underpants. I don't care. I'm trembling with cold. As my boyfriend buttons my shorts back up, I wonder if they'll have to amputate my frostbitten fingers.

The rain gets worse, and the trail becomes vague. I notice that there actually is no trail. I notice that we're lost. We're lost in the middle of the Alps. I've seen enough TV specials to know that this is not good. I suggest to my boyfriend—who takes great pride in his navigation skills—that I think we may be lost.

"We're not lost," he says, pointing down a rocky ravine. "There's the trail, right down there. Let's just traverse the hillside."

"Good thinking," I say.

Traverse the hillside??!

I watch him first, the way he digs in with the front of his boot with his body almost flat against the steep mountain. He's smiling with the joy of the challenge, the star of his own reality TV show: *Adventure in the Alps*. With mud gushing all around me, I follow closely behind him. My legs are just beginning to shake uncontrollably when we regain the trail.

After another silent hour, during which time I understand fully the difference between a Yale grad with a focus in theater and a Dartmouth grad who went out for the ski team, I notice the brook just below us has become so swollen that it is now a rushing river. I see whole enormous tree branches being carried away in it.

"There it is," my boyfriend says proudly. "Grindelwald. We've reached the halfway point."

When we get back to the hotel room, I throw myself on my side of the bed and turn my traumatized body away from him.

"Wasn't that awesome?" he says, spooning me. "You did great! I'm so proud of you."

I attempt a comment but fail to deliver. He gives me a little squeeze, and I wonder if he wants to make love, but moments later his grip on me loosens and he begins to rhythmically snore ever so faintly.

I close my eyes but don't fall asleep. *Why am I doing this?* I ask myself. *Why am I here?* Is it to prove to myself that I can keep up with an earthy, unspoiled guy? Is it to prove to myself that I can push my body to its limits? Or is it because I'm desperately trying to land a ring on my finger before my thirtieth birthday? Perhaps a little of each, I decide, or a lot of each, depending on how I'm calibrating things. Either way, I'm clearly somewhere I don't belong, doing something I shouldn't be doing, with someone I shouldn't be with.

Red Flag #7, January 1997—Greenwich Village

We're living together now, and it's Friday night and my boyfriend calls to say he'll be home around seven. Seven comes and goes and eight o'clock stares me in the face. I leave messages on his cell phone, but they go unanswered. I order in Chinese food even though we had tentative plans with another couple, and hunker down in a chair with a book and my anger to wait.

He comes home at ten, drunk and defensive.

"Why didn't you call?" I demand.

He tells me to stop pestering him and claims he lost track of time and didn't know he has to report in to me every time he wants to grab a beer with a buddy.

"You do," I say. "You do because I sat here waiting for you and worrying about you and you need to be considerate of me because I'm the woman you live with."

He rolls his eyes and turns on the TV.

I'm staggered by his rudeness and can't understand how he can fail to see his behavior as such. To compound things, he falls asleep on the couch in a pattern that has become a routine. Wasn't the point of living together to get in bed beside each other every night?

"It's time for bed," I say, pulling him up. "Let's go. *Up.*" And like a petulant four-year-old being dragged by his mother, he follows me into our bedroom.

Red Flag #8, April 1997—West Virginia

I'm sitting at breakfast in an ornately decorated dining room listening to the Head of Banking address the "spouses/significant others" of the Managing Directors who are currently at a business meeting. There are roughly two hundred women in the room and one man.

"Please be understanding when your husbands, wives, or boyfriends come home late," the Head of Banking says, "even if it's two in the morning and they've been at a gentlemen's club. It's just a work thing, ladies. Nothing to get alarmed about."

There's a smattering of giggles from the audience. The Head of Banking is pleased with himself and smiles, too.

"Please be understanding if they're playing golf all weekend. Conversation is highly overrated. Believe me."

There is another smattering of laughter and the Head of Banking places a *New Yorker* cartoon on an overhead projector that shows a couple: the man in a tie, carrying a briefcase, checking his Palm Pilot; his wife, in a headband and pearls, pushing a stroller while simultaneously holding the hand of a toddler and trying to get his attention. The line beneath the drawing reads, *Do you have any openings next month for a family dinner?*

I turn to the woman on my right, a slender brunette about my age with a giant diamond on her finger, and whisper, "Do you think this is funny?"

She whispers back, "Well, it certainly does hit the nail on the head."

The Head of Banking continues: "Become your own community, ladies. Support each other. Get your nails done together. Take your speed walks together. Have a girls' night out. Because we consider the work that you do on the home front to be as important to the success of the firm as the work your spouses are doing for us."

I whisper to the woman on my right, who eerily resembles the woman in the *New Yorker* cartoon, "This whale bone corset is really digging into my rib cage."

She looks at me like I'm from Mars and whispers, "Pardon?"

I shake my head and apologize for disturbing the speech and instantly emulate her attentive pose, hopeful that it will enable me to better appreciate the message from the Head of Banking. It doesn't. It only makes my neck stiff.

After our talk from the Head of Banking I return to our plush, pink, green, and gold room. I'm scheduled for a massage after lunch and tennis at four. I take my suitcase out of the closet where the chambermaid stored it and start to pack all the outfits I put in so carefully the day before: the cocktail dress for the semiformal Friday-night dinner, the tennis skirt, the gown for tonight's black-tie ball, the bathing suit for the whirlpool my boyfriend and I hoped to soak in together. I'm collecting my toiletries when he comes in and asks what I'm doing. "Going home," I tell him. "This isn't for me."

He tells me to calm down, and I tell him about the lecture from the Head of Banking. "The Head of Banking is a moron," he says. "He has nothing to do with us and you have nothing to do with anyone else who was in that room. Ignore it. It's bullshit. He was just trying to be nice." There's a stare-down. Then he says, "Besides, what are you going to do? Hail a cab? We're in rural West Virginia."

He has a point. He has several points. And suddenly I regret my reactionary hotheadedness that now seems to have been ignited by the sparks of identification with the other women in the room as opposed to my ostensive assurance of our differences. My boyfriend is right. He's usually right. He's a real individual, and I'm too easily swayed by group opinion. I thank him for helping me be a better person. I thank him for helping me recover my sense of humor. I make a joke about the Head of Banking and he laughs, and I paint on a fresh coat of lip gloss, brush out my hair, and out we go to meet the others in the Orchid Room for lunch.

Red Flag #9, June 1997—Union Square

I have a drink with my ex-boyfriend, a fellow writer, who asks if my current boyfriend is my soul mate.

"Definitely not," I answer flatly.

"Does he understand you?" my ex-boyfriend asks, alarmed. "Does he get that you're an artist?"

"He doesn't understand me at all," I explain. "But I feel protected by that. I feel like he'll never be able to mess with my creativity if he doesn't even get it."

My ex-boyfriend gives me a reprimanding look that melts into sympathy. Then he says, "*You* know what you want for yourself. I just hope you're not with this guy because you think you should be."

That night I flip through the pages of Edith Wharton's *The Age of Innocence*. When the main character marries the boring-but-appropriate May Welland instead of following his heart and running off with his soul mate, the scandal-ridden divorcée, Ellen Olenska, I cry so hard I'm unable to join my boyfriend for a business dinner. I tell him I'm coming down with something, climb under the covers, and sob myself to sleep.

Red Flag #10, August 1997

I'm no longer interested in sex. It's been weeks now, maybe months. I'm depressed because my boyfriend hasn't asked me to marry him yet and we've been together for more than two years, and I'm depressed because he might ask me to marry him and I know we aren't right for each other. Everyone else in our social circle has gotten married. I've even caught the bouquet a few times. My thirtieth birthday is looming. I'm paralyzed with fear.

The Reasons I Ignore the Red Flags

I ignore the red flags because I really want to get married. I want it to be *my* turn to try on the wedding dresses I see in the window at Vera Wang every time I pass by. I want to *register*, whatever that is. I want to have a reason to buy all those lovely bride's magazines, especially the Martha Stewart wedding issue, which always features the most gorgeous floral bouquet or wedding cake on the cover.

I ignore the red flags because I'm terrible at math and my boyfriend is a math genius. He also has a great sense of direction, and I have no sense of direction whatsoever. I get giddy when I think of all the genetic gaps I'm going to fill. What's more, he can skip a stone across the water, drive stick, work a grill, make a fire; he appreciates the smell of honeysuckle; he loves the Hamptons and knows all the back roads; he thinks ahead, he thinks calmly, he thinks in a linear progression, while I live in the moment, get overwhelmed easily, and think free-associatively. And let's face it: it would never even *occur* to me to scale a mountain.

And then there's the fact that he knows the difference between a Bordeaux, a Burgundy, a Merlot, and a Syrah; he's admired by his co-workers and gets invited on golf outings and dinners at impressively beautiful places and sometimes I get to come along; he's read more fiction and nonfiction than I and often suggests great books to read; when the sink broke in our country house, he got beneath it, creepy as it is down there, and fixed it himself; he runs twenty miles at a time and still has energy to go to a nice dinner and out to the movies; many of his friends are interesting and fun; he's Jewish even if his mom does throw a Swedish Christmas party every year.

And of course, we've invested a lot of time getting to know each other, and my mother keeps nagging me, "When is he going to propose?"

Have I mentioned that I really want to get married?

Let me share a small fact that I like to pretend didn't affect me: For my twenty-fourth birthday, one of my aunts gave me the gift of my horoscope being done by one of the leaders in the horoscope industry. Despite a profusion of great attributes and predictions for my future, the guy also said—and please notice the quotes—"Bad luck for you in the house of marriage and relationships."

There is *no way* I will let this prediction be right. Mind you, I know it's just a horoscope. I know there is no validity to it. I know I'm a fool for letting it affect one millisecond of my life. But it does. I won't lie. It has haunted me through my twenties. And I am going to disprove it by getting married.

And I *will* get married. I'm a Taurus. We're a very stubborn, determined bunch.

October 1997—Kent, Connecticut

The suspense is killing me. Will he ask me? If so, when? Should I get a manicure once a week, just in case? Should I wear makeup before I leave the house in the event that we'll want to take a picture to document the moment?

On a magnificent Saturday in early October, my boyfriend suggests we go for a hike. It sounds like a nice way to liberate myself from the prison of engagement anxiety. I throw on some boots and army fatigues and a ratty old T-shirt and we set off in the car for Kent, Connecticut, where the leaves are apparently at their peak.

Once you know about the little white blazes, the Appalachian Trail stops being a mystery and becomes something you think of as your friend. "There it is!" I shout as we round a bend in the road. We pull over and park on the side of the road near a telephone pole and plunge into the sweet-smelling otherworld of the woods.

We get to a clearing high up with a beautiful view. Another couple is already there. "It's the height of fall foliage season today," they tell us. They've just finished a picnic and show us a blow-up pillow and explain that they will now take a nap. My boyfriend becomes agitated and suggests we walk farther. I begin to complain. I don't want to walk farther. I'm tired and sweaty and feel we've gone far enough. But something in the urgency of his tone makes me relent, so off we go, into a beautiful, leafy glade.

We stop for a moment while my boyfriend appears to be tying his boot. He isn't. He's getting on one knee. I begin to laugh. This seems ridiculous. But I bite the inside of my cheek and warn myself that a man is about to propose and I better shut up and let it happen.

My boyfriend tells me he wants to climb all of life's mountains with me—the real ones and the metaphorical ones—and will I marry him? I laugh and apologize for complaining. He says that isn't an answer to his question and asks me again if I'll marry him.

I say, "Of course!" and he laughs with joy and relief. I wish I could feel some kind of honest thrill, but I don't. I'm not entirely sure I feel anything other than a sense that the whole thing is a little silly. I'm aware that we are going through a ritual, but it seems remarkably phony to me. I feel like I'm in a play about getting engaged rather than in my own life. I think it's sweet that he came up with such a lovely sentence, but telling him that seems too academic so I keep it to myself.

The next thing I know, he's taking a diamond ring out of his back pocket. It's gorgeous. I love it. (Of course I love it. It's the ring I designed myself. I designed it myself and then I left a piece of paper with the jeweler's number on top of his briefcase one morning while he was in the bathroom.) I tell him it's magnificent and slip it onto my finger—which, of course, it fits since I tried on countless little ring samples until I found the perfect one.

My boyfriend, now fiancé, pulls two plastic cups and a demi-bottle of champagne out of his fanny pack, and I love him for his resourcefulness and feel more reassured that I've just agreed to become his wife. He pops the cork and sets the camera on a rock, and we take a self-timed picture of ourselves smiling and clinking glasses. The setting is exquisite. We couldn't look happier in the picture. So why is it, when he pulls a cell phone out moments later and says, "I thought you might want to call your mother," I feel like I will share the news right away so she can stop bothering me about when I'll be getting engaged rather than sharing the news because I'm so happy?

The Engagement

I become both obsessed with planning my wedding and disgusted with the entire process almost immediately. I get heartburn. I have insomnia. You can see my rib cage I get so thin. There is terrible tension between us. My parents beg me to postpone the wedding. I won't. All of my Christofle silver has arrived, and I don't want to return it. I want to get to the other side of this wedding so my fiancé and I can resume our calm lives. I try to remember: did we have calm lives before? I have no clear recollection.

The Wedding, June 1998—the Plaza Hotel

I don't like my dress. It weighs eight hundred pounds, and I can barely move in it. It feels symbolic of the life I am signing on to: the life of an indentured servant, the life of a banker's wife. I cry during the ceremony. (Everyone thinks it's because I'm so moved by love, but I can tell you now it was out of pure terror.) My fiancé starts swaying while the rabbi recites the seven blessings. He told me earlier that day if you think you're going to faint, a good way to keep yourself conscious is to sway back and forth on the balls of your feet. I can see him fighting to remain erect through the recitation, but he clearly almost goes down while the cantor takes his time singing the seven blessings in Hebrew. I regret having the cantor *and* the rabbi. The seven blessings somehow feel like seventy. They're endless. They give me too much time to reflect on what's happening.

What's happening is that I'm not happy with the white carpet they put down so I could walk down the aisle on a white runner. It has wool loops in it, and they kept catching the heel of my shoe all the way down the aisle. It was so treacherous, I had to clutch on to my parents like a cripple. I'm also angry about the lighting. It's too dark and I don't like the shadows being cast on the white carpet. The chuppah, too, is not what I had expected. It's much more elaborate and overdone. It definitely could be considered over-the-top. I didn't want to go over the top. It's clear that I have.

The Honeymoon, Bali

I cry halfway to Frankfurt because the band played the theme from *Titanic* during the party and I specifically asked them not to. I cry because the light on the bandstand was purple and orange and I wanted everything to look classic, not contemporary. I explain to my brand-new husband that purple and orange lights are clearly contemporary colors. He turns away from me, disgusted, and delves into his book. I know my behavior is, in fact, disgusting, but I can't seem to control myself. I think about my sisters who cried through their weddings out of joy. I wonder what's wrong with me as I ask the stewardess for another glass of wine. It goes a long way at thirty thousand feet.

When we get to Bali we play a lot of gin. I try hard to make friends with some of the other honeymoon couples so we can break up the monotony of our trip together. We find one couple with the same itinerary and play hearts with them every night after dinner. Thank God.

While we are reading lethargically on a giant, thatch-roof-covered, outdoor bed that overlooks a magnificent view of the southwest Pacific Ocean, nibbling absentmindedly on fresh, still-steaming spring rolls that one of the waiters placed by my side when I wasn't looking, my husband asks me what's wrong. I put down my book and tell him that I'm anxious about our upcoming move to London, even though really, somewhere inside my confused mind, I know I'm anxious about the fact that we just got married and we are clearly not a perfect fit.

He reminds me that I will write a novel, and I tell him I'm afraid I'm not a good enough writer to write a novel without guidance of some sort. He tells me there are plenty of other writers in London and repeats for the six hundredth time that it's going to be great.

"It *will* be. I *know*," I agree. I agree because he has an amazing ability to shore my anxieties with his steady, deep voice. I agree because I know, theoretically, that most people would love to live in London in a three-story town house with a garden in the back in posh Chelsea with a successful banker who runs marathons and climbs mountains. I agree because really I have no other choice other than annulment, and I wouldn't dream of doing that. I've done it. I've gotten married. I pulled off a huge, successful party. It's behind me now. Two years of hiking and biking and running and skiing and watching eighteen rounds of golf and arranging dinners with friends and going through all the talks—all those endless talks! Eight months of preparation for a twenty-minute ceremony and a three-hour party.

I got what I wanted. Didn't I?

June 1998—London

I huddle on the sofa in the TV room all day shivering in one of my husband's sweaters. Our boxes haven't arrived yet, and I only packed shorts and T-shirts. I think about ending the marriage, but I realize we haven't even gotten the photo albums and the wedding video yet, each of which cost a mint and took countless hours of labor-intensive work by me to assemble.

I call my husband at work and complain because the hot water won't come on and it's cold out and drizzling. I call him at work and complain because I can't put together the desk I bought at Peter Jones that arrived with an Allen wrench and instructions that make no sense to me. I call him and complain because I'm alone and lonely and I can't find a decent chef salad anywhere.

My husband's secretary begins to tell me he isn't in. He starts running home from the office instead of taking the tube, which gets him in around 9 p.m. He comes home at 10 one night and finds me seething in anger, the curried chicken I made for us now dried out and cold. He tells me maybe he can't make me happy anymore. He leaves the house to take a walk, and I'm bereft until he comes back, and then I hold on to him like a life raft, terrified of what would happen if I actually did let go.

I go to the gym. I shop. I write. I give him what I've written to read.

He says, "What's the *point* of this?" He hands it back and suggests I think about things a little longer before I write them down. I tell him I'm blocked and can't write anymore, and he tells me he wrote his senior thesis in forty-eight hours and got an A. He predicts that if he took the summer off he could write a best seller. I tell him to go ahead.

I hatch a plan. I will write a screenplay with my best friend. My best friend lives in New York. I wish I knew someone to write with in London, but I don't. So I commute between New York and London, and I write a screenplay. When I'm in London I try to be the perfect wife: I plan trips across Europe and to Africa, I make reservations at great restaurants, I revive the pear tree in the corner of our garden and serve poached pears with vanilla and cinnamon for dessert at our dinner parties. I go on road trips with my husband in our BMW Z3 convertible; we go to theater in the West End, to football games in Chelsea, to a rugby match in Dublin. I can't wait to get back to New York, though, where I feel my dreams becoming reality.

As I get happier, I expect my life with my husband to follow suit. It does and it doesn't. I find him colder and more impatient than ever, and I can't stand his lectures on the state of the world, brilliant as his analysis always is. Still, our lives can only be categorized as great. He's proud that I've written a screenplay and now that I'm trying to raise the money for it, he's interested in the meetings I'm taking. We've also made great friends in London, some of whom have lavish country homes with names like Donbery Lodge, which we visit for "weekend parties." We go to National Trust estates like Polesden Lacey and Sissinghurst and congratulate ourselves for getting around England and seeing what there is to see. We go to Paris sometimes just to say hello to it, and to Milan and Prague. We ski in the Alps and swim in the Indian Ocean. But night after night I curl up and face away from him while he delves into another book. Night after night I tell him I'm exhausted. Sometimes I'll coax myself into sex because I know it's something we should do, but my heart just isn't in it.

I wonder if this is how it is with all newlyweds. I ask some of my friends. Many agree it's hard to keep passion alive. So I feel okay. I feel like I'm part of something larger than myself. I'm participating in a cultural ritual, and I'm doing just fine.

September 2000—London

I find a company in New York to produce the film, and they also agree to let me star in it. I tell my husband that I'm moving home to make my movie. Our two years are just about up anyway, and the original deal was two years. He tells me the original deal was that we would give it a try for two years and see how we felt. I tell him that if he wants to remain married, I recommend coming back to New York. I'm sorry it's come to threats. It feels cheap. I know he's angry because he wants to stay in London. I love London by now, too, but my career is about to begin and I've waited too long not to go for it.

I'm asked to tea by the wife of the Head of Banking. She cautions me to stop being so competitive with my husband. She tells me that she likes to play the harmonium and that she has satisfied her career dreams by being on the board of the harmonium society and also by playing frequently at her dinner parties. She tells me how much the firm values my husband's contribution and suggests that there may be a way for it to help fund my movie if I agree to let him spend another year or two in London.

For a few moments I find the bribe tempting. But then I look at her and thank her for the tea and tell her I need to be going.

"You're a very lucky girl," she says in a final attempt to ring truth into my hard head.

"Aren't I?" I reply, silently laughing. She doesn't realize that my luck, financially speaking, was in my birth, not my marriage: my parents took good care of me. No one will ever be able to buy my devotion, certainly not the wife of the Head of Banking.

September 2000—Manhattan

While I'm making the movie, there is a lot of time in the makeup chair to think. What I think about is this: I'm thirty-two years old and I want to have a few children. My husband and I have been married now for two years and we've been together nearly six. Against all odds and a constant low-grade fever of anger running between us, we seem to be surviving. The wedding is a distant memory. We've had our London adventure. It seems like time to start a family. I'm way behind my sisters. I don't want to be an old mom, and I'm already not going to be a young one.

We wrap the film the last Saturday of November, and my husband and I head out to the Hamptons for our first weekend together in close to two months. I've been using an ovulation kit, so I know the timing is right. Two weeks later it's confirmed by the double blue line on the little stick I peed on with crazy hope and anticipation: I'm pregnant.

I'm not as elated as I thought I would be. Instead I become depressed. I become depressed because when things aren't great with my husband, they're tense and miserable, and they're tense and miserable most of the time. He tells me I'm too needy, and I tell him he's selfish. We go to bed angry. I start to feel insane for bringing life into the world with someone I don't like most of the time.

I make lists about why I *do* like him and read over old lists. My husband and I see a marriage counselor. I cry hysterically and tell my husband I don't feel connected to him; we never really talk.

He says, "Let's go out to dinner then and talk."

We go out to dinner and I say, "You start."

He tells me about a nursing shortage in Ghana. He goes on for some time about it—twenty minutes at least—giving me details and numbers. After a while I interrupt and ask him what this has to do with the fact that I'm feeling anxious about the pregnancy and the state of our relationship. He says it has nothing to do with it: I told him we never talk, so he's talking.

I say, "What about the baby?" and he tells me—with exasperation that I confuse with passion—that he loves me and is thrilled at the thought of becoming a dad. And I'm suddenly way too exhausted to fight our marriage anymore. I decide I will accept what it is and what it isn't. I decide to feel reassured by his excitement and delight. I decide it's not good for the baby for me to be so upset. I decide to calm down. I decide to be happy.

It's amazing, all the things you can decide to do when you really want something to work.

September 11, 2001—TriBeCa

It's a magnificent morning. At 8:46 a.m. I tell my baby nurse the plan for the day: I'd like to go with my newborn daughter to the Baby Gap in the Winter Garden, which is attached to the World Trade Center, as soon as it opens. Our conversation is interrupted when a huge plane flies by the eleventh-story window of my living room. A moment later it hits the North tower. We run to the nursery, which faces the nearby towers, and stare at the huge black hole near the top. Angry black smoke pours out into the brilliant, aqua sky, and we watch, dumbstruck, as a half-circle of debris arcs out all around the hole. It's strangely beautiful, the arc, and I think, for a moment, that it's a ticker-tape parade. I'm unable to make a connection between the hole and the debris and the plane. I run downstairs to see if my doorman knows what's going on. No one knows anything. I run back upstairs, and my baby nurse points to the sky and says, hysterically, "Those are people." I try to calm her down, telling her it's only debris, but then I look more carefully and realize that, in fact, the things that are flailing this way and that are arms and legs and men's suits and their ties.

I think about the plane and I think about my proximity to the towers. My husband took an 8 a.m. commuter flight to Washington, D.C., for a meeting near the Pentagon, so I know he isn't reachable. I decide that if a piece of the plane hit something on the ground, the whole neighborhood could go up in flames. I decide that the building could keel forward if there is major structural damage. If so, I will be an ant beneath the foot of a giant. "Let's go," I say to the nurse. We are still in our pajamas, but we leave—my daughter tucked under one arm, our bulldog puppy under the other—and I lead my little family to safety.

En route to the Upper East Side, I hear that an 8 a.m. commuter flight has flown into the Pentagon. I have been trying, unsuccessfully, to call my parents to let them know I'm coming. When I hear the news of the plane crash, I lose control of my muscles and drop the phone. Is my husband dead, I wonder? My mind is blank as I pick up the pieces of the broken phone and try to fit them back together.

My husband isn't dead. He sends an e-mail to my father from his BlackBerry many hours later: He's fine; he managed to pay a taxi driver some insane amount to drive him from Potomac to Princeton where he then got a lift with a friend down to his parents' home near South Orange. There is cheering and general rejoicing at my parents' apartment now that we know he's safe. Intellectually, I know that I'm relieved, but I'm still too numb to feel *actual* relief. As usual, I feel nothing in the actual moment at hand; I feel nothing at all.

That night I stay in my parents' bed. We lie awake most of the night watching the news. One station keeps playing the frantic phone message of a thirty-two-year-old woman to her fiancé who she was set to marry in two weeks. The message goes like this: "I'm stuck in this stupid building and I can't get out!!! This is so absurd!!!!!! Honey—I—there's no way to get out!!!!!" The bereaved fiancé is tawny-haired, square-jawed, in his early thirties, wearing a light-blue Oxford that matches his eyes—that matches my husband's eyes. "She's my soul mate," he tells the newscaster between sobs. "I don't want to be alive without her. I don't want to be *alive* . . ."

I want to feel that way about my husband, but I know I don't. What I do feel is a complicated tangle of resentment and respect and fear and partnership and love . . .

What *is* love? I begin to wonder. *Really*. What on earth is it? When my husband and I first met and talked, I felt the first tinges of an emotion I thought could become love. When we first kissed and slept together, I felt what I thought was love. I distinctly remember going around telling people, "I'm so in *love*." After every fun dinner with friends, or a walk at sunset on the beach in the Hamptons, I felt I must be in love. After getting to know each other so deeply, after surviving fights, and deluges in the Alps, after sitting together through funerals of friends and celebrating at the brisses of my sisters' sons, I felt certain that what I felt was love.

And yet, when I examine the reality of my emotions, or lack thereof, I know that I don't feel the kind of love that the bereaved Romeo on the TV set before me feels for his lost Juliet. I know there must be more to it. I know I'm missing out on something that has been written about by all the great poets and writers, and sung about by all the great balladeers, and painted and expressed in countless ways. I'm missing out on love. I don't even know what it is.

I fall in and out of a miserable sleep. When I open my eyes, picture after picture of young firemen flash on the TV screen. The number of deaths in the NYPD and NYFD are staggering. My mind can't contain the magnitude and I sleep again.

I wake once more around 2 a.m. as reports begin to filter in about the structural flaws of the towers themselves. Had the flaws been corrected at the structural level, the implosion could have been avoided, the newscaster tells us. The architect of the towers is being interviewed now. There are blueprints on the screen. There is a discussion about fireproofing and asbestos and things my mind can't take in because the station keeps alternating views of the blueprints with views of the towers caving in on themselves, rushing to oblivion in one bizarrely neat, massive, vertical crumble.

How do you fix a structural flaw? How do you even *know* there's a structural flaw until the structure topples? Can my husband and I ever correct the structural flaws in our relationship? I ask myself in the solipsistic, but often helpful, manner many people—especially unhappy people—have of personalizing tragedy. There *must* be a way to make repairs; *must* be a way to open up the walls of our relationship and fireproof the staircases of our escape routes and strengthen the steel of our individual stubbornness so it doesn't melt under the heat of our explosions and smash us to dust. There *must* be a way, otherwise I know we will implode, just like the Twin Towers, caving under the weight of our repeated angers and frustrations and all our unmet, individual needs.

I will give myself one year. If one year from today we haven't made deep, structural improvements, it will be time to move on. Life is short. There is no way to hide from that fact after today.

September 12, 2002—Bridgehampton

Lying in our bed—the bed in which we conceived our daughter; the bed in which we shared so many moments of passion, exhaustion, happiness, sadness; lying in our bed on the hard mattress I've always hated but chose anyway after testing several others because my husband prefers a hard mattress for his back; lying in our bed, holding my husband's capable hand—this is what goes through my head before I utter the words that will usher in a new chapter between us: Am I about to make a huge mistake? Do we really belong together and struggling through things is really what marriage is all about? What will become of me? Will I ever find this so-called love I think I'm missing? What will happen to all of our friends? Will they take sides? Will I have a normal social life? Will I ever have another child? Will I be lonely? Who will I go to the movies with on the spur of the moment? How will we explain this to our daughter? Will it create problems for her? What will my family think? Will the pain and confusion I feel ever go away? Will I ever meet someone who is as brilliant and great at instigating adventures? Will I ever ski again, hike again, bike again, explore the world again with someone as grounded, brilliant, loyal, and attractive by my side?

Lying in bed, holding my husband's familiar hand in mine, my right leg thrown over his left in the position we've slept in for almost eight years, I keep the words in my throat for many long moments. But I think, too, about the prayer I made in temple while I was there for a September 11 memorial: a prayer for relief; a prayer for an end to all the fighting/tension/angry silences/lonely togetherness/name calling that has come to define our lives together. My husband is an amazing person; I have no doubts about it. But for some reason, we don't make each other happy. We've tried, and we're people who usually succeed. There is no other way to view it: we've failed.

"I'm no longer thriving in this relationship," I say quietly but clearly. "I think we need to consider a separation."

There. I've said it. It's as if my water is breaking all over again: *What is this new feeling?* I remember asking myself that morning in August when our daughter decided to arrive almost a month early. *What, exactly, is happening?* I wondered as the water gushed from between my legs.

I think we need to consider a separation.

The words surround us and we bathe in them for a moment. Then he says, "I agree." The water rises and I start to sob, and then we make love with the desperation of two people who will soon be separated by war.

Labor

My metaphorical water did, indeed, break when I uttered those words. What next? Labor. My husband and I try to figure out what course to take. Should we stay together and try counseling? Should we separate in the hopes of reconciling? We decide on separation leading directly to divorce.

We labor for many months to create the right terms. We promise to do it amicably. I can't say we are always successful, but we are mostly successful. Amicability is like getting an epidural: you're still pushing hard, but the edge is off the pain and it's a real relief. As my sister said before I went into the hospital to give birth, "It isn't absolutely necessary, but I *highly* recommend it."

Infancy

And so I begin my new life: the life of a separated person. Like any newborn, there is a lot of wailing in the beginning. I cry every day for a few weeks, and then every few days for a few months, and then every so often, and eventually there are no more tears left. But in the beginning, I cry. I cry alone and I cry to my mom, I cry to several girlfriends and I cry on the shoulder of my cleaning lady. I drink wine alone at bars and cry to bartenders, and I drink wine with other divorced women as we plot how to meet men. One thing is certain: as I listen to these women tell me their ex-husbands are "worthless fucks" and that "no one is out there," I vow not to ever become like that. I will not be bitter. I will learn how to live on my own again.

But first, I have to learn how to sleep through the night. Several divorcées recommend Ambien. I prefer self-scrutiny, which doesn't lead to nights of peaceful slumber but it does lead to several insights. And I don't mind the sleeplessness. I learn what it feels like to be tired all the time and I take refuge in it. The tiredness numbs reality for me, like a natural Valium. Still, through the fog of my exhaustion, two things remain crystal clear. One, my ex and I must remain amicable, always; and two, we are making the best decision for our daughter, who will be spared the trauma of growing up with parents who are constantly either fighting or trying not to.

Taking the High Road

Somewhere tucked between the Crying phase and the Liberation phase, comes the Placing Blame phase. This unfolds while you tell people "what happened," naturally from your wounded point of view. It feels good but gets you nowhere. I learn this: It's best to keep certain details of your private life private. The phrase I use over and over again is: "It just wasn't working; we weren't the right people for each other." And I'm telling the truth.

The Aftermath

The heart is not a rational muscle. Of course, there comes the inevitable day when I find out he's with someone new. Even though I'm with someone new, too, I feel betrayed. I feel disgusted. I cry over the phone and ask what she has that I didn't that enables him to be happy with her and not with me.

He says, "Stop comparing yourself to her. You're two different people. You both have strengths and weaknesses. The difference is that you and I annoyed each other and she and I don't."

My therapist tells me that I need to cultivate indifference. It takes me two years to reach this stage, and to stop worrying that some other woman is spending time with our daughter. Once my ex-husband starts living with someone, though, something in me honestly and truly lets go of the perverse dream that we will one day be a "normal" intact family. I'm not sure if it's the fact that someone has moved in with him or if time *does* heal all things. Well, not all things. If you're in a bad relationship, time only makes it worse.

I've been asked by every man I've dated since my divorce why I got married in the first place, especially if I knew there were real problems between us going into the wedding. I've reduced the answer to the basics. Timing: I wanted to get married. Fear: I didn't have the character to call it off. Indecision: I could never truly decide by what criterion you choose your life partner.

And quite frankly, I'm still not sure I know even now. I've spent countless hours asking myself just what ingredients are necessary in the recipe for a perfect couple. How do you know *for sure* that you're making the right choice?

Personally, I think without chemistry, you're doomed. But then there are all the other factors that need to be in the right place: Do you have the same goals for the future? Do you have the same priorities? Can you make each other laugh? Is there mutual respect? Are you in a comfortable place together financially? Are you intellectually compatible? Do you enjoy socializing together? Do you have enough time for each other? Is there deep mutual trust? Can you honestly, truly, communicate? Can you fight and come out intact? The list, of course, goes on.

Of course, one person will never have every single quality you desire; my mother told me that long ago and I believe her. So here's what I've concluded. If there's one red flag, march on. If there are two or three red flags, proceed with caution. If there are more than ten red flags—and I left many off my list—don't just stand there watching them wave in the wind. A red flag at the beach is a warning to stay out of the water, a warning to protect your life. Take care of your heart with the same vigilance. Otherwise, no matter how nice your bathing suit or how fit your body, you're going to drown. Take it from me. I've tasted the sand on the ocean floor.

Love Me Do

Ann Hood

I leave things: dishes in the sink, clothes on the floor, magazines on tabletops, empty coffee cups in my car. I leave movies that are boring and parties that aren't fun. Once, in college, I left a waitressing job after an hour because they recycled the rolls from the breadbaskets. A few years later, in a bout of perpetual unemployment, I worked for thirty minutes in a travel agency before walking out. I leave the places I've called home with an ease and efficiency that is hard for some people to understand.

In 1981, I rented the first floor of a renovated Victorian house in Marblehead, Massachusetts. A week before Christmas, I began to notice strange disappearances: the two sweet potatoes I left on the counter for that night's dinner, the silver icicles hanging from my Christmas tree, my springer spaniel Molly's kibble. One afternoon, while I was staring at the missing pages of a paperback book, a rat almost the size of Molly sauntered past me. The rat paused to check me out before continuing into the kitchen. I packed a suitcase and left, returning a month later only to salvage what the rats had left behind. Not only did I leave that apartment, I left Massachusetts for good.

It's probably no surprise that I also leave people. When I quit a job or moved away, I usually left the people who came with them: neighbors, co-workers, roommates. Sometimes I stayed in touch, but more often, either to put the bad stuff behind me, or just eager to move into a new phase of my life, I simply left. When boyfriends got sullen, or disagreements grew too frequent, I broke up. Sure, I cried when "our" song came on the radio, called just to hear his voice on his answering machine, but that didn't stop me from walking out the next time a relationship hit some bumps.

There have even been a handful of times when I have left friendships that I had thought would endure, not blithely but after feeling betrayed. I know that another kind of person, one who sticks things out, works on problems, has some character trait that I lack, would have fought to the bitter end to salvage even these relationships. That same type of person, I suppose, sends chatty Christmas cards to former neighbors and roommates; cries when she packs up her china to move; does her dishes and cleans her car; stays at the same job until she retires. Me? I leave.

The one place I thought for certain I would never leave was New York City. The first day I moved into my tiny sublet on Sullivan Street, in a former convent painted pink, I walked the maze of streets that made up my new neighborhood and actually felt the cells in my body shift and settle. Standing on the corner of Bleecker and Third that hot June day, I knew that I would be leaving jobs and lovers and even the apartment where I had just dropped a Hefty trash bag full of belongings, but I would not, ever, leave New York City.

A dozen years later, almost to the day, I was driving a rented U-Haul up the West Side Highway, watching my beloved city growing smaller in the rearview mirror. At thirty-five years old, I had fallen in love, hard and fast, and the man who was about to become my husband lived in Providence, Rhode Island. The night Lorne told me his plans for us—that I would move to Providence and live with him in a quaint historic house, that we would get married and have children and grow old together, I laughed and said, "I will never leave New York."

But I leave things. Even things I love. Even things I promise never to leave. So, with my cats screaming in their travel cases beside me and the truck bumping beneath me, with my future ahead of me, I left.

———⚬⚭⚭⚬———

The thing about marriage is, you're not supposed to leave. You stand up in front of a hundred of your best friends and closest family members and promise them and the person you're marrying that you will stick it out. No matter what. I know people don't. All the time. I was even one of those people a couple years earlier, a person who left a marriage after five years. And having left one, the pressure to stay in the next one is even greater.

The thing about this marriage of mine was I wanted it to work. I really love my husband. He is handsome and kind and thoughtful and romantic and passionate and smart. Every year he makes my anniversary present out of our wedding picture, translated into paper or glass, whatever material tradition deems that year's gift is. It gives me real pleasure to watch the shelf where they sit gather more of these gifts—me clutching a bouquet of white tulips, both of us looking younger as time passes, our faces free of the pain and loss waiting for us just up ahead, those grins captured in tin and wood and cotton. I am happy to watch these accumulate, marking off another year together.

Still, for some time, I missed the life I had left behind. I missed walking down Bleecker Street before the city woke up, the quiet of Manhattan in the early morning, the smell of espresso and sugary pastries drifting from old Italian cafés; I missed the ballet class I took two mornings a week with its crazy array of NYU students, injured ballerinas, and plain old New Yorkers like me; I missed the noise from the street that played like a lullaby when I went to sleep at night; I missed the graduate students who crowded my apartment every Tuesday night for pasta and wine and discussions about writing fiction; I missed the friends I met for coffee, the friends I met for beer, the ones who fed my cats when I went out of town and the ones who walked for hours with me on Sunday afternoons.

I missed all of it. I struggled to navigate the car through the strange and sudden one-way streets that littered my new city. I struggled to make friends. I wondered where a person bought good cheese here, where to find a movie theater that played foreign films, where the good independent stores were. I loved my husband, but every day when he put on his suit and walked out the door, I missed my real life, the one with lunches with magazine editors and book parties and other writers flopping on my sofa wondering if our new manuscripts would ever get finished.

I had promised my husband and all those people at my wedding that I wouldn't leave, but whenever we had a disagreement or a full-out fight, I imagined packing my bags and getting on Amtrak to Penn Station. Sometimes, I said it aloud: "I'm leaving! I'm going back to New York!" And later, when we had kids, I imagined bundling them up and moving us all into an apartment not unlike the one I'd left in the West Village. But after a while my husband, who is calmer and even more sensitive than I, pointed out that I had to stop threatening to do that. When you're married, he reminded me, leaving means divorce and emotional damage. He had no intention of leaving me, he said.

Both of us had parents who had stayed married to each other forever, and happily. Somehow they had worked out their differences. Was I really going to uproot my family and our lives because my husband liked to spend Saturdays cleaning instead of loafing? Or a dozen other reasons both small (how can he refuse the fruity olive oil I brought home so happily and drench his salad with bottled dressing?) and large (how could so many of his friends be so conservative?).

The truth was, despite all of this, I had no intention of leaving him either. I just couldn't find my way in this new place, in my new life. Even after we had our son Sam, I struggled with the other mothers I met in their workout clothes and with their talk of home renovations. I didn't fit in here. That's what I felt. That's what I knew to be true. At night, when it was just my new little family, things seemed right. Eventually, we had our second baby, Grace, and Sam went off to a nursery school where I met women who were not unlike me. Some of them were also displaced New Yorkers. Some of them were writers.

Slowly, slowly, I began to make my way. I thought about leaving less. And when I did leave, to teach or give readings, I missed my family and home more. Arriving back at our little red colonial house after a week away, seeing Sam and Grace and Lorne waiting for me on the stoop with flowers in their hands, shouting, "Welcome home!" sweeping them into my arms, made me understand why people stick things out.

This is where I was three years ago: busy taking Sam and Grace to school, to ballet, to the rehearsal for *Oliver!*, to play dates. They layered potatoes for potatoes au gratin and apples for apple crisp. They set the table together, deciding which color Fiestaware plate each of us should get: Sam always took purple and Grace always took pink and Lorne and I got whatever they decided for us. After dinner, we put on a bad dance tape and together we did the chicken dance and the macarena and the twist. At night, I read them Greek myths or Roald Dahl books. They fell asleep holding hands, and Lorne and I would stare down at our happy sleeping children. Then, on a hot April day, Grace spiked a fever and died thirty-six hours later from a virulent form of strep. She was five years old.

Some statistics say that fifty percent of couples who lose a child get divorced. Some statistics are even higher. It is easy to understand why. When your life is ripped apart, all the rules no longer apply. There is no order anymore: in your family, in your life, in the world. A week earlier, my mornings were all the same. I made my kids their lunches—ham on white bread, a yogurt, three cookies, and an apple for Sam; sliced cucumbers, cheese and crackers, blueberries for Grace—searched for clean underwear and matching socks, struggled to untangle Grace's hair and find Sam's homework, then drove them to school. Now, I didn't know what to do when I woke up. The life I had struggled so hard to create didn't exist anymore.

Eventually, Lorne went back to work. He put on his suit and went to his office. But my office was a tiny room off our dining room. It didn't provide an escape for me. My work was a blank page that needed filling. But I couldn't think or form sentences. Suddenly, the woman who ran away when things got tough had nowhere to escape to. Our house filled with my friends. They held my hand and did our laundry and picked Sam up from school. They climbed into bed with me if they had to. In the evening, when Lorne returned from work, he came home to a house full of people.

These are the kinds of things that tear grief-stricken couples apart. I craved noise and conversation; he needed solitude. Lorne took comfort in sitting at Grace's grave and talking to her; I hated going there, hated the idea that my little girl was there, and avoided it. Church became a refuge for Lorne; but I hated God. The different ways two people grieve are enough to make them seem like strangers to each other. But losing Grace did the opposite for me. I saw the man I married as more precious.

On a New Year's Eve six years earlier, we conceived Grace together. Except for the midwife, we were the only two people there when she was born. He's the one who put on the Simon and Garfunkel CDs, and sat with me in the whirlpool until we climbed onto the king-size bed and, with me pushing and Lorne coaching, brought Grace into the world. My husband is the person who, when Grace's head emerged, said, "Here she is! She's the most beautiful baby in the world." He cut her umbilical cord and walked with the midwife across the room and weighed our baby daughter. Together, we held her and said her beautiful name over and over, whispering it to her, announcing her to the world.

Lorne and I were by her side five short years later, in a cold room in an intensive care unit at the children's hospital, whispering her name again, this time desperately trying to keep her from leaving us. I watched my husband climb onto the hospital bed, amid tubes and machines and monitors, press his lips to our dying daughter, and sing her the Beatles' "Love Me Do." We stood together, banished from her room, pounding on a Plexiglas window, as they tried one more futile time to save her life. We pounded on that window and together yelled her name: "Grace! Grace!"

We have been crying in each other's arms ever since. At first, after friends went home to their own families, we fell into bed together, exhausted and so filled with grief that we could only cry; words were too difficult, too meager. But slowly, our crying framed our stories. "Rerember?" we would ask each other, using Grace's mispronunciation of "remember." Rerember the night she was born? The way she used to crawl, dragging one leg behind her? Rerember when she stuck the goldfish cracker up her nose? When she wouldn't leave the stage after she danced in a ballet of *The Polar Express* but instead stayed there, bowing and bowing, alone in her white tulle?

These memories are ours, Lorne's and mine. We are the only people in the world who hold Grace's history. I used to think that leaving was the thing to do when times were hard. But having now lived through the hardest time, having made it because Lorne was by my side, holding me, and I was there holding him, I understand the virtue, the necessity, of staying.

I am writing this on the eve of my eleventh wedding anniversary. Tomorrow night, Lorne will give me a gift. It will be our wedding picture cast in some new material. I am holding a bouquet of white tulips; we are both grinning out at the world, our faces hopeful and happy; we are facing the future arm in arm.

What Happens in Vegas, Stays in Vegas

Alice Randall

Reader, I married him." It's a boast, it's a confession, and it is a good-bye. After intimately narrating her childhood, her coming of age, and her troubled courtships, after revealing all the significant hopes and violations of her life before the altar, with these four words Charlotte Brontë's Jane Eyre announces: I won't be telling you what happens next.

Marriage is about learning to keep secrets.

No one knows much about what goes on in someone else's good marriage. Bad marriages are an altogether different beast. People talk about them, often incessantly. They tell details of what happened. They quote, as close as they can come to verbatim, what was said. Shock and disappointment are common themes, opportunity lost, how could I, how could he, wrong heart chosen, I married my mother, my father, my fill in the blank, who I wanted to love me but didn't. All of these stories are familiar to anyone who has married friends, if some of the couples are unhappy—and some of the couples are always unhappy.

After the honeymoon, you don't tell what happened on the honeymoon. Everyone knows, of course, but then again, they don't know. The *Kama Sutra* suggests there are sixty-four postures of carnal knowledge. Outsiders never know which have been chosen. If whatever happens leaves the newlyweds deeply satisfied, it is not spoken of—except between the two of them.

What happens in Vegas, stays in Vegas.

A good marriage is a lot like Las Vegas. You take risks. You act a bit of a fool. If you are lucky you're going to be up, and you're going to be thrilled, and you're going to feel alive—when you're up. But when the wheel stops turning, the card has flipped, or the last play has been made, the last second has run out on the clock, when you've lost so much you thought it would kill you, but you're not only still alive but feeling more alive than you have ever felt—you know you're coming back to Vegas, you know you will gamble again. The house, it seems, must always win.

That's marriage's sole obligation—to thrive and to profit by providing you a sheltered place to play. And when you play again, it thrives and profits.

What happens in Vegas, stays in Vegas.

It's a promise friends make to each other when leaving on a trip to that strip in the desert—and it's the promise you need to make to yourself on the trip to the altar. Or, another way of describing this is to say marriage is a little like the Central Intelligence Agency in a sixties espionage flick. I could tell you all about mine, but if I told you, I would have to kill you. It's not that I can't put words to it, it's that I shouldn't.

I didn't always know this. In 1985, I married one man. Twelve years later I married another.

Between these events were a divorce and a seven-year period of living as a single mother—in a little pink town house with my little brown daughter. Ours was a happy house full of music and books and love. I remember dancing around the living room to the sound of Aretha Franklin back when we still had a stereo. I remember countless bubble baths, finger painting at breakfast, face painting and tutu wearing. I remember my daughter and her friends unleashing pounds and pounds of powdered sugar in my kitchen, enough, if I remember correctly, to break the vacuum cleaner, in pursuit of the climactic scene of the first movie my little daughter ever directed. I remember reading the *Iliad* with her at the front door while we waited for the carpool, and bribing her to memorize line after line of Blake with the possibility of a puppy hovering in the distance. I remember sweet mother-daughter trips to France, and Antigua, and Hawaii, holding hands as we snorkeled and swam, being terrified the boom would knock her off the boat into the warm but careless Caribbean.

I could tell you all about raising my daughter, Caroline. I could tell you all about it because good families are largely transparent places in which the sharing of history strengthens the bond.

Marriage is something different. It's the walled box within the glass house. For me, marriage is a private place within family. It's a haven. It's a pleasure box. It's a sanctuary. It's a place where my husband David and I can step out of the world, and step out of time. It's an everyday Sabbath—safe, sweet, and inviolable. Within our marriage there are no chains on our imagination, no truth that may not, in time, with love, be spoken. In our marriage passion is servant to love. Love is the roof above us, and respect is the floor of our pleasure palace in the desert, of our marriage in the modern world.

My first marriage—wasn't a marriage at all. It was a tent set up in the middle of a three-ringed circus, his family, my family, the world—his work, my work, his old lovers, my old loves—everyone was invited to the show, invited to ride the elephant, smell the elephant dung, take a turn at pushing a broom. Everyone was invited to watch us on the flying trapeze working without a net. All and sundry were invited to clap. The clapping was essential. We had almost as much fun hearing the applause as we did flying through the air.

We were not careful, and we were not private. We thought our wedding license gave permission to say anything (with the exception of I want a divorce), or do anything we wanted (with the exception of having sex with other people). It was, here I am, and you have to deal with me, because you promised. It was, now, let's hear what you want. And now, I'll tell you what I want. And, I am so angry with you, and me, that they are not the same thing. It was, O God, send us riches, power, and fame so we can eat in great restaurants, and sit with pretty people, and get drunk enough to fall with our pretty bodies into bed, and somehow it will be fine that life is this brutal. We barely lasted five years.

One night, when we were in one of those fine restaurants, and he had drunk so much fine wine he had to excuse himself from the table, I started staring at the gold and diamond bands on my hand, the one his mother had worn when she cut her wedding cake with the silver cake knife Langston Hughes had given her for a wedding present, and the one that had appeared on my pillow in the little blue Tiffany box as we sailed off the shore of Mustique after dancing in Bailey's Bar. Staring at my rings, across a distance of time I started hearing the voices of the first couple of country music, George Jones and Tammy Wynette, singing . . . "Golden ring, and one tiny little stone . . . by itself it's just a cold, metallic thing, only love can make a golden wedding ring."

We both had drunk quite a bit of wine, but the evening wasn't cruel or sloppy, it was quiet and brittle and angry and cold. When my first husband sat back down, I slid the rings from my finger and threw them at him.

"One thing's for certain, I don't love you anymore," I said, quoting the song.

My first husband understood. He was a brilliant man who knew the lyrics to obscure country songs and the laws of many foreign lands. He had the sophistication to be amused. He did not lose his equilibrium.

"I must be the only black man in America to have his wife an-nounce that she's leaving by quoting a country song."

He didn't think I was going anyplace. I had promised. He knew me to be a woman of my word. He could afford to applaud the fine performance.

It wasn't a performance. I wasn't going, I was gone. It had come to me in an instant. If I stayed, one day some man would treat my daughter the way this man treated me. Someone would ask her to pretend to be a brown, Harvard-educated version of Laura Petrie—while earning funds from a career she made invisible—and get very angry when she thwarted those expectations. And she would let him because I would have taught her to. I had had a very close encounter with a marriage that was a cross between a Johnny Cash prison and Sartre's hell, and I didn't want my little girl to know anything about it.

When I was deciding whether or not I would try to flee from prison or wait to be redeemed from hell, I read three books over and over: *The Awakening, The Age of Innocence*, and *Wide Sargasso Sea*. To this day they are the books I recommend to anyone contemplat-ing a divorce, or an engagement.

The Awakening ends with the suicide of a woman who would rather keep walking into the sea than return to tend children and husbands and lovers, with the other women who seem to enjoy tend-ing children and husbands and lovers. It's a strange tale in which the only way the heroine finds to be true to her children and to herself is to die.

The Age of Innocence, Edith Wharton's novel that won the Pulit-zer Prize in 1921, explores a season in New York society in which one privileged New Yorker falls in love with a passionate woman after having married a conventional girl. It examines the golden chains of society, while giving a glimpse of the velvet chains of sexuality and feminine knowledge. It ends with a line I have always loved. When

I recall the line and sing the words aloud to myself, I speak, "The problem with doing your duty is that it unfits you from doing anything else." Wharton wrote something a little different. She wrote, "The worst of doing one's duty was that it *apparently* unfitted one for doing anything else."

Wide Sargasso Sea changed my literary life. Reflecting on the untold tale Jean Rhys revealed in Charlotte Brontë's novel *Jane Eyre* inspired me to unshackle the untold tale cowering in Margaret Mitchell's *Gone With the Wind*. *Wide Sargasso Sea* tells the story of a woman, the first Mrs. Rochester, whose life is vanquished by marriage. Bertha Rochester, the first woman to marry Mr. Rochester, is a creature who, until Jean Rhys picked up her pen, was merely a monster—the mad woman in the attic. When I read *Wide Sargasso Sea* in my early twenties before my first marriage, I understood *Jane Eyre* to signify that we each had to betray and to help murder our wild selves before we got our happy ending. I did not ache for marriage.

And yet I married again. Read in a certain light, *The Awakening*, *The Age of Innocence*, and *Wide Sargasso Sea* are ironic meta-masterpieces. All three authors, Chopin, Wharton, and Rhys, were married. Though each woman announces throughout her text the limits of marriage proclaiming the shallowness of the bond—the very beauty and complexity of each of their texts announces the secret that each carved out for herself, a herself, an independent identity, a freedom the other side of duty, a freedom far more illuminating and powerful than the wildness it replaces.

All three texts announce it is an extraordinary and married thing to have books and babies and breasts.

<hr />

I, Alice Randall, took David Steele Ewing, to be my lawful wedded husband, sometime between one and three o'clock in the dark early hours of morning (all involved were far too exhausted, excited, bewildered, or young to note the specific time) on April 20, 1997.

When we are sweetest to each other, we wake up and celebrate our wedding at 2 a.m., the hour we have appointed as "the hour." We feast on champagne and smoked salmon and each other, and then we go back to sleep. When we are sweetest to each other we are perfect. Some years we are too tired or too bitter to play with each other in the middle of the night. When pressed to pick a date to celebrate during normal dinner hours, I always prefer to choose to celebrate our anniversary on April 19.

It was on an April 19 that I got zipped into my wedding gown, on April 19 that I showered and scented my body, April 19 that I began my strange long second trip to the altar.

David, being a lawyer and legalistic, prefers to celebrate on the twentieth. If this was my first marriage I might be irritated, but it isn't, and I am not, and that has something do with how it has come to be we are so very often sweet to each other.

There's an old country saying that goes, upon finding oneself to be lost in the woods it is a great advantage to have been lost in the woods before. Marriage is a forest and it is always night. I have been lost in it once, and I am lost in it again. This time I know how to make a fire without burning down the forest; this time I know where I can find ripe berries and where the alligators will try to find me. This time I'm not so busy starving, and shivering, and getting stung, that I don't have time to enjoy the pleasures of the forest.

The last time, when I was getting all that education, I barely survived.

That's the problem with the old saying about getting lost in the woods—it only applies to people who didn't get killed the first time. Getting lost a second time requires that you survived your first experience. It also requires that having been lost in the woods before, you are bold enough, or fool enough, to enter the woods again. I am both.

I wore a black gown to my wedding to David. I had a good excuse. We had gone to a ball before the wedding. Looking back, I suspect I planned my second wedding as an elopement from a ball, so that I would have reason to wear black. I was in mourning for the innocence I lost in the first marriage; I was in mourning for the freedom I feared I was losing again. I was sober and I was solemn; I was full of love and full of doubt. I didn't know if the marriage would last forever, five years, or five minutes. Having been so certain, and so wrong, the first time, that I was making promises I would never break, I was humble speaking my vows the second time.

We were both kneeling in the little A-frame church that looks like a ski chalet on the Vanderbilt University campus, in the middle of a loud fraternity and sorority row. Suddenly, the street went quiet that Saturday night when it became known a couple wished to exchange vows, so that after blaring chords of Southern rock guitar, all I could hear were the words from the 1928 Book of Common Prayer, spoken by our young minister, a woman who was stopped by the police and almost arrested when she left our wedding breakfast. The officer didn't believe anyone performed marriages at that early hour, and the tags on the car the minister had borrowed had expired. As I gazed into that grace-filled priest's face, illuminated only by cheap votive candles, she asked me if I took this man. At that moment I heard the strains of a single violin, imported from the symphony, and the sounds of friends sobbing in joy, in relief, and in fear, as I trembled, repeating after the priest, with my virgin daughter and her two best friends standing with me as true maids attending. There was precious little certainty.

The second time I thought, I want this man now. I love this man now. I believe we can build a happy home. I believe he is grown. I know I am. I believe this man may be my child's last best chance at happiness.

David proposed two months after we started dating. We were at Bill Clinton's second inaugural. It was freezing cold. A black woman opera singer, Jessye Norman, was singing. We were on some part of the Capitol lawn when David dropped down on his knees. I thought he had been shot. I had no idea in the world what he was doing. I thought he was having a heart attack. It was only when the people around us began applauding that I understood what was going on. David had popped the question. All I could think to say was, "If I ever marry again, I will marry you."

I didn't think I would marry again. Barely a month before my eight-year-old daughter had surprised me with a question as I tucked her back into bed just after the stroke of midnight on New Year's Eve.

"Mama, do you ever think about getting married again?"

"No," I answered.

"I think you should start thinking about it," my daughter responded.

"Do you have someone in mind," I asked?

"Him in there," she said.

Him in there was a six-foot-five, brown-eyed handsome man who had not yet turned thirty. I had already seen thirty-five. Him in there was stunningly beautiful. On my best days I am quirkily pretty. Him in there had a law degree but earned less than thirty thousand dollars a year. On my best days I am not inexpensive.

I remember walking from the relative bright of Caroline's room—she liked to sleep with a light on—back into the dimness of my room. David was sitting on the floor of my bedroom on a patchwork blanket with the remnants of a feast around him. I hadn't been able to get a sitter for the big night. Him in there had decided we didn't need to go out. That we could have a good time right at home. Then and there I knew I might tie a second knot.

For me marriage is all about two things: taking care of family (children and the old folks in particular) and consecrated consummated erotic love. I married David because I thought it would bring more joy to my child rearing and old-folk tending. And I married David because I think sex with someone willing to commit to being tender until the last minute of their life and willing to forsake all other consummated erotic adventures is far superior to any other kind of sex.

———◆———

Nine years later, we have discovered marriage is more. Day after day we create for ourselves, and each other, a space to bring our best selves, and a place for our most broken selves to be known. Knowing mends. Day after day we remember it is never wise to attack your partner, that you will live with the injuries you inflict. Day after day we try to be wise.

Nine years of privacy and gentleness, nine years of willingness to hear any news that needs telling, and nine years telling most news that needs to be known, braided in with nine years of exploring how to worship another person's body (without being guilty of idolatry), is nine years of learning how to allow the walls of love and respect that began by confining, to turn outside-in, into a skeleton of love and respect that sustains.

My second marriage is nothing like Jane Eyre's. Let her tell you about it:

I have now been married ten years . . . I know no weariness of my Edward's society: he knows none of mine, any more than we each do of the pulsation of the heart that beats in our separate bosoms; consequently, we are ever together. To be together is for us to be at once as free as in solitude, as gay as in company. We talk, I believe, all day long: to talk to each other is but a more animated and an audible thinking . . .

My second marriage has much to do with inviting all the raw passion and abiding difference and ever wrapping these with ribbons of compassion, respect, patience, and knowledge that the house has to survive if you are to play again.

The first time I got married I was looking for Jane Eyre Rochester's marriage, the marriage that Edna Pontellier wanted and could not have so she walked into the sea, the marriage I suspect doesn't exist—outside of novels—and barely exists inside of good ones.

My first wedding was held at High Noon on a bright blue fall day at St. John's Lafayette Square in Washington, D.C. St. John's is an eminent edifice with a golden roof. The reception was at the Cosmos Club. It was a small wedding, fewer than one hundred and fifty guests, but the guest list included at least two ambassadors, a Supreme Court justice, and a White House official who biked over from the Executive Mansion for the occasion.

The day after the wedding, I was in a little Porsche with my first husband headed for Vermont. I remember reading the *New York Times* that Sunday morning and seeing a picture of a pretty girl named Mari-Alice Williams. I remember thinking how strange it was that she was in my class at Harvard and black and I didn't know her—then I realized I was looking at a picture of myself.

In my first marriage I was a stranger to myself, some girl who wanted to try her hand at playing house, someone who wanted to forget she had ever gone to Harvard, or had a career or a thought, because the beautiful creature she had fallen in love with wanted a woman who had never had a career or a thought.

When I look at the pictures of my second wedding, my marriage to David Ewing, I recognize the woman in the photographs. I look like me in my black dress. I am not in costume or disguise. There is an old Southern phrase that makes a fine motto for second marriages: Begin as you mean to go along. Do things at the beginning the way you want to be doing them over and over for the next forty years. I began as I meant to go along—the second time.

I will never forget the worst argument we ever had. It was shortly before the wedding. David was, to my mind, being stupid, silly, incompetent, and insensitive. I cursed him. I repeated the two-word curse three times. *Fuck you. Fuck you. Fuck you.* Could I have said that? I remember my beloved staring at me. His face looked so sad, then it looked so concerned.

He asked, "Oh, Sweetie, what is wrong? You must be sick, or so tired, to talk to your Sweetie that way. I know my Sweetie wouldn't talk that way to me unless something was very wrong."

Something was very wrong. I was scared I would be betrayed. Scared we would both morph into monsters once we were married; scared the ghosts of my adolescence would move into the house as soon as I moved a man in; scared that getting married would be locking two wild people into a house and inviting them to have a go at each other—scared my second marriage would be like my first, like many of the marriages I knew. Something is very wrong with most marriages, and something was very wrong with me until David, who had just turned thirty years old, took what he had learned in his family home and threw it back at me.

He was kind, and he was patient. He invited me to remember who I was when I most enjoyed being me. He offered to give me any assistance necessary to regain my equilibrium, including his certainty I was not elementally a bitch. If I was acting like a bitch, according to David, I had a reason. I desperately wanted this man to be my husband.

I wanted this man for my life. I wanted this man to be my daughter's stepfather. One day, I wanted my daughter to be as certain of the elemental goodness and value of men, as David, who had been rich in good mothers in his childhood, was unshakably certain of the elemental goodness of women. I did not wish to disillusion the one I loved. Been there done that. Found no pleasure in it at all. I decided then and there if David thought it would be impossible for me to be less than sweet . . . it would become impossible. *Fuck you* turned to *Fuck me, darling*.

And he is sweet to me. A few nights ago I woke up in the middle of the night coughing. David got up and found me liquid Benadryl. He fed me a dose. He reassured me. He got me a cough drop and then he got back into bed. I do not take the small kindnesses for granted. I remember when I did not have them. I perform small kindnesses when I can.

I entered my first marriage a bold, willful child. I entered my second marriage a grown woman. I had buried a parent. I had started and sold two different companies. I had achieved a measure of success as a songwriter and as a screenwriter—and I had experienced a significant failure—I had failed to provide my daughter two parents living in one happy home. And I had achieved a great success—a content, evolving child.

Somewhere along the way I had sacrificed my wildness of my own free will and volition. I had gotten up with the baby seven days a week, most of 365 days a year. I had gotten up in the middle of the night to take her to the bathroom, to change sheets, to discuss a nightmare, to cuddle, to put stuffed lambs back in the bed, to call the doctor about a fever that had crawled in on invisible microbes. I had written trash TV to pay her private school tuition; I had found the pleasure and honor in doing my duty.

In the final chapter of *The Age of Innocence*, there is a line that I didn't love when I first read the book, or when I next read the book, a line I did not truly understand till recently: "It seemed to take an iron band from his heart to know that, after all, some one had guessed and pitied. . . . And that it should have been his wife moved him indescribably."

Someone had guessed and pitied, someone had understood the passion he felt, the love he desired, even the love he could not have. Someone had been silent witness to his most profound and unmet wishes, his wife. And it moved him indescribably. Now it moves me indescribably. Another secret.

Marriage provides a witness. A discreet and compassionate witness provides wings. Doing one's duty only *apparently* unfits you for anything else. Appearances are often deceiving. In my experience, a good marriage allows you to do your duty while pursuing a deep if not broad personal freedom.

The good marriage is all about the freedom to discover who we are, coupled with the responsibility to be kind. The good marriage is all about private engagements and private pleasures, about taking the time to know someone more and more, year after year. It's about learning your love's true language and learning to speak it, at the same time you teach your love your true language. It's about noticing and respecting the differences in your languages even as you become bilingual.

Of course, there are moments when one or the other of you is horrible. There have been times when David and I have fallen out of love. When we fell out of love, it was a comfort to find ourselves in a consecrated and kind garden of truth and *politesse*. We have discovered that a kind garden of truth and *politesse* is a fine place to fall back in love.

I believe my husband has only raised his voice at me once. He has never raised his hand. There have been a few occasions when I have beaten him over the head with a pillow, and once when I poured warm chai on him while he was driving. On both occasions we quickly resorted to the regress of giggles.

What we have never done is braid our intelligence to our intimacy and use our intelligence and our intimacy to hold up a vicious mirror, each to the other. In my first marriage, we did that over and over again. It was a long swim in an alligator pond.

My first husband and I were bright and angry and confused. We thought marriage meant the end of freedom. We were furious with each other for being the reason we couldn't have all the kisses in the world, couldn't have all the money in the world, couldn't just do what we wanted to do, when we wanted to do it. We both confused marriage with growing up because they happened, or tried to happen, at the same time.

And then we were not married, not even legally, and we still couldn't have all the kisses in the world, or all the money, and we could do less of what we wanted to do, when we wanted to do it. All grown-ups sacrifice wildness to discipline if they wish to achieve. If they are lucky, they discover their wildness reborn and transformed into freedom.

The second time around I know that I have ended my own freedom because I have chosen to cultivate, to nurture, and to commit. The limitations are not something my beloved has placed upon me but something I chose for myself. The forest turned into a garden with walls. I have stopped swimming in alligator ponds. This is cause to celebrate. My wild roses have begun growing on trellises. This, too, is cause for celebration, and this is marriage.

David knows everything there is to know about me, every hope, every fear. He doesn't try to fix a thing. I know more about him than anyone else in the world. It's not the same thing, but it's good enough for us. Last year we had a particularly sweet anniversary. We decided to go back to the Vanderbilt campus and have a picnic just before midnight. We got hot chicken from a local soul food joint. We ordered a small version of our wedding cake. We loaded our feast into a little red wagon. Beneath that moon, I thought of an old soul song I hummed along to when I was a small girl in Detroit, a song I often hear played by society bands in Southern ballrooms, "My Girl."

"I don't need no money, fortune, or fame. I got all the riches, baby, one man can claim, I guess you say, what can make me feel that way, my girl . . ." When we're out on the dance floor I always change the words and sing, "My Man." David looks at me as he mouths "My Girl." We both wonder how many on the dance floor are in on our secret, happy club. We are amused to know that some people probably think that we shouldn't be up dancing. The years have been materially good to us. But we know. We know without anyone applauding.

I will tell you a secret.

It rarely snows in Nashville. When it does, David rushes home and we get on the little sleigh bed I slept in before I married him. We get on the bed we didn't get into until we were married, the narrow bed where we literally had to sleep on top of each other the first six months after the wedding, the bed where I once lay and wondered if any man would ever touch me again. We open the French doors to our bedroom, letting in blasting cold, then we cuddle beneath a blanket and we watch the snowfall. Sometimes we make love. Most times we just lie under a patchwork quilt of trust and truth, of Eros and silence, with the cold and the beauty all around.

I've Got to Be Bad

A. R. Baumann

As I lie back in the chair getting readied for my Botox and Perlane injections at the plastic surgeon's office, I wonder how I can cover up the marks on my face so my husband won't see them, because I told him I never put any in my lips—a big fat lie! I am a recovering drug addict and alcoholic and have been sober for quite some time, but I'm still, after twenty-two years of marriage, juggling the good girl with the bad girl.

Why can't I just stand up to my husband? Admit to my clandestine doctor visits? Because I am still scared of him leaving me. Because I am vain. What can I say? I live in Los Angeles, a city for the enhancement of face and figure, a city for the self-obsessed. And, finally, because to feed the addict in me, I still have to get away with something—I've got to be bad. It quiets the addict beast inside of me, and I need it. I love getting away with things—like Restylane injections or smoking behind the pool house—that my husband doesn't approve of. My husband plays guard dog to my addictions. I know he's right, but I often can't stand him for it. I love to be the errant child to his parent, but I am at the same time always scared of being caught in the game.

When my husband decided he wouldn't be married to a smoker,

his will won over mine, and I pretended to quit. I don't dare smoke anywhere near him. I mean, fuck! I can't argue with him, because he will immediately launch into a lecture about the perils of smoking. I know it is useless to try to defend my bad behavior because, with this and most other topics, I can never win a debate with him. I always come from my gut while he comes from his head. I lose it emotionally, while he coolly builds a logical argument and delivers it in that big German voice. I cringe. *No!* I scream inside.

Sneaking, of course, always appeals to my addict side. My assistant smokes too and when she comes over, we hide out in the back of the house and light up laughing and creeping around like twelve-year-old thieves. She's also in AA, so we talk about our feelings and who, what, or where if anyone or anything fucked us over that day. I always put on a black turban so my husband won't smell it in my hair. Sometimes I take my purse with me to the back of the house because it holds all the tools of the trade: Listerine mouthwash, and perfume, Coco by Chanel, which I rotate with Opium. Jean Patou's 1000 and Guerlain's L'Heure Bleu are my evening favorites that I pour over myself because I can't smell anything as the result of my cocaine abuse twenty-five years ago. After I crush out my cig in the dirt of a plant, I mess the dirt up so it looks like it hasn't been touched up. Then I rinse with Listerine and spray with Opium. My assistant and I make sure no one sees us tiptoeing back in the front door. Now my teenage son is a surfer, and he's often outside on our deck looking at the ocean, so I have to make doubly sure he is nowhere around because I know he would rat on me to his dad.

Today, after dragging those cigarettes out of the car window (I don't want to have a smoker's car!) all the way home to Malibu from the plastic surgeon's office in Beverly Hills, I get my accoutrements out and rinse and spray before I zoom down our driveway.

For the first twelve years of our marriage, I was sober. Then about ten years ago my husband quit the music industry and sold his record label. He wanted peace. So did I. He and I and our three kids followed his dream to Cabo San Lucas where he bought some land. His dream—a high-end, silent retreat way up in the mountains with black palms, a delicious breeze, a running stream and peace, peace, peace. There would be yoga, clean gourmet vegetarian food, some fasting, and dharma speakers from all over the globe.

Unfortunately, the investors bailed after some of the project had been built with our money. The silent retreat failed and so did my AA program. I got sick with pneumonia and didn't know it. I thought it was just a bad cold, and I started swigging cough medicine. I loved the energetic and slightly trippy feeling. Because of the cough syrup's addictive ingredient, dextromethorphan, I started with a sip and soon was drinking a whole bottle every day. My cold didn't get any better, and I ended up in a Mexican hospital run by nuns. When I complained of chest pain, they started me on morphine shots twice a day. With the morphine, I became very animated and humble and asked in broken Spanish how the nun who was attending to me realized she was Jesus' bride. I remember, in my narcotic haze, romantically thinking about her conviction to God, her saintliness, her lack of materialism. She didn't need *things* to make her happy. I was seconds away from renouncing my wealth and following her into the nunnery when she turned to me and in perfect English explained that she was sick of being poor and that there was nothing *happy* about it! From then on, every day when she gave me the beloved shot, I tipped her a hundred U.S. dollars, which she said she would send home to her family on the mainland (in Mexico). I told her how kind she was to her family, but I think that the money went into her white headdress and stayed there.

When my family in Houston found out I was in the hospital with pneumonia, my eldest sister Beth, the family caretaker, perfect in every way, flew down to see me. "You're taking morphine for pneumonia?" she exclaimed, astonished at my state.

I smiled. "Of course, for the pain in my heart," I said with slurred words and then proceeded to fall over the side of the bed laughing.

My husband was so involved with his business venture he didn't notice that my stupor was not the result of pneumonia, and since I'd been sober long before we met, he didn't know to read the signs.

The day after I was released from the hospital, I moved the family into the dream house we had built on the ocean. Within days of the move, I developed double pneumonia—back to the hospital, the nuns, and the morphine shots.

When the doctor realized what was going on, he decreed, "You're an addict!"

Well, yes.

My husband, not an addict, cried, "What's wrong with you?"

But God love him, he took care of business. I was having a hard time in Mexico, and he grudgingly moved the family back to LA. It took two years of slipping on and off the cough medicine before I was finally ready to kick it. But during that time, he'd say things like, "Why don't you get it? You can't take that!" Finally, I realized he'd never understand what it meant to be addicted. And that I'd have to get sober myself, and when I failed—leave it to the rooms of AA, not to my husband.

With all of it, I wonder how we have survived our marriage. My husband and I don't get bored with each other, that's for sure. With the desperate years long gone, we're still completely different. He is disciplined, organized, methodical, rational. He conducts his life smoothly, everything functioning perfectly—another world from my stumbling though the day. He's careful what he eats. My husband made a decision that for a year, he will exercise six days a week and eat only three meals a day—no alcohol, sugar, or white flour, and very few grains.

Now me, I go on binges. Big, ugly ones. I'm good in the day, mostly. But I awake often in the night, and, like a zombie being conducted by my master, I move mechanically over the bedroom carpet to the limestone in our hall, across the planked mahogany wood in the foyer to the limestone in the kitchen. My arms and legs feel as if they don't belong to me. I stand in front of the fridge and eat anything with fat or sugar, anything crunchy, doughy, or icy sweet. Maybe a trillion calories afterward, on my way back to the room, I awaken from my spell and want to beat the shit out of myself. My husband recently put a lock on the refrigerator door, so now I won't be able to make any more midnight rendezvous with the kitchen.

When I do muster up some abstinence and lose weight, I replace food with shopping. Like eating, it's as if I'm in a hyper trance running from store to store. I'm very organized with this. I know what fits and what doesn't. I get a saleslady and dash through the clothes, grabbing mountains of dresses, shirts, pants, and skirts. Once I get my clothes, I square away the shoes and bags and then scamper through the store for belts, hats, and nightgowns. I repeat this behavior in a few more shops, then, winded, drive home happily and a little guiltily —for, as the Ghost in *Hamlet* said, "Oh wicked wit and gifts that have the power so to seduce won to this shameful lust."

I sometimes sleep too late—my husband gets up at five every morning. I try to meditate after I get up like my best friend who does it for hours, but I can barely sit there for five minutes without looking at the clock. My prayer is: "I WANT THIS! I WANT THAT!" So having failed to empty my mind, I give up and proceed to my dressing room and the "vitamin" drawer: Zypan, progesterone, testosterone, estrogen, LipoGen, Omni-Vim, Muscle Aid, Quantum Digest, DHEA, pregnenolone, vitamin C, vitamin E, Perque Energized Double Zinc Guard, and calcium magnesium.

I go to AA, OA (Overeaters Anonymous), or Al-Anon meetings, driving too fast when I leave them, so I'm a mess by the time I get home. But once there, just to get more stressed, I have a really huge chocolate, sugar-free cappuccino. Then I try to de-stress by exercising with my trainer (though I usually ask her to walk the dog while I'm on the elliptical machine, so perhaps I don't get as much exercise as she'd like). This completes my spiritual and beauty regime. My writing comes next and, of course, the kids. I have three, but now the oldest and the youngest are on the East Coast. I miss them terribly. I never felt I was a good enough mother. I was lax on the discipline and magnificent on the love, but I worry that won't take them through the hard times.

I still, after many years, see a psychiatrist—a shrink to the stars—and inevitably it turns out to be a phone session because I convince myself it's not worth my time to go there. After all, it is at the other end of Malibu. But we talk about his problems, too, and I always hear about his best friend who is one of the Beatles. Antidepressants are my current drink or drug for the day, while my husband knocks back about two and a half glasses of wine in the evening (when he's drinking—he often goes without for a couple of months probably to prove he isn't like me—an alcoholic!). Sometimes, he leaves a little bit in the glass, and that pisses me off. How can he leave some? Hell! When I was drinking I could never even leave a drop.

I don't know how we got here twenty-two years later. We didn't fall in love until we were older. We just coupled after a party I gave for the movie I was in, with the lower-echelon actors, of course, because I had one line, and even that was cut out. I swore I wouldn't have sex with my husband-to-be on the first night. But he was conniving and weasled his way in by confiding, "We can just sleep together. We don't need to do anything." Well, of course, I slept with him and did all the rest with him, too.

I always had to prove I was the brilliant, talented artist, while my husband made his first million in a hit rock band. He didn't have any of his gold records hanging on the wall, while I, after doing two short films, had everything displayed in my office. And sometimes

I've been known to open a conversation with someone I've just met by telling them of my small achievements. My husband never mentions his. After we married, his record label became very successful. But when he was through with it, he was done. He sold it and never looked back.

I hate that thing in me that needs so much approval. I come from a super-wealthy Texas oil family with generations of uber-successful, driven people—including my sibs. I always dreamed of being famous to prove I belonged to this family, but I despised the most important component: competition. I was lousy at it. When I was acting on the stage in New York, I suffered from spastic colon, and when I got big movie auditions, I sabotaged them with alcohol and drugs before I even made the second callback.

I make a joke out of my vanity comparing myself to Lucy. My husband is Ricky, a musician, pleased with himself and his life; and I am Lucy, fumbling through my life in a fog of self-centered fear while I fight my addictions. But, in the end, we each complete each other. I am spontaneous, compassionate—I had to find compassion, a lot of it, to live with myself. I make my husband laugh.

And thank God I have him, because I'd be dead without him.

White Knight

Anne Landsman

I should have married a doctor. Every time I get sick or hurt, or sit at one of my children's bedsides in the middle of the night as they wrestle with a burning fever, a stomachache, or a rasping cough, I wonder why I didn't. I grew up in a small town in South Africa with a doctor in the house. For many of my growing years, my father's "rooms" were right off the hallway, smack in the middle of our home. As his practice grew, he moved his operation across the street, to a small house with a jacaranda tree in front of it. All through my childhood, a doctor's services were never more than a few feet away. I remember him extracting a rose thorn deeply embedded in my knee, piercing my ears when I was a teenager, and treating every cold and virus and stomach complaint that came my way with unswerving attention.

Instead of marrying a doctor, I married James, an architect, who can barely distinguish a virus from a bacteria, grippe from croup, staph from strep. His world is the world of aesthetics, measurements, details. He is passionate about green design, finding the right wood stain, the right white, the most beautiful ceiling fan, light fixture, doorknob. He loves doing origami, and our home is full of paper stars, cranes, frogs, polyhedrons. The words I grew up hearing—the names of diseases and orifices and body parts—are foreign to him, and what absorbed my childhood household, day in and day out (and sometimes at night too, as my father was often called to do house calls) is of little interest to him.

As different as we are regarding matters of the human body, so are we different regarding our larger dwelling places, the homes we've lived in together. I secretly aspire to the glorious mess described in John Bayley's *Elegy for Iris*, the chaotic newspaper- and book-ridden crumbling English houses he and Iris Murdoch lived in together, the same haphazard chaos C. S. Lewis lived in, named "the midden" by one of his contemporaries. I'm a pack rat, a trait shared by my doctor-father, who loathed throwing away old newspapers, collected stamps and coins, and hoarded all kinds of peculiar things including toys that were given to him by pharmaceutical companies, marrow bones from the soups my mother made for him, and a miscellany of other objects that he referred to as "collectors' items." I know there is a Grey Gardens lurking somewhere in my soul, a wish to leave everything in my immediate presence in the same hallowed spot for the next forty or so years, so I know exactly where it is. Thankfully, I'm also practical, and live in a household with another adult, two young children, a dog, a tortoise, and a fish tank, and that lifestyle would mean a kind of familial insanity I'm not willing to embrace.

However, just as I secretly own this vision of unrepentant squalor, so, too, does James own an equally powerful dream of himself in his own natural setting. His dream, though, is a glistening, spotlessly clean modernist castle, true to the principles he learned from his teachers at architecture school. In this immaculate airy place, there will be no clutter of any kind, no old newspapers, letters, magazines. All the detritus of daily life will be gone, and the space will express itself in its purest, most pleasing form. It's a vision that was fine-tuned by his semester spent in Denmark as an architecture student, where even the lunch boxes are designed with separate compartments to fit the right-sized sandwiches. Just as I don't live my dream of filth and mayhem, so, too, does James not cut our children's sandwiches into lunch-box-sized shapes.

In reality, he's just as fond of their old art projects as I am, and clings to all kinds of odd bric-a-brac, including a trophy his parents had made for him after he was bitten by a stray dog, inscribed with the words, "Jimmy Wagman, Bravery and Courage in the face of 14 rabies shots." He's fascinated, as I am, by a long, curling tooth that Snowball, my daughter's late, best dwarf hamster, once sprouted, which was snipped off and given to us in a tiny glass vial by our veterinarian. (Who knew that hamsters' teeth can become ingrown, a condition that, if left untreated, can become fatal?) So, although we don't live in a midden, our home does contain a fair amount of these artifacts, known only to us, beloved only by us.

Most of the time, we coexist between the extremes of his latent modernism and my latent clutter. We fight sometimes about how to manage the influx of paper into the house, where and how to put things and find things, but for the most part, we manage reasonably well. However, every few years, James is overtaken by a desire to improve the way the house works, bringing us all closer to his vision of a seamless, perfectly organized life. In the very beginning of our marriage, we renovated a loft downtown, which we later sold, and we have been renovating new places ever since, roughly on a four-year cycle. Over time, I've come to see these bouts of renovation fever as the acute manifestations of a disease that's been in remission for a while. They can be ugly, but they're not fatal. We also have the good fortune—and perhaps good sense—to be able to air these conflicts with our therapist, whom we consult over issues both big and small.

However, I did not know where renovation would take us the first time we tore down walls, moved plumbing stacks, waited for contractors who never arrived, chatted with carpenters who never left. Unlike deleting a sentence or shifting a comma, or perhaps rearranging a chapter or two (the kind of change I perform in my work life and am most comfortable with), the changes brought on by renovation are epic. Nothing is where you left it; you can take no wall, no faucet, no toilet seat for granted. Everything exists in a swirl of possibility, a delirious dream of what your life might be like if you just get it right this time. When we entered the loft we had stripped down to four bare brick walls, James whispered, "Look at the light, the space. Wish we could keep it like this forever." He saw a luminous cathedral, and I saw Dresden.

Time and time again, he wanted to visit the empty shell of our new home, to drink it in. One Saturday night, between dinner and a movie, he dragged me into the space for yet another look at the studs, the rough plumbing lines, and the electrical conduits. When I fidgeted, looked at my watch, and mentioned we might miss the movie, he answered with, "I'm checking to see that the sliding door hardware is installed properly." For a moment, I even tried to dredge up some enthusiasm for the raw beams, the hanging outlet boxes, the piles of wood everywhere. But it was impossible.

"We're going to be late," I said with an edge in my voice.

James didn't answer.

"You're ignoring me," I went on, more loudly this time.

"It'll only take a minute," James answered.

"It's already been ten minutes," I said.

He stopped, looked at me. "If you stop bothering me, I'll be able to finish what I'm doing!"

As he tromped around, clouds of plaster dust rose into the air, rubbing off on our clothes, getting up my nose.

"I don't want to be here! I'm allergic to dust!" I finally shouted.

He hissed at me, eyes big black orbs. "There are no walls. The neighbors can hear everything. You're embarrassing me."

I screamed back, "I don't care!"

Then he shouted, "Get out!"

I dug my heels in, parked my five-foot-three-and-a-half-inch self right in front of him. "I'm not leaving unless you're leaving."

Suddenly James's face seemed to twist into the long visage of the evil Joker, as he towered over me. He shoved me out of the way, and I fell against the framing. In seconds, he was at the door and running down the stairs. I sat down on the floor, sobbing.

"Come back!" I screamed through my tears. And, half an hour later, he did. .

Of course, there's a history behind both our foolishnesses. I grew up in a home where we never even painted the walls once throughout my entire childhood, so afraid were my parents of change in any form. The furniture never moved an inch, and even on the occasions when an eccentric great-uncle came to visit and left his trademark banana peel draped on the light fixture in the dining room, the peel stayed where it was for several weeks, slowly turning browner and browner. Now that I've lived through several renovations, I also know that my parents' testy marriage could never have withstood the onslaught of such unremitting chaos. Not for them the skeins of plaster dust, the sharp tang of polyurethane, the clump of workmen's boots.

James, on the other hand, was raised in a home where to renovate was to live. He grew up doing some of the work himself; he painted walls in his childhood home, fixed up his father's offices in downtown Philadelphia when he graduated from architecture school. Over the years, he has guided his parents through several renovations. To him, to pick floor tiles together is to be in a family.

So, shortly after we were married, we began our first renovation. What I quickly learned was that the seemingly easygoing man I had married was a design Nazi. His ironclad opinions ranged from the big-ticket items like heating systems and where the walls should be, all the way down to the plates, knives, and forks. I was shocked to learn that he had a whole range of dismissive adjectives ranging from "too suburban," "tacky," "old ladyish" for sofas, wood stains, curtains, bathroom tiles, paint colors that offended his artistic sensibilities so much that to ask him, even for a minute, to consider living with them would be like asking him to tear his heart out of his body. When faced with such zealotry, I couldn't dream of backing down. I had been raised in a household where righteous anger held sway, and I was determined to meet every design belief he held with an equally passionate one of my own.

A case in point was the death struggle we had about the windows. I've always loved the idea of billowing curtains, softening and framing the window and filling the room with an orangey-red glow, much like the color of sunset. Big, long curtains, hanging from a wooden rod, on big wooden rings. A neighbor of ours had curtains like that in South Africa, and I've liked them since I was a child. "So sixties," James said with a grimace when I described my vision. He despised window treatments of any kind and particularly hated the wooden rods I liked, insisting that they ruined the frame of the window, obstructed the way the window expressed itself. I could care less about the window expressing itself. What I loved was fabric, and lots of it.

He countered my gauzy curtains with bottom-up shades, insisting that they didn't interfere with the lines of the window and gave both light and privacy. I couldn't help feeling that they looked like shades installed upside down—which they were—but he stuck to his guns. I remember the installer coming to the loft to install them, muttering, "These shades never work properly, but architects love them."

So—on and on we battled, from the fight over the shades, to the light fixtures, to the bathtubs, to the faucets, to the kitchen sink, the sheets, the doorknobs. We fought about everything. I felt that I capitulated more often than not, and James would claim the same was true for him. I began to learn over time that it was true I cared less than he did, had far, far less energy for home improvement than he did, that it was sometimes wiser to let him have his way instead of fighting as a matter of principle. As much as he loved visiting the lighting stores on the Bowery, Gringer's Appliance Heaven, and AF Plumbing Supply, I hated those places. Looking at twinkling halogens and incandescent lights and floor lamps and desk lamps made me seasick, light-sick. Being in a showroom filled with bathtubs and faucets was a kind of existential horror, as was our visit to the appliance store. At all these locales, James was in his element, clearly well liked by the salespeople he had done business with in the past. I was neither client nor architect, but one step removed—the architect's wife.

That first renovation shook our fledgling marriage to its roots, but we survived, and finally moved in to our (almost) finished home. Slowly, we began to heal, to unpack, to live with the things we liked, and didn't like. The anxiety about the soaring cost of everything began to subside as the workmen finally left and we were left in peace. We had a dog, Esther (whose rust-red color matched the wood stain on the floor and some of the walls), and now we were finally ready for a child.

When I became pregnant, the differences in our personalities and our passions became apparent yet again. During our Bradley birthing classes, James always seemed to be nodding off, lulled by the late hour, the slightly stuffy classroom we were in, the deluge of information he had little interest in. Ever the doctor's daughter, I strained to hear everything the instructor said, determined to ace the upcoming test. At home, when we tried to do the relaxation exercises together, this difference reared its ugly head again. I wanted to do everything by the book, and James had a more laissez-faire approach, very comfortable with the idea that we would manage once we were actually in the throes of childbirth. As I grew more and more pregnant, I began to worry that my nonmedical husband would have trouble advocating for me in the hospital, dealing with the know-it-all doctors and their strict protocols.

"Shouldn't we think about working with a doula?" I suggested. "Someone who has navigated this before?"

James was indignant. "I don't want anyone else there," he said. "I am your doula."

I was moved but still skeptical, afraid that when once we were in the hospital setting, the doctor would take over and that I would end up having an epidural, an episiotomy, a C-section, all the interventions that we had been working so hard to avoid. Precisely because I had been raised in a doctor's house, I felt I knew both the shortcomings of modern medicine as well as its extraordinary innovations. I wanted the best for my unborn child—a natural childbirth but in a hospital with the best possible neonatal care in the world, in case it was needed. Throughout my pregnancy, I remembered my father coming home from the hospital after delivering a baby, tiny bloodspots on his shirt and his tie, his face radiant, his voice rising with excitement as he proclaimed, "It's a boy!" or "It's a girl!"

I also remembered the authoritative, brusque way my father spoke to his patients, definitely a style of doctoring that's as outmoded as the Nelson inhalers he had us breathe into when we had bad colds. My brother, sister, and I were all well schooled in worst-case scenarios—the boy who put his hand on the red-hot filament of an electric heater, the man who was electrocuted by his own vacuum cleaner, the family whose car collided with a train on the rail crossing just outside of town—all the boils, lesions, fits, and chills caused by a thousand different diseases.

Despite my imagining all the things that could possibly go wrong, I wanted to rise above my past; I wanted to make a fresh start. I wanted to be safe, and I wanted my baby to be safe, but I didn't want someone making all the decisions for me. I toyed with the idea of having a midwife, and then picked a gentle, soothing female obstetrician instead. Clearly, I wanted a doctor present, but not someone who was going to boss me around. In some ways, I wanted James to be the authoritarian doctor figure, channeling my father's gruff tones and making sure that the real doctor didn't mess up.

I grew bigger and bigger. The month I was due to deliver was a very hot June, and it became harder and harder for me to lie down in our bed at night. I took to sleeping upright, in a big armchair with pillows under my arms and legs. I watched James sleeping peacefully, his mouth open, dark lashes shading his cheeks. He seemed little more than a child himself. Perhaps I should tell him what to do in case the baby came early, and too fast for us to get to the hospital in time. A friend of mine had given birth like that in South Africa, her husband catching the squealing, blood-soaked infant, all three of them crouching on the bathroom floor. What if the cord was wrapped around the baby's neck, right there on the floor in the bathroom? Would James know which page to turn to, which book to find? What to do? Oh, how I wished I'd married a doctor!

The night my water broke we were having dinner at the Bowery Bar. When we got up to leave, I felt something trickle down my leg. We called the doctor's office and they paged Dr. M., our doctor's partner. Dr. D. had apparently gone on an early Fourth of July vacation. I suddenly had a sinking feeling in the pit of my stomach. Dr. M. was Scandinavian, and something about her suggested the coolness of fjords, the chill of an Arctic winter. She came from a stock of reserved, hardy people. She was never going to understand the tortured coils of my Lithuanian–South African–Jewish mind, how I was capable of imagining every possible negative outcome in the world, but how badly I wanted to be fully conscious during my child's birth. I wanted to sail through the shoals of my fears and come out unscathed at the other end, holding a baby whose senses weren't dull by pain medication, who had come into the world the natural way, every inch alive.

On the phone, she told us to time the contractions and wait until they were regular and fairly close together before we called her again. If nothing happened during the night, we should come to the hospital in the morning, and she would make sure it was, in fact, amniotic fluid that was leaking from me. James was beaming from ear to ear, and I remember him going to sleep with a bucolic look on his face, the smile of an innocent.

I lay awake that night, going over a conversation I had had with my father days earlier about whether or not to ask Dr. D. to induce me, since she was going away on vacation. "If you do that," he'd said, "the die is cast, my girlie." I understood that to mean that one intervention leads to another, and that I would have lost control from the outset. Still, perhaps I should have asked her to induce me. At least I wasn't afraid of her, the way I was afraid of Dr. M. I also remembered the story my father had often told of a man who fainted at the birth of his first child, and how he and the nurse left him lying on the floor, stepping over him occasionally as they attended to the needs of his laboring wife. Was James going to faint? I'd really be on my own then!

By the time Dr. M. examined me with her cool hands the next morning, I had spent a long, sleepless night.

"Yes, it is amniotic fluid," she confirmed. "Take a walk in the park to try to get the contractions going," she told us. "If nothing happens by three, come back to the hospital and check in. We have to deliver the baby within twenty-four hours of your water breaking in case an infection sets in."

June 30, 1995, was a gorgeous late springlike day in New York City, the sky robin's egg blue, no trace of humidity, perhaps even a whiff of sea air if you sniffed hard enough. In the park, there were children playing in the playground already, and we watched them dancing in and out of the sprinklers.

We walked and walked and walked, as if in a dream. In the sylvan setting of the park, James was in his element. A few years earlier, he had taken a street-tree pruning class with the NYC Parks department and still had a "citizen pruner" card in his wallet, which allowed him to prune any street tree in the city, if the need arose. He admired the generous canopies of many of the trees, and how they were maintained. At the base of an impressive oak tree, we noticed a knot of people pointing upward, to one of its long branches. A red-tailed hawk had just landed, bearing a rat in its mouth. It was bringing lunch to one of its fledglings, a smaller, fluffier hawk. On the ground was a hawk feather, which James picked up and gave to me.

As the countdown to 3 p.m. began, I couldn't help searching James's face for clues. Did he have any idea how much I was counting on him? That I wanted him to be a doctor-doula-husband all rolled into one? That I had set the bar impossibly high? Did he remember anything from the eight-week Bradley class? As the minutes ticked away, I began to walk faster and faster, hoping to jump-start the contractions. My body wasn't having any of it, and nor was the baby, seemingly asleep at the wheel.

I barely remember the process of being admitted to New York Hospital later that day. I do remember, though, the first, lazy contractions I began to have, as the Pitocin dripped into my veins through the IV.

Soon all I became aware of was James, his honey-dark eyes round like a lemur's, his voice, a little shy at first, then gradually more confident, as he talked me through every contraction, telling me to relax each part of my body, to feel warm and loose and heavy, to let go. I closed my eyes, and he told me to imagine the beach in the little town in South Africa where my family would go on holiday, the waves rolling in to shore, then receding. He reminded me of the muscles of the uterus, as they contracted and released, contracted and released, just like the sea coming in and going out. My usually reticent husband talked a blue streak that long, long afternoon.

As the hours wore on, and the sunlight began to fade in the windows, James started to experiment with his monologue, going for some light relief. I'd finished the first draft of my first novel two weeks earlier, and it took place in a town famous for its ostrich feather trade at the beginning of the twentieth century. James decided to expand his repertoire from the seaside to the interior, to the scrubby Karoo where the ostriches roamed. At this point, I was also trying something new. I was leaning forward and squatting. His hand was near me on the squatting bar, and when he mentioned the ostriches waltzing on the veld, I didn't find it funny at all. Since I had long since given up speaking, all I could think of doing was to bite him. He yelped, pulled his hand away, and that was the end of the ostriches.

The spaces between the contractions got shorter and shorter, and suddenly my body seemed to be thrown into an entirely different gear. I knew from my Bradley class that I was moving into transition. I clung on to James, my body wracked and tossed by regrouping muscle systems, raging hormones. I lost all sense of modesty, and even the sound of James's voice seemed to disappear in the storm. All I could see was a patch of his shirt, his arm.

The first time I registered the time was when Dr. M. came in at 7 p.m. and said, looking at her watch, "You should have had the baby by now." I looked at James; he looked at me. Had we missed something? Was there a deadline for this? Then Dr. M. said she was going to examine me, to see how far the baby had descended.

I remember her peeling off her gloves after the examination, announcing that the baby was turned around, in the posterior position, and she also had her arm up, as if she were sleeping on her crooked elbow. "I want you to lie on your back and turn onto your right side," Dr. M. said. There was a silence. I knew how uncomfortable I was lying on my side, my nights of sleeping upright because of agonizing muscle spasms. I was at a crossroads here. I could trust Dr. M., or listen to my body.

I looked at James beseechingly. "Remember what it said in the Bradley book about back labor?"

He looked blank. Oh God, why couldn't he just be Dr. Bradley himself, right now? Just for one minute?

Then I suddenly found myself saying, "Take out the Bradley book. It's in the bag." I could sense how embarrassed he was, how he hated contradicting the doctor, but he fished the book out of the bag anyway. Between contractions, I hissed, "Turn to the part about back labor." He rifled through the pages, his discomfort increasing every second. "Give me the book," I growled when he couldn't find the right page.

I took the well-worn copy of *Natural Childbirth the Bradley Way*, written by Susan McCutcheon Rosegg and Peter Rosegg, and found what I was looking for. "Here it is . . . page 157. Pushing on hands and knees!" I said triumphantly.

"It's an old midwives' trick," Dr. M. said, shrugging.

So I scrambled onto all fours, just in time for another contraction. At 8:54 p.m. our daughter, Tess, was born, and handed to me from behind, like a football passed between my bent legs. My first glimpse of my baby was her lying on the pillow beneath me, staring up at me with limpid blue-green eyes, her head covered mysteriously, miraculously with a mass of wet blond hair. (James and I are both dark haired, dark eyed.) She looked sanguine, speculative, and has looked that way ever since.

More than a decade has passed since then. We had a son, Adam, two and a half years after Tess was born, and he came so quickly that I had no time to agonize over which position to assume. We also sold our loft and moved uptown to an old town house, which we gutted and rebuilt. For the most part, we fought less this time, until we came to picking a white for the stairway. My white, Pearly

Gates, was a soft white, with yellow undertones, a hint of tea stain and parchment. His white, Downy Gray, had cool blue undertones. My white was an old white; his white was a new white. Never had we fought harder than we did over those shades of difference. Finally, our therapist suggested that we blend the whites. I remember watching one of the painters pouring Pearly Gates into the bucket of Downy Gray, and mixing the two colors with a stick.

Whenever we face the specter of renovating again, I fear that one day James will leave me for a lady architect, a fellow believer in bottom-up shades and Downy Gray. Perhaps they will even work together and become one of those chic husband-and-wife architect teams.

I'm also still given to endless worrying about my family's health, listening for the heartbreaking wheeze of asthma in every bad cough my children get, looking for bull's-eye rashes, testing for strep with every sore throat. On occasion, I still wish there was a doctor in the house, particularly when one of my children is sick. Once I frantically asked James to listen to my son's breathing in the middle of the night—again fearing asthma—and tell me if he thought he was wheezing.

"I am not a doctor," he said sleepily.

"I don't care," I answered. "Just act like one! Just pretend!"

Even more recently, I noticed welts on my midriff, which I showed James, asking, "Do you think I have shingles?"

"Shingles?" James responded. "Aren't shingles what they put on rooftops?"

Despite these moments, I haven't forgotten that when both my children were born James was the only person in New York Hospital who could take care of me, who could make the pain of childbirth bearable. Both times, the sound of his voice was the only medicine I could take.

Welcome to the Club

Leslie Lehr

Club: n. A group identified by some common characteristic.

—Merriam-Webster Online

I have never been a joiner. I ate more Girl Scout cookies than I sold. Wearing pantyhose was too high a price for sorority membership at UCLA. And fifteen years after joining *Club Mom*, I cannot believe I created human beings who don't know the difference between the floor and the clothes hamper. Yet now I find myself in another club, one of the fastest growing clubs in America. It has no sales quota, no dress code, and no extra laundry. Sound perfect? I spent a year kicking and screaming—and okay, crying hysterically—before joining. Now I'm glad I did: welcome to Club Divorce.

The day my husband left, I thought the world had ended. The world as I knew it certainly had. How could this be happening to *me?* Me, the girl who pretended those were not my parents screaming at each other in front of the junior high school. Me, the girl who stole the family car from the police impound lot to visit my mother in the hospital after her divorce-induced overdose. Me, the girl who refused to go to Princeton to spite my dad for being unfaithful. My marriage was *fine*. Even our children thought so—wasn't hiding in your room when your parents fight normal?

The D word had come up before—my husband often tossed it out when he ran out of alternate vocabulary during everyday arguments. I begged him not to talk like that, but he insisted *divorce* was just another swear word. Once, he threatened to leave as we fought over how I was painting the white picket fence of our new house; we had to stop when our neighbor, a divorcée who happened to have the same name as me, came outside for her mail. I ignored the omen. We loved each other, as much as anyone knows what that means.

Then one infamous June day, reality erupted like a volcano in front of grown witnesses. Every breakup starts with some horrible scene, and mine was no different. Due to the nature of my husband's freelance job in the film industry, we never knew when or if he would be in town. So, when I had to commute to an intensive ten-day graduate school residency, my father and his third wife flew in from Ohio to help ferry our twelve- and fifteen-year-old girls to and from school. I was published and produced and taught in the Writers' Program at UCLA, but that week, I was an MFA student buried with thesis work. As it turned out, my husband was home recovering from an unusually stressful job. He was brilliant in his work, and he took it very seriously, which was part of my initial attraction to him.

But he cared about his work so much that his frustrations sometimes spilled over at home. Years earlier, I had given him a punching bag, only half as a joke, for his anger. On this auspicious day, my six-foot-four-inch husband had no interest in taking his anger out on the punching bag. Instead, after some drinking and arguing with me, he wanted to beat up my father. My husband often blamed my father's shortcomings as a parent for our marital woes. Our daughter's bedroom door locked shut as I tried to block him in the hallway by her room. He shoved me against the wall and stormed on, raging as

I caught up and tried to lock the door to the porch where my father was relaxing outside. My husband was a Vietnam vet, a Marine who knew seven ways to kill a man with his bare hands. My father, a nine-time Ironman triathlete, kept his distance on the couch across the porch. But he and his wife were horrified by the scene.

My husband didn't actually go after my father, but yelled awful things at us both and then grabbed his keys to sleep at a friend's house a few blocks away. He was not himself, and I wasn't sure how much he had had to drink or what medications he had taken, so I was nervous about him driving. I couldn't stop him, but when the front door closed, it was as if the Tasmanian Devil, a spinning, whirling mass of pain, had left. I was glad. I was distraught. And I was embarrassed. I burst into tears. This was my life, but having witnesses, my father and his wife, react so strongly, made it real. I was tempted to pack my husband's bags, but I couldn't. He was a good man having a rough time, that was all.

He had a lot of rough times. The man I loved was a conscientious objector—the first sergeant to declare himself one after being in active combat. He fought and won the right to not carry a gun. I had the letter he carried in his pocket behind enemy lines framed on my office wall to prove it. He was a hero, my hero. He deserved a safe haven. Maybe now he would agree to go to counseling with me.

He called to demand that my father be gone when he returned. So my father left two days earlier than planned, and I skipped a class to buy my husband's favorite cut of pork chops, a meal the rest of us hated. I wanted to please him, to end this and move on. When I got home, our older daughter was waiting for me in the kitchen. Not only did she help me unpack the groceries without being asked, but she, a vegetarian, made no disparaging remark about the pork chops.

After the last bag was emptied, she caught my eye and said, "Daddy moved out."

I was so furious that he would pack up while she was home, then use her as a messenger, that the pain of rejection was slow to sink in.

"He said to call him," she added, as if I would naturally do as he asked. He Who Abandoned Us. For the first time, I imagined myself joining the unspeakable Club. I couldn't even say the D word. I refused to follow his orders: I didn't call him.

An hour later, I picked up our younger daughter from softball practice and pretended everything was fine. I was good at that.

She stopped to take her dirty cleats off in the kitchen and spied the pork chops on the counter. "You said we could have pizza tonight!"

I overlooked the dirty cleats and pulled her into her sister's room. She looked around, surprised to be allowed past the Keep Out sign, while I yanked the headphones out of her sister's ears. I patted the denim quilt on the trundle bed for them to join me, then wrapped an arm around each girl. I looked from one innocent face to the other. I took a deep breath to keep from bursting while I considered what words to engrave in the younger one's memory, words that would split her life forever into Before and After.

"Daddy moved out," I said.

I gave them each a squeeze and recited that universal speech about how he left me, not them, but they already knew that. They had lots of friends with divorced parents. It wasn't as if our life would change on the surface. Despite our agreement not to travel after he missed most of my first pregnancy for a movie job out of state, the film business had fled LA for the tax breaks in Canada. The girls were used to their father being out of town, speaking to him long distance at night. No, the tragedy was that I had failed to provide a perfect family for them. We were a cultural cliché. Our girls would now be like so many others on the school rosters that got longer every year: two addresses, two phone numbers, and no idea where they left their history books. For a moment I imagined that it would make no difference. But just yesterday we had felt sorry for a little boy carrying his Star Wars pillow across a parking lot to his father's car. That was us now. Our hearts were broken.

We took turns crying and consoling each other, shrieking in solo, sobbing in harmony, and reprising a perfect chorus of woe. We emptied an entire box of Kleenex, then the sticky travel pack stashed in my daughter's book bag. When those were gone, we blew our noses through the rest of the toilet paper on the roll in the bathroom adjoining their rooms. When the girls sniffed and started pulling at my sleeves, it was time to move on.

We got in the car and rode aimlessly through our hilly neighborhood for over an hour. We listened to the Beatles and sang all the words we could remember. We pointed out stars as they burst out into constellations—little families on fire, like us. We peered in kitchen windows where fathers smiled over plates of pasta. We identified the breeds of dogs being walked and hoped our pound puppy—the one their father had nursed to health—had found the pork chops by now. None of us were hungry, not even for pizza.

We didn't want to go home. We wanted to join the stars and fly about the earth and pretend this never happened. We were in a new country that night, an alternate universe called Girls R Us, just like me and my mom and my sister so many years ago. I had created a new generation, only to repeat history. I wanted *this* to be over, to go home and forget about it, but what was home now, exactly? When the gas gauge edged into red, we reentered the earth's gravity and I heard stomachs growling. We went to Baskin-Robbins and buried our grief in ice cream sundaes. I would always remember this night.

The next day, after I dropped off my younger daughter for a ride to her softball tournament, I took my older daughter to my Saturday seminar at graduate school. My cohorts raved about my fabulous daughter and wished me a great summer.

"My husband left me," I said, and tried not to cry.

After I drove home, fixed my daughter lunch, did a load of laundry, shopped two stores for my younger daughter's favorite flavor of Gatorade, and begged my hairdresser to squeeze me in for a haircut so I could feel human enough to make it to my daughter's all-star game, my cell phone rang. It was my husband.

"I'm ready to come home."

I came to a halt by my car in the blazing hot parking lot outside the hair salon. But when I opened my mouth to answer no words came out. It wasn't just that he had put us through the wringer like dirty bath towels, but that he could so easily do it again. How could I pretend it never happened? Even if I could forgive and forget, this time there wasn't just me to consider. I would do anything in the name of love, but what about our impressionable girls? What kind of role model would I be to take him back after the long sleepless night the girls and I spent elbowing each other in my bed? He had been gone so often I no longer thought of it as "ours."

I stood there, melting in the waves of heat rising from the asphalt. I wasn't trying to punish my husband. This was the worst fight we'd ever had, but it wasn't the first. The honeymoon periods following every homecoming had gotten shorter. Ever since the Gulf War began, his nightmares and all the trauma of war had returned; he had far larger demons, but I was the one within reach. And I wasn't innocent—it takes two to mess up a marriage. A few years earlier, he said I was unlikable. I remember lying on the bed that afternoon, sobbing and shaking, until it was time to pick up the girls at school. When another mother smiled at me, I was surprised. Maybe I wasn't unlikable after all.

I went to therapy and learned to stick up for myself. (He paid for it, he liked to remind me.) I was no innocent, but at least I fought fair. For the past year, I had been sticking Post-its on the bathroom mirror and on my office door that said: Be nice. Still, when he was gone I did everything; when he was home, I did everything wrong. I got criticized for how I loaded the dishwasher and backed out of the driveway and didn't answer my cell phone when I was with the girls. I married the rebel, but lived with the Marine. But I would never have left him. He Left Me.

I was late for the softball game, but he was still waiting for my answer. Which made me realize that I had a choice. What would be best for the girls? If on that fateful June day, my father's wife (who was close to my age) was so shocked to hear me called names, names I had gotten used to—what had our children gotten used to? I would never allow my girls to be treated like that by any man. Ever. And neither would their father. Why did I count less? How could they respect me if I let him come back so easily? How could they learn what was acceptable?

My husband said he had a nervous breakdown, and I don't doubt that's true. But "I'm sorry" didn't cut it anymore. I had been teaching our children about behavior and consequences all their lives. Things had to change for Daddy to come back. Call it a time-out. I had no intention of joining the dreaded Club. But I needed to be able to trust that this wouldn't happen again. This was an opportunity to make our marriage better. I gripped the cell phone tightly, took a deep breath, and said: no.

When I got to the softball tournament, I felt like I radiated failure and everybody knew. I waved at my daughter, told the coach there was trouble at home, and asked him to go easy on her. He nodded, his eyes unreadable behind mirrored Ray-Bans. Did I look different to him? No longer the good mother, the good wife? Not only did my husband leave me, but I didn't let him come home. I was both pathetic *and* evil. At least my reflection looked okay; I had lost weight due to marital stress or maybe fewer pork chops, and my khaki shorts were a respectable length. When he turned back to the girls on the ball field, I looked for a spot for my folding chair amid the overweight wives wearing sloppy T-shirts and diamond eternity bands. How could they be so lucky and I so wrong?

At the end of the row, a thin blonde woman sat in a beach chair, hugging a toddler in her lap. Her ex was an assistant coach, elevated to a place of honor for his three hours of devotion every other weekend. She was there for every practice and game, but she was a little too thin, too blonde. I smiled when she looked up at me, but I sat with the married women. I didn't want that scarlet D on my forehead.

The next morning, I took off my engagement ring and wedding band and looked at the eighteen-year-old tan line on my left hand. I thrust a toothbrush in a cup of Palmolive and scrubbed the diamond. I wanted my life to sparkle that bright. But how could it? My husband left me.

I was the one who had proposed. I had worked my way from film school through a few freelance gigs to a staff job as the West Coast production manager for a company making Clio-winning commercials and popular music videos. I thought it was only a matter of time until I was running Paramount Studios. After all, at twenty-three, I had an upstairs office and assistants to fetch my coffee. I cut off my long hair and wore thick glasses to look older. That's where I met my husband. I held my engagement ring to the light, admiring the marquis diamond he charged on my credit card and paid off month by month. I refused to be wrong about my choice, even if I was too young to know what to look for. My husband was a hardworking crew guy, the silent romantic type, who was rumored to go home with the buxom blonde models. Yet he picked me, a petite brunette who read the *Wall Street Journal*. He took me on picnics, plied me with art and antiques, and spent his last dime on our first romantic rendezvous. Our twelve-year age difference gave him a history that made him stand out from the parade of boys in my past. He was making his stand in Vietnam when I was in second grade. He wanted to make babies; I wanted to make movies—I thought that together, we could do both.

Over the years, when other couples split up, we felt superior. We were loyal, like the Marines say, Semper Fi. In the mid-seventies, my parents were the first in our Midwestern suburb to divorce. My mother bore the brunt of her own parents' divorce back East and was blackballed from neighborhood picnics; some of my friends weren't allowed to play in my "broken home." My mother did not miss my father's eccentric ways, but she would never forgive the loss of fathers—and families—in general. She always told me to be nice to my husband. I never confided in her. I was too ashamed. I thought I could handle it. Divorce was ugly. I jammed the rings back on my finger.

Two days after he left, we had a family meeting to tell the girls Daddy would be living apart from us while we worked on making things better. A week later, the summer session began at UCLA and I was teaching a new class of aspiring novelists. I wave my hands a lot when I talk, and each glimpse of those golden shackles distracted me from the topic. They gave me a stomachache. My husband had stopped wearing his ring; he was free and unmarked. During the break, I listened to a message he left thanking me for the leftovers the girls took him from a barbecue we had without him. He said it was the first real meal he'd eaten all week. He was being nice, agreed to see a counselor, but I wanted him to be the one to set it up. I was tempted to remind him how he used to complain about my cooking. Instead, I pulled off my rings and put them in my wallet.

After the break, I asked everyone to introduce themselves. I wondered who would notice the tan line from the missing rings on my wedding finger. I asked my students, lawyers and engineers and other professionals, about their home situations. I pretended to be concerned about writing time, so I'd know how much homework to expect. Really, I wanted to know who was married, who was divorced, and where I fit in.

Several months later, I still hoped that we would get back together. We went to a counselor who gave us handouts on anger and depression. I read my Al-Anon book every night. I called an old friend from my girls' preschool days, and she took pity on me. She invited the three of us to have dinner with her family. She was a gourmet cook, something I respected in others but couldn't fathom myself. She and her husband were polite, but there was a cold war in that house that curbed my appetite. The hostility in the air between them, the jabs and insults were so strong that it was all I could do to make it through the main course. I couldn't wait to go back to my peaceful home.

An hour later, I crawled in bed with a cup of frozen yogurt and stared at the framed wedding photo of my husband and me under a flower-draped gazebo in front of the sailboats in Marina del Rey. He was so handsome with his long hair and blue eyes and black tails. I was so young, with a strapless gown, upswept hair, and lavender eye shadow. We had decided on poetry for our vows, but he didn't memorize his part. He had planned to have musician friends play, but ended up making a tape that the DJ ignored. On the video you can see the fishing boat glide by in the background and hear someone call "Don't do it!" I didn't listen; I was in love. Now my husband had a short military haircut, lived in an apartment complex with all the other estranged husbands, and my gown was in a vacuum-sealed box for the girls. Would it bring them bad luck?

Buttercup, our kitty, jumped up and nudged her head beneath the bed covers of the bed I'd slept alone in for half of my married life. She was the one I cuddled with and cried to. My husband didn't remember what kind of flowers I liked. After three years in this house, he didn't know where the flashlight was kept. When I told him we ended up at Baskin-Robbins on the night he left, he didn't believe

there was one so close to home. Last year, he had been in New York
for three weeks when Valentine's Day rolled around. He called that
morning—to see if his new cell phone worked. He realized it was
Valentine's Day only when I told him I made the girls pink pancakes
in the shape of hearts for breakfast and forged his name on their
gifts. He complained that the holiday was invented by Hallmark,
but it had always been my favorite. Here in LA there was no way to
avoid the Cupid signs—how could it be so different in New York?
He asked if I minded him having dinner with a female business associate, since it was the only night they could do it. I said yes—unless
they went to McDonald's, every restaurant was set up for romance.
I spent that night watching *The Vagina Monologues* with a glass of
wine and a box of chocolates that my mother sent the girls to give
me. I tried to masturbate and failed. When he called from the emergency room with food poisoning, I laughed. He didn't understand
why that was funny.

Epic rains fell in Los Angeles during the months following our
separation; it seemed that even the sky was crying with me. The wall
between our family room and our garage buckled and cracked and
finally fell down. Our younger daughter's allergies kept her home
from school several days each week. My mother sent me tapes of
women like me on *Dr. Phil*. I read every book on relationships at
Barnes & Noble, from how to save your marriage to how to have
a good divorce. There wasn't much out there about how to decide
between the two. Did everyone else automatically know? Click the
switch and game over? For me, the ambivalence was worse than despair. Neither of us was innocent, but neither of us was happy, either.
I conjured up all the times he said, "I hate you" just to stay strong.
And I knew he didn't mean it, so I waffled. Every phone conversation began with words of love, but ended with swearing. He wanted
to come home. I made lists of pros and cons, but they kept changing:

Things like eating yogurt in bed versus wanting to have someone in bed with you did not equate on any level.

The girls started bunking with me. One snored and the other kicked, but no matter, I was always staring at the ceiling by 3 a.m. After a month, the girls became urgently interested in our family scrapbooks, oversized Hallmark albums with expansion rods and plastic pages that lifted off with sucking sounds then stuck over all the pictures. I was no modern scrap-booker with all the fancy scissors, but I was a master at collage and I'd filled up an album for each year since their birth.

One night after dinner, they begged me to look at them together. We all smiled so much when they were babies, and had strangers take a zillion pictures of us during the toddler years. As the girls got taller and my hair got shorter, there were fewer pictures of us together. I was behind the lens as the family photographer. My husband mostly appeared at formal holidays. One shot of him frowning behind the trick-or-treaters reminded me of the many I'd thrown away. I had cut pictures out to make our memories pretty in more ways than one. Our scrapbooks were edited like a reality show: only happy faces allowed. The next few years were almost all of the girls.

Then we found a double-page spread of me in the kitchen with a rolling pin in my hand and a Christmas apron smeared with flour. I remember how happy my husband was that day, taking all those pictures of me in the kitchen. It was five years ago, the year my movie was produced and my first novel was published, a banner year, by all accounts. We also snorkeled in Hawaii and went to my high school reunion in Ohio. Four years of pictures followed, with all my birthday pictures taken by a waiter at my favorite beach restaurant. They are nearly identical—right down to the missing husband. Rod Stewart sang that "every picture tells a story," but that story is fiction. It takes pages of pictures to recognize the truth. Now it was all too obvious. I was relieved the day the girls got bored of reminiscing and put the scrapbooks back on the shelf.

There were many days that summer when I thought it would be easier just to let my husband come home and be done with it. He said he wanted to come home, he said he loved me, but mostly he complained about his studio apartment. And I couldn't blame him. Then I would overload the dishwasher without being criticized, back the car over a sprinkler head without being ridiculed, and grill a piece of halibut exactly the way I liked it. The girls would ask if they could invite a friend over, and I didn't have to find out what kind of mood their father was in before answering. The thought of seeing his car in the driveway gave me a stomachache. I knew marriage was hard work, but just how hard was it supposed to be?

My husband and I went to counseling as much as his schedule and inclination allowed. But it was difficult to change our behavior when we still had grievances to air. I would never be the wife he wanted, and I was tired of trying. Clearly he wanted to stay married. But it didn't seem like I was the reason.

Meanwhile, our savings hemorrhaged from the cost of two places. Our roof leaked and our plumbing was shot, and while we had been too stingy to fix those things before, now it was a gamble. My husband was never relaxed about money. He never adjusted to the uncertainty of working freelance. Meanwhile, I worked 24/7: We were incorporated, so I managed the books, the house, the kids—and wrote and taught and studied every spare moment. When he was home, even when he was between jobs, he couldn't understand why I didn't drop everything to make dinner. But, I thought, if he wasn't working, why didn't he pick up the slack?

I was getting sinus infections way too often, so I went to my doctor at the Motion Picture TV Clinic, where most film union families go. He asked if I was still taking birth control pills. It was bad enough swallowing a daily reminder that we weren't having sex when we were married, now there was no point at all. I told my doctor I'd stopped a few months ago. He jumped up to get me a pregnancy test. I broke down and bawled. I managed to tell him that my husband and I were separated, our sex life a distant memory. He hugged me, then handed me a Kleenex. I was touched. Then he nodded about all the temptation on location. "It's not what you think," I told him. "My husband is faithful." For a minute I wished he wasn't—my decision would be so much easier. The doctor went on to sympathize about the traveling—Club Divorce has a huge Hollywood membership and we had made it far longer than most. The doctor sat quietly until I stopped sobbing. Then he said something about my immune system and scheduled me for every *other* test in the book.

When school started in the fall, I dropped my daughter off at school after a doctor's appointment, finished my MFA thesis, researched the next chapter of my novel, and went grocery shopping in time for our counseling session before the afternoon carpool. My husband had mentioned he might have to work, but he never confirmed, so I wrote the check, slipped on respectable pumps, and rushed over. There I sat, smiling at Dr. K. and watching our dollars dwindle with every click of the clock. Why didn't he call? I was tempted to call him, but stopped myself. I wasn't his mother. Nor did I want to be.

After twenty-five minutes, Dr. K. suggested that I stop waiting and step back. He suggested that I put aside my marriage for a moment and consider it from a different perspective. "Marriage is not your life," he said. "It's a part of your life." I knew that my life had veered drastically from the path that I had intended. But, for the first time, I realized that the identity crisis that fueled my writing was never going to end.

Dr. K. asked me what I had dreamed of, what I wrote in my journal.

"Nothing," I said. I stopped keeping one ten years earlier during a crisis, when we almost split up. Back then, the girls were reason enough not to, they were so young that our oldest was just learning the alphabet. That's why I put my leather journal aside—I realized that one day she might read it. So I switched to flowered books for the girls, in which I wrote nothing more revealing than the details of each birthday, what their favorite colors were, and which My Little Pony dolls were sleeping on their beds. Dr. K. said nothing. Funny, how silence makes you listen to yourself.

Then he asked why I was getting my MFA when I was already a successful author. This one was harder, since I measured success in dollars, like my husband did—and he was very supportive. He envisioned an idyllic retirement in some cozy college town where I would teach. It sounded nice, but . . . not yet. I was already teaching enough. I just wanted to be a better writer, to see what I missed in film school. Mostly, I wanted those initials behind my name. I needed them for self esteem. And I was lonely, even when my husband was home. I craved the company of other writers, a community outside the suburban PTA. My husband was looking at the end of his life, while I had half a life to go. I don't know if it was the dozen years he had on me or the way he looked at life, the way he was raised. He had all those extra years of freedom before we married—I was jealous. I used to want to run a film studio and to earn an Oscar. He said he saved me from the film business, but that's what I had trained for, that had been my dream. I didn't know what I wanted now, after fifteen years at home, except for *my* turn to live large. I wanted to listen to the Stones, not Sinatra. I wanted to move back to the beach, not some little college town.

When I got home, I opened my closet to change, but there was nothing I wanted to wear. When had my wardrobe become a sea of khaki and white? Here and there was a splash of color; the fuchsia silk dress on our anniversary when we had such an ugly fight that the waitress never came back; the blue Hawaiian dress I wore for his birthday dinner when we had a fight and he left me at the table; the strapless teal gown I wore in New Orleans when my novel won a prize—but he never never saw me in it, because he wasn't there. All of my nice clothes had bad memories. With beige I could be invisible. What happened to my silk lingerie and garter belts, my vintage sweaters and hats?

On the wall hung a photograph of me in a red strapless sequined dress. For a study of color opposites in photography class, my sister posed me leaning in a backbend over the turquoise railing of a lifeguard stand on the beach, my dark hair flying upside down past the sparkling red hem. It was the second and last time I wore that dress. I'd seen it in *Vogue*, saved for months, and bought it to surprise my new husband on our first New Year's Eve. After hours of primping, I made my grand entrance looking like a movie star. My husband took one look and said, "I hate sequins."

I dug deep in the closet past his clothes and found the dusty wardrobe bag. Inside, the red sequins still sparkled. It was too beautiful to give away, too full of dreams that I couldn't let go. I stripped then and there and wiggled into it. While I zipped it up, the girls got home from school and burst in. They screamed in delight and begged for a turn. They were older now, almost old enough to date, so while they each twirled in my red sequined dress, I lectured. I made them promise to get premarital counseling, to think ahead twenty years before letting hormones control their destiny. I wanted them to understand that I gave them life—we gave them life—to contribute something to the world. They were not to squander their happiness for a moment, or for a man. The trick was learning how to do it. The girls weren't listening anyway: One brushed my hair while the other zipped me up. They wanted to see me twirl in that dress.

What would they see me do next?

After that counseling session when my husband hadn't shown up, I started buying oil paints and concert tickets, things I used to enjoy before we married. I started hiking with a single friend and taking the girls to the theater and having picnics on the beach by myself. I went to literary events and political fund-raisers; I bought a sequined skirt and went salsa dancing. I had put my life on hold every time he left town, only to be disappointed when he was back. For years I had begged him to take me to San Francisco for my birthday or our anniversary, but he never wanted to go. Anywhere. Of course he needed time to recuperate from all his hard work, and he was tired of crowds or worried about the next job canceling and being short of funds. But it was my life, too, and I was missing it! He avoided my literary events and hated my beloved palm trees and couldn't bear the sand on the beach. My husband assured me that he would never go salsa dancing. He would never do any of those things; he wouldn't stand in line for a movie even to be with me. I wanted a companion, not a roommate.

My best friend from England flew in with her kids to see Eric Clapton, just as we had in high school. I wasn't sure if I was regressing or getting back to who I really was. When she left, she gave me a vibrator, a big purple plastic thing that I recognized only from reruns of *Sex and the City*. Was this my fate? When I went to a specialist for one of my medical tests, I mentioned that I'd just been to a rock concert. The doctor insisted I start carrying condoms. She said newly single women were considered high risk—and she wasn't talking about pregnancy. You know you're a member of the Club when . . . you and your teenage daughter are both at risk for STDs. I had to laugh.

When my sister announced she had to work on Thanksgiving, I bought tickets for San Francisco. Three tickets. I had enough mileage on my credit card to pay for the flight and a room near the wharf. I didn't have to wait for my husband to take me, I could just go. We would have an adventure, just the girls and me. We volunteered to help feed the homeless in Santa Monica on Thanksgiving Day, partly to make sure we deserved it. My estranged husband had asked me to go to dinner that week, but I didn't want to be alone with him, so I invited him to join us. He was posted at the dishwashing station while the girls and I mixed vats of instant mashed potatoes.

"In a perfect world," he said, "I would be going to San Francisco with you tomorrow morning."

"In a perfect world," I replied, "you would have taken me when I asked."

The girls and I had a fabulous time in San Francisco, dashing wherever we wanted to go at any moment, all together, like a happy family. Then, on the way home, we realized my younger daughter's beloved bear was still in the hotel room. I was more devastated than she was. After weeks of tears and phone calls, it was never found. She learned to make do. We all did.

Soon after, my sister sent me a magazine with an excerpt from the new AARP study. Statistics showed that the majority of people who initiated divorce over the age of thirty-five were women. It stated that most women were better off emotionally afterward. Happy, even. And I could almost believe it, me who had a steady boyfriend ever since fourth grade. My generation of women was the first to be educated with the expectation of a career. Maybe our mothers didn't plan for us to have it all, but certainly they paved the way for more options. But what about the option of love? What if no one else would ever love me? I wasn't quite ready to take that risk.

The week before Christmas, I walked our black Lab, Scout, past the home of a couple I knew from the PTA. People were used to seeing me alone, but at the last Parents Night, most were shocked that we had split up. This couple knew better. They had seen us argue during a barbecue the month before my husband left. Yet, tonight their driveway was full of cars that spilled out to the street. All the twinkle lights were on, and through the kitchen window I could see heads bob beneath a sprig of mistletoe. They were having a party, and I wasn't invited. Surely, they didn't believe I was a threat to married women. Was I a threat to their marriage by virtue of being a bad example? Or was the truth that we really didn't have that much in common beyond the PTA? If we weren't a couple, we'd have even less in common. I was separated, not divorced—I still had hope I wouldn't be. I waited until Scout finished peeing in their beautiful roses, then yanked her toward home.

Six months passed, then seven and eight. We still went to counseling whenever he could make it. He still sent his checks home, and I still did the books. He was waiting, as if he had done his penance and that should be enough. He was around to ferry our daughters when possible, but for the most part we went about our daily lives as if he were working out of town. Our older daughter felt sorry for him; our younger daughter just wanted to know what was going to happen. So did I. "Should I Stay or Should I Go," the '80s tune by the Clash, became our theme song. I couldn't make a decision about what to eat or what to wear, let alone what to do with my life. With our lives—all four of them. It was too much responsibility.

Finally, I found a book called *Too Good to Leave, Too Bad to Stay*. There were dozens of questions by which you could determine if you'd be happier in the marriage or in the Club. I whizzed through the big questions, thrilled at scoring so many points to Stay. We really were in love, we really did have happy times and important values in common. But when I got down to the details, identifying things I was not willing to live with, I knew the key to the Club was in my hand. There was one thing that had to change for me to even consider staying. He had to stop drinking. That was my bottom line. He was by no means a drunk, and had every right to a few beers after a hard day of work. But I hated hearing the slur of his words; our worst fights always followed. Fear was my bottom line. At our next counseling session, I drew a line in the sand: Thirty days dry and I would continue to work on the marriage. I knew he could walk the line. But thirty days later, he crossed it. No big deal, he was in New York out with the crew after work. My husband said he didn't think it counted if he wasn't with me. He wanted credit for his honesty. I blinked and wondered if I was invisible, if my words vanished as soon as they came out of my mouth. Did I not make it clear? I panicked. Did that mean our marriage was over? Was it over because I had to stand behind the stupid line I drew, or did I really want it to be over?

A moan came out nowhere, and I realized it was coming out of my mouth, from the deepest part of me. My husband tried to put his arm around me, and I recoiled. For the next twenty minutes, I wailed like a banshee. Then I wiped my eyes, went home, and put on fresh mascara and drove to my next graduate school residency. This time I hired a college girl to help. I wanted to curl up in bed, but I attended seminars and conferences and workshops and volunteered at the evening activity, just as I'd promised. I *kept* my promises. He didn't. He didn't mean to cross that line, I told myself, he didn't understand. He just wasn't thinking of me. But that was the whole point, wasn't it?

Still, I wasn't ready to give up on our marriage. It had been only six months since he left; it felt sudden. I couldn't believe he hadn't taken me seriously. Yet I was afraid to call it quits simply because I had said I would. We still spoke, about the plumbing problems and the kids' schedule. He went the next thirty days without drinking, but it didn't mean anything to me. He didn't do it when I asked for proof that he would make changes. And as soon as he realized he'd gone thirty days without drinking, he saw no reason to go for thirty-one. He didn't want to change, he just wanted me to change my mind.

I spent New Year's with two divorced friends at a big party in Topanga Canyon at a place called the Mermaid House. We wore feather boas and paper tiaras. My red sequined dress would have been perfect. I wasn't ready to dance or to date, but I toasted to a better year ahead. When I got home and toasted the girls with sparkling cider, I realized I still wasn't ready for the Club. I still couldn't say the D word out loud. All I knew was that my fear of the known was now greater than my fear of the unknown. Call it progress.

Another Valentine's Day passed without any card or gift or flowers—only a passing sneer about the holiday when he called for the girls. The next day during our counseling session, he protested about not finding anything perfect, or anything that would please me, but there he was, empty-handed. I was relieved. I told him I thought I wanted a divorce. It was the first time I'd ever said the D word out loud.

"Fine" he said, and stormed out.

I only said I *thought* I wanted one—leaving room for discussion. We still had ten minutes left, already paid for. Dr. K. looked at me and shrugged.

A few nights later, my husband called, when I had just gotten home, all relaxed, from yoga. He was angry that his next job had been canceled and warned me to forget about getting the plumbing fixed. What a waste of a yoga class. After all this time, I still felt his anxiety, his anger, as if I were attached. I couldn't bear living like this, but after ten months apart, the only thing that had changed was the number of lines on my face. I ran to the shower without waiting the requisite five minutes for warm water to squeeze through the corroded pipes that were exactly the same age as me. The cold blast woke me up. I didn't have to be upset; I didn't have to bathe in cold water, either. It was a revelation. I decided to go ahead with the plumbing—and the roof—and the divorce. I changed his name on my cell phone to "X."

I got a loan and hired the plumbers. They had to rip through the walls, so I finally took down the old wedding picture. I painted twenty-six different shades of blue on the wall and couldn't make a decision. When had I become so unsure of myself? I realized I was looking for perfection, and there was no such thing. No one would be there to criticize me. There was no right or wrong answer, only what I wanted. And I didn't have to figure everything out by myself. I asked for help and got it. But I didn't have to do what anyone else suggested; they knew what they liked—I was still figuring it out. Finally, I hired painters to cover all the beige with three shades of blue. They painted a hot pink wall in my bedroom to frame the French doors and the pink roses outside. They took away the punching bag. My estranged husband took everything else—the leather furniture, the king bed, and the high-thread-count sheets. I bought a small bed, a cheap comforter, and an electric blanket.

When softball started up again, the tan line on my finger was gone. I chatted with the married moms, but sat with the blonde. By the second game there were four of us, all laughing at the same jokes. Sometimes there weren't so many things to laugh at, but we were friends all the same. Divorce is awful—there's no getting around it. For my children's sake, I wish things had worked out differently. Their father and I have shared custody, but they still live with me ninety-nine percent of the time. They are adjusting to having the occasional dinner with Dad. When he cancels or forgets to cancel, it no longer bothers me; I am no longer waiting for him. The girls have lower expectations than I did. And they are old enough to say yes or no on their own. It's hard to know how much adolescent angst is normal and how much is due to divorce, but I am doing the best I can to be a good mother. And a good role model. There are no mistakes in life, only lessons. And mine produced two wonderful girls.

Their father and I are not friends yet, and if it happens, it will be a long time coming. I went through all those stages of grief, and now, over a year later, he is just beginning. He won't admit to having left me; he said I made him go, and maybe there is truth to that. He did me a favor. Every time he opens his mouth in anger I know I made the right decision. If he hadn't left, I would be looking in the mirror, wondering who that woman was. Now, I'm starting to remember.

My mother's divorce still haunts her, but mine has taught me to be strong and move on. My only regret is not leaving earlier, starting over younger—but I'm not looking back. No matter what happens, I am better off. I wake up happy even when it's raining. I have a future that I can blame no one for but myself. Best of all, I am not alone. My mother's generation kept their dirty laundry to themselves, and she will scream when she reads this, but with so many women today starting our second act, the Club is going public just when we need it most.

Last week, membership got me a double discount on a coffee table. Last night, it got me an extension on my Whirlpool warranty. And I don't mean from sympathetic or lecherous men, but from other women who've experienced hell and are happy to help out. Just this morning, I took a second look at the beautiful thirty-something trainer standing behind the desk at the gym. She wasn't wearing a wedding ring, but I didn't feel sorry for her. I pushed my way back inside those heavy doors—I just had to know. "Excuse me," I said. "Are you divorced?"

She smiled as if we were already friends. "Almost," she said, and laughed.

We exchanged a few intimate details, the kind that would bond us and so many others, forever.

"Welcome to the Club," I said. She waved as I left.

I want to fall in love again someday. I'm not so sure about marriage. Mostly, I want to feel comfortable in my own skin. I want to smell the flowers and to dive in the waves and to have a voice in the world. I am proud of being a member of the Club.

We have courage in common, and those inalienable rights: life, liberty, and the pursuit of happiness. Now when I see women with rings on their wedding fingers, I don't feel jealous or resentful. Instead, I wonder if they are happy. Or if they have to go home to cook pork chops.

In Sickness

Pamela Bol Riess

I want a divorce." The words ricochet around in my head, insistent and tempting. At the slightest provocation, they gather in my mouth like a tiny special-forces unit assigned to liberate me. Sometimes, I actually say it. The words burst out like a dare and a challenge, and for a moment, I feel dizzy with the idea of it, that we might, that we could, call it quits.

But I don't really mean it. What I mean is, "You hurt my feelings. I'm lonely. I wish you would really listen to me, instead of listening with half an ear, your mind elsewhere, thinking about a call you need to make, an e-mail you forgot to send. I wish you would ask questions, probe beneath the layers of what I'm saying, climb into my life with me, as though it's happening to both of us." What I mean is, "I miss you. I miss us. Who we were years ago, back in the beginning."

I find this thought ironic since our marriage did not get off to a particularly good start. I should have known we were in for trouble when it rained on our wedding day. My mother had spent the summer and many thousands of dollars ensuring that her lovely English garden was at its absolute loveliest for our outdoor ceremony. Hours before the guests were scheduled to arrive, a skinny high school kid fluffed the grass with a leaf blower and the landscaper gave the flowers and plants a final trim with a pair of nail scissors. The rental company set up rows of white chairs, and the local contractor installed a wooden platform built for the occasion. My mother, as usual, had outdone herself. And then, the sky opened up. This was not a light shower. This was a full-on deluge that lasted several hours. The landscaper went home, drank a bottle of wine, and cried herself to sleep.

Eight months later, I did the same thing. Not because of the rain, but because Jack was weathering a psychotic break in the psych ward at St. Vincent's hospital.

You would think that having one's husband suffer a complete mental collapse would destroy a brand-new marriage. But it did not. From the moment Jack began his slow decline, I was completely committed to helping him get better. Although I wouldn't have phrased it that way, because at first, I didn't even realize he was sick. A stressful job resulted in anxiety and sleeplessness, which in turn led to a kind of wakeful stupor that, despite Psych 101 and years of my own therapy, I did not recognize as depression. I labored under the delusion that all he needed was a few solid nights of sleep and everything would be fine. I became single-mindedly focused on this goal.

At the time, I was earning about $15,000 a year working part-time as the in-house writer for a nonprofit that provided assistance to crime victims. I was also, halfheartedly, writing a novel. After a brief and unhappy stint in the hospitality consulting practice of a Big Six firm, Jack had returned to his true love, the restaurant business. With his master's from the Hotel School at Cornell in hand, he'd taken a job as the manager for a new high-profile Brazilian churrascaria in midtown Manhattan. This was his chance to make a splash in the big pool of New York City dining and put everything he'd learned at school to work.

Most nights, I stopped by the restaurant to have a drink before heading home. I loved sitting at the bar, chatting with the waiters, the girlfriends of the other managers, the owners, and briefly, with Jack. To anyone who didn't know him, he looked fine. To me, he looked exhausted, thin, and pale.

"Get out of here as soon as you can," I'd say, hugging him, feeling the bones of his scapula through his chic black suit. At home, I'd go to bed at ten and then wake up when Jack came home at two or three or four. Each night, I tried to convince him to go right to sleep, but he'd just shake his head. By then he was barely speaking, but his muteness had descended so gradually it seemed almost normal.

I flung myself wholeheartedly into the great quest for sleep. I scrambled eggs with cheese melted on top and made toast with lots of butter. Jack would sit on the sofa in the living room with the plate balanced on his bony knees and push the food around with his fork. I whipped up concoctions of warm milk and Kahlúa. I rubbed his back and his feet. I ran baths and gave blow jobs, hopeful he'd drop into a post-orgasmic slumber. My father, a physician, prescribed very low-dose sleeping pills. Nothing had any effect.

Over the course of three weeks, Jack slept less than a total of twenty hours, and then, one Sunday, he couldn't get out of bed. He couldn't speak or tell me anything at all about how he was feeling. I called his father, a Jungian analyst in Seattle, Washington. "He sounds depressed," his father said, and it was as though someone had flipped on a light switch. If I had been a comic strip character, my thought bubble would have said "Duh."

I felt stupid for not having realized sooner what was going on. Early in our relationship, Jack told me he'd had a breakdown when he was twenty-two, just before his graduation from college. But both he and his family presented the event as an aberration, not the norm. That time, drugs failed to have an impact, but ten rounds of electroconvulsive therapy finally seemed to cure him. He hadn't had any problems, nor any follow-up care, in the eight years since.

This time, a visit to a psychiatrist resulted in a diagnosis of major depression with psychotic features. The doctor asked if we wanted to admit Jack to the hospital.

"Do you think he needs to be hospitalized?" I asked. I still didn't understand just how sick he was.

"Not necessarily. But he's admitted to suicidal ideation, so someone needs to be with him at all times."

"Suicidal ideation?" Jack had never told me he'd been thinking about killing himself, but evidently, he'd told the psychiatrist. How could my smart, handsome, athletic, funny husband want to die? We were sitting next to each other on an overstuffed leather couch. I found his hand and squeezed it, but he didn't squeeze mine back.

"Yes," the doctor said. "Can you manage to have someone with him?"

"Yes," I said, though I wasn't exactly sure how.

We left with a prescription for a trio of pills meant to induce sleep, reduce anxiety, and eventually, lift Jack's mood. But the drugs didn't kick in fast enough, and a week later I found myself riding with Jack to the hospital in an ambulance. My father-in-law, Michael, rode along with us. He'd flown out from Seattle when the situation appeared to be devolving.

We spent the entire day in a hallway in the emergency room. Jack lay on a gurney, and his father and I tried to get Jack to eat a slice of pizza or drink a soda, but he wouldn't; he was convinced the food was poisoned. Finally, after seven hours of waiting to be admitted, Jack lunged at a resident who was asking him a series of questions and filling out an intake form. "Give me a pen. Give me a pen," Jack screamed. He told me later that he was simply tired of waiting, that he'd only wanted to sign himself in to the hospital; but at the time, he seemed scarily out of control. As a result of his outburst, he ended up drugged and restrained in a "quiet room." He wouldn't be allowed onto the psychiatric ward until the next day.

"You should go get some rest," the nurse said. "He's out for the night. Come back in the morning."

So my father-in-law and I left the emergency room and went out to dinner and then back to the empty apartment. The day had been long and surreal, and we were both completely exhausted. While he made calls to the Pacific Northwest, I watched *Beverly Hills 90210*, escaping into that sanitized and comforting drama. When the show was over, I began to get ready for bed, but then stopped. I couldn't stand the thought of Jack sleeping alone in that strange place. For the past three weeks, he'd been waking up nightly, anxious or fearful about one thing or another. I didn't want him to open his eyes in that white, sterile room and not know where he was.

I pulled on jeans and a sweatshirt and headed back to the hospital in a cab. It was early May, and the air was cool and hazy with moisture. Out on Ninth Avenue, the world continued on as usual. People strolled down the street and sat eating dinner in restaurants. Cars honked, and the traffic lights changed just as they always had. But that world didn't have anything to do with me, or with Jack. Our world had contracted down to this one problem, his illness. Getting my husband back. At that moment, it was all I cared about, all I could see.

Visitors were only allowed in the emergency room for the first ten minutes of every hour. At eleven, I went into the quiet room and stood over Jack, stroking his brow. He looked more peaceful than he'd looked in weeks, and for a moment I let myself believe when he woke up in the morning he'd be himself again. For the next fifty minutes, I sat on the steps in front of the hospital and sipped a cup of coffee. I didn't know what was going to happen to Jack, or what was going to happen to me.

Jack had started working at the restaurant in early March. Now it was early May. Though Jack was still technically employed, I didn't know if or when he'd be able to return to work. I wasn't sure what kind of insurance he had, whether or not it covered mental illness. My measly salary wasn't going to be enough to pay the rent, let alone pay the doctor and hospital bills we were racking up. I needed to call the insurance company, meet with the hospital social worker, perhaps fill out an application for Medicaid. I needed to call the restaurant about sending his paycheck, even though he hadn't worked for the past ten days and hadn't really earned it, and if they wouldn't do that, I needed to fill out forms for disability and/or unemployment. I made a to-do list on the back of a grocery receipt and carefully folded it into my pocket.

At midnight, I went back into the quiet room and decided not to leave when the nurse announced time was up. A sheet crisscrossed Jack's chest and secured his wrists and ankles to the stretcher rails. It reminded me of the complicated rope contraptions my father engineered to secure luggage to the roof of the car on family vacations. I untied the sheet and made a provisional bed on the cold tile floor. The chill seeped through my clothes, but there was nowhere else in the world I wanted to be. At some point, I got up and turned off the fluorescent lights. An hour later, a nurse opened the door and turned them back on again. "Who's asleep on the floor of the quiet room?" she yelled down the hall. "The girlfriend," someone yelled back. I didn't protest. I didn't care who they thought I was or what they called me. I only wanted to be with Jack, to reach up and hold his hand, dangling over the side of the bed.

At St. Vincent's, we decided to skip the slow trial-and-error process of drug therapy and move right to ECT, because it had been successful in the past. At first, ECT was terrifying to me. I thought it somehow shocked your brain into resetting itself. But the doctor explained the shock lasted only a few seconds and was designed to induce a seizure. The seizure, in turn, caused natural antidepressants to flood the brain. It was a blunt, but organic, and therefore extremely effective, instrument.

At that time, St. Vincent's was a dispiriting, derelict place. Jack ended up there because the psychiatrist we'd originally consulted was on staff and I'd thought that this would somehow make a difference in his treatment. It didn't, but moving him to a nicer hospital proved complicated and expensive, so I decided to leave him there among the mostly poor, indigent, minority population.

Meanwhile, I kicked into high gear. It's ironic that one of Jack's worst moments turned out to be one of my best. I wasn't happy to have a sick husband, of course. I would have given anything to go back to the way things had been before. But my life had a purpose and a direction that it had heretofore lacked. I had vowed to love Jack in sickness and in health, and I wasn't going to let him down.

Every day, I went to work at my part-time job and then spent the late afternoon and evening visiting Jack. I tried to ignore the smell of piss wafting from the bathroom off the common room, tried to ignore Bob, an old white guy with a fringe of gray hair who stood against the wall asking, "Am I real, or am I an illusion?" much to the consternation of the many patients who had a good deal of trouble telling the difference. Sometimes my oldest sister, Jennifer, joined me there. She'd show up after work in her Hermes scarf and Prada loafers bearing bags of snacks for Jack. Invariably the other patients hit her up for money, because more than anyone else in the room, she obviously had it. Sometimes they asked her to buy them pizza and once she said yes, a mistake, because then they expected her to buy food every time she stopped by.

During these visits, Jack and I talked, but not about anything important. The ECT made him forgetful, and the anti-anxiety medication made him groggy, so it was a challenge to have a real conversation. Sometimes I talked to his roommate's mother, a tiny Italian woman who believed all these men were in the hospital because they watched too much television.

Sometimes we played cards or checkers or made origami frogs. When it was time to go, I felt relieved to step out of that smelly room into the fresh spring air, but also terribly sad to be leaving Jack in such a dump.

At home, I was always struck by the dark and silence of the apartment, by not having anyone to speak to once I got there. People called to check in, to ask how things were going, but by then I was too exhausted to report or explain. I drank wine by myself, and more than once made myself throw up before I went to sleep so I wouldn't be too hungover to go to work the next day. Sometimes I cried, but not a lot. I feared if I started, I wouldn't be able to stop.

After two weeks at St. Vincent's, the doctors decided to release Jack from the hospital. He'd had only three rounds of ECT. I later learned that a full course of treatment was ten, but I didn't know enough to argue. Compared with the rest of the patients, Jack probably did seem healthy enough to go home.

He went back to work on a limited basis, and at first seemed to be all right. But then, about two weeks later, he called me at work and said he was sure the doorman was whispering about him when he walked by. He thought perhaps the owners of the restaurant were going to kidnap me and hold me for ransom to recoup some of the money he believed they'd lost as a result of his absence from work.

"Don't go anywhere," I said, and raced home, my heart beating in my throat.

The next day, we went to meet with yet another psychiatrist. By this time, a friend of my sister's had offered me a job with her head-hunting firm. I'd never worked full-time and didn't know anything at all about recruiting financial services executives, but she said I was smart enough to figure it out. Besides, the salary was $50,000, the same amount Jack had been making at the restaurant. It felt like a fortune to me. Enough to keep our apartment, to buy groceries, to pay the deductible for doctor visits, the only charges, it turned out, insurance didn't cover. But I was due to start my new job in less than a week, and I couldn't afford to take time off to look after Jack.

We sat in the psychiatrist's office discussing our options. The place was decorated with tasteful mission furniture and Turkish kilims. Books lined the entire length of one wall. I can't remember his name, but I remember the psychiatrist's reddish-brown beard, and his calm voice as he picked up the phone and called Payne Whitney, the psychiatric unit at New York Hospital, to see if they had a bed. This time, we didn't need an ambulance. This time, we simply walked a few blocks from the doctor's office to the hospital and Jack signed himself in. On the way, we stopped at Super Cuts because he wanted to get his hair trimmed. Because of his paranoia, I worried Jack would think the hair clippers were some kind of device designed to torture him, but he sat still and passive as the stylist sheared away his curls.

Payne Whitney was a vast step up from St. Vincent's. The visiting room was clean and bright and contained an exercise bike as well as an array of magazines and newspapers. The television was in a separate room, so its blaring didn't overwhelm conversation.

By then it was June, but it felt like summer never really came. The weather never turned hot, and Jack was absent. During past summers we'd spent weekends at his grandfather's lake house. There, we'd get up early and water ski while the water was still smooth and glassy. Jack was an excellent skier, sent up great plumes of spray as he cut sharp slalom turns and then raced across the boat's wake. His legs were so strong and lean, you could see the striations of his muscles.

Walking the long blocks from the subway to the hospital each evening, I passed by young couples and groups of friends sitting in outdoor cafés sipping gin and tonics and glasses of cool chardonnay. They all looked carefree and happy, oblivious to me, trudging along by myself. I wanted to sit down at one of the tables, join a group, or take a table for one and order a simple plate of pasta. But it wasn't food that I really wanted, or even companionship. I wanted the feeling of freedom and relaxation that I'd always associated with summer when I was a child.

Entering the lobby of the hospital, I was hit with a blast of cold air. Riding up in the elevator, I was self-conscious, knowing I was watched by a security camera. I smiled at the nurses at their station, said hello. I wanted them to see that Jack had a well-dressed, pretty young wife. That he hadn't always been, wouldn't always be, a delusional psych patient. I popped my head into Jack's room to see if he was there. Most of the time he wasn't. His roommate, Phil, a television producer in another life, would glance up and ask me if I had any pot. "No," I'd say, then head into the common room to find Jack. He was usually sitting on a plastic-covered sofa waiting for me. Sometimes he was watching television or scribbling thoughts and plans on a yellow legal pad. I held his hand and asked him how his day had gone, how he was feeling.

Because the ECT impacted his short-term memory, he often didn't remember my visits.

"Why didn't you come yesterday?" he'd ask. He looked so worried.

"I was here for three hours. Don't you remember?"

But he didn't. I tried not to cry in front of him. Falling apart wasn't an option. I had a job to do, money to earn, a husband to take care of.

Sometimes we snuck into Jack's room and lay down on his narrow bed. The plastic mattress cover crinkled as we settled onto the pillows. We just held each other, kissed each other chastely, as though we were acquaintances or blood relations.

Several friends asked me if I was going to leave Jack. But the thought never crossed my mind. I did, on more than one occasion, fantasize that Jack somehow managed to commit suicide. After the meeting with the first psychiatrist, Jack admitted to me that he'd spent a few hours one Saturday walking around the city scouting for a building he could jump off. I imagined my life if he'd actually found one. Then, instead of being that poor woman married to a lunatic, I would be that poor woman whose husband had killed himself. I'd speak at the funeral and be brave and eloquent, and people would come up afterward and offer me hugs and words of condolence. As long as Jack was alive, though, that wouldn't happen. All but our closest friends seemed to feel that mental illness was somehow private and unmentionable and something they shouldn't really get involved in. And since Jack's father had flown back to Seattle to prepare for a long-planned sailboat race (I remember being galled at the time . . . why did he quite literally get to sail off into the sunset while I was sitting in the piss-smelling visitors' room at St. Vincent's?), and since no one else in his family offered to get on a plane to help me (and because I certainly wasn't going to ask), I opted to take on the demeanor of uber-wife and proceeded to handle whatever came my way with a kind of determined efficiency.

I saw myself as doing nothing less than saving his life. This was in part a grandiose construct, and in part the truth. That same month, an acquaintance's husband jumped to his death during a paranoid episode in which he believed the IRS and the FBI were after him for some unclear and unarticulated transgression. His wife, fed up with his mental state, left him alone in their apartment. When she returned several hours later, he was dead on the sidewalk and there were cops all over the place.

Even now, Jack will sometimes say, "Without you, I'd be dead or homeless." I don't know that it's true, but I suspect that some of our current problems are rooted in the idea. I hate to admit it, but some part of me feels he owes me. I've never needed him in such a large and obvious way. But I need him in many small and daily ways, and when he doesn't come through, I feel unreasonably angry.

Recently, he left me standing on a sidewalk holding my two-year-old nephew on my right hip and a large plastic toy shovel in my left hand. My five-year-old niece and my four-year-old daughter teetered on the edge of the curb knowing they were not allowed to cross the street alone, but also knowing I didn't have a free hand to offer them. And there was my husband, charging into the road alone.

"Jesus, Jack," I called, and he spun around. "What the hell are you doing?" I barked. I hated how I sounded. I hated the person that, over the last ten years, I have become. Sometimes I think I want a divorce just so I can stop acting this way. In the car driving home I began to cry.

"Are you thinking about getting a divorce?" Jack asked. We have become this predictable.

"Yes," I said quietly so the kids strapped into their car seats wouldn't hear me. But I really wanted to scream, "I saved your fucking life. I'm not even asking for a tiny fraction of the thought and effort and focus and concentration it took to do that."

His illness has taken its toll in other ways. Jack was eventually diagnosed with bipolar disorder, and I've helped him get through several minor and one major manic episode that lasted three months. Our daughter Lydia was six months old when it began and nine months old as it tapered off. Though Jack managed to stay in his job and out of the hospital, he wasn't someone I liked, let alone loved, for most of that summer.

With an infant on my hands, I didn't have the energy or the interest to take care of him the way I had before. I already had one child. I didn't need another. And furthermore, I wanted him to take care of me. I felt abandoned and betrayed and completely convinced that our relationship would always be imbalanced, that Jack couldn't stand to have the focus on me.

Something snapped in me that summer, some feeling of trust or hope that I haven't been able to regain. When Jack got sick at the beginning of our marriage, I assumed it was simply one scene from our marriage that we could get through and then put behind us. I could handle it because it felt transient and exceptional, not something we'd have to live with in any ongoing way.

But I was wrong about that. Jack's illness has the power to undermine his reliability, his stability. When he doesn't get enough sleep or is under pressure at work, I can see, through a glitter in his eye or a slight twitch in his face, the disease pushing up against the medication, and sometimes, very slightly, breaking through. These interstices where the disease wins, however briefly, are terrifying to me and recall the whole history.

Sometimes, I feel like a survivor of the Great Depression (no pun intended) who hides money in the mattress and stocks canned goods, always preparing for the worst. Over the years, I've lost and regained my husband several times. I've trusted him, depended on him, only to be betrayed, not by him so much as by his disease. Now, he's appropriately medicated and has been on a relatively even keel for the last five years. But what if the medication stops working? What if I let myself love him again, really love him? What if I let myself depend on him, need him? And what if, once again, he disappears?

When he doesn't really listen to me, when he doesn't remember what I've told him, when he leaves me standing on a sidewalk with three young children, I feel micro absences that recall the macro absences I've experienced.

A month after Jack was released from Payne Whitney, we celebrated our first wedding anniversary. My mom treated us to a night at the four-star inn where we'd spent our wedding night. We checked in and luxuriated in the enormous bed. The sheets were cool and creamy, so different from the scratchy hospital sheets, gray with age.

We played tennis, napped, went out to dinner. During the meal, we talked and laughed and cried a little bit. We toasted ourselves, proud for having survived our trial by fire. For dessert, we ate the top of our wedding cake. It was perfectly preserved, tasted exactly as it had 365 days before. But we were different. We were not quite as innocent as we'd been. Still, we had reason to be hopeful. Our marriage, and more important, our love, was intact. We were still open to each other, willing to risk being disappointed.

But I'm not so willing to risk it anymore. I've become what I've always disdained in other people: someone who can't really open up because she's terrified of getting hurt. I've built myself a little bunker designed to keep Jack out and myself safe. But it's lonely in here. If our marriage is going to survive, I've got to find a way to chip away at the bricks.

The Last Gasp

Andrea Chapin

Something happened this week that gives me hope. It came after my husband, Jeffrey, and I had a major blowout, that followed another even more major blowout a few days earlier. And the thing that happened was this: I came home after going to the gym and leaving my husband in charge of the homework hour, pajama-ing, teeth-brushing, and bedtime reading, and when I went into the bathroom, the back of the toilet and the nearby wall were a gallery of jack-o'-lanterns—pointy teeth, scary eyes, the whole bit—and I burst out laughing. Earlier in the evening when I'd been trying to get dinner on the table, our five-year-old son had come to me and asked if we could make Halloween decorations and put them on the toilet.

"On the toilet?" I had asked, wondering what issue of *Martha Stewart Living* this might be from.

"The toilet," he nodded.

I'd said something to defer the project and went on my way in the kitchen. What struck me now, as I looked at the artwork, were not only my son's wonderful scary faces, but also the jack-o'-lanterns my husband had made. They were works of art, and I had never seen him do anything like that before. I tried to recall past kid/parent art projects, and I couldn't remember if he had ever created any art alongside our children—if he had it hadn't been remarkable.

For many years, my husband came home for the evening once or twice a week. But since 9/11 that changed, and now it was rare that he missed dinner, though he regularly went back to his music studio when the kids were in bed. So it was not that he had done the Halloween project that was so astounding—because he now spent a lot of quality time with our boys—it was that the renderings of the pumpkin faces were so good.

During the rest of the week, every time I walked into the bath-room and was confronted with those glaring faces, a question lurked in the back of my mind: Can we middle-aged adults really change? Can both of us, my husband and I, tap into the long-dormant skills and abilities that are necessary for our survival as a couple? I know I have to change, but if he doesn't, can I respect and live with him?

Ten years ago, when we hit another rough patch in our marriage, we went to a couples' therapist, and with her help, we navigated our sinking relationship to safer shores. Ten years ago—when we'd been together for nine years and married for four. Ten years ago—when we didn't have two boys ages five and nine. Then, we'd fought about the same issues we were fighting about now: money, art, financial and emotional dependability, intimacy. Ten years seemed like a cen-tury ago.

Though I can't recall what exactly started the fight that forced us to call in a professional then, I'll never forget the moment we knew something had to change. We were standing in the middle of our living room (the same rental we are still in) with our hands balled into fists at our sides—ready for a brawl.

"You're driving me crazy!" Jeffrey had shouted.

"Well, you're driving me crazy," I countered.

We lived a bohemian life in Manhattan in a small walk-up in the Village. My family called our way of life hand-to-mouth; I preferred calling it day-to-day. Neither of us was good at planning for the future. Jeffrey, a musician turned songwriter and music producer, had always been self-employed. I had—after a decade of work in magazines, as a freelance writer and editor, and a recent MFA in creative writing—taken a full-time job editing. I was providing the health insurance and getting regular paychecks. I had finished a novel that an agent was trying to sell. Jeffrey had money sometimes. When he didn't, he didn't seem to worry about it. This drove me crazy.

Part of what had drawn me to Jeffrey was his ability to concentrate and his undivided delight in writing music: He could sit in his studio for hours at a time, reworking the bridge of a song, fiddling with the chorus. But what had seemed charming in the first beats of our relationship was now making me furious. "Okay, write your songs, but for God's sake go out and earn some money, too," I nagged. The time I suggested bartending, he reacted as if I'd punched him.

I was thirty-five and Jeffrey was thirty-seven, and he had started to bring up the idea of children.

"You know," he said one day over breakfast at a diner. "Being a father, having children, is not something I want to miss."

I'd responded by smiling faintly and turning pale.

"Don't you have anything to say about that?" he pushed further.

I wasn't sure I did. All I could imagine was me at a magazine job all day and most of the evening, with no time to spend with my kids, let alone work on my second novel, while he waltzed in and out humming his tunes. And then there was the fact that ever since I'd met him he'd worked every day until at least three or four in the morning, a schedule that extended from his musician days, and the thought of being alone with a baby when a fever spiked didn't make me feel any better. I expressed my fears not at that breakfast, nor in any direct way, but the fights about money, always started by me, went from once every six months to once a week and then, quickly, it wasn't just money we were fighting about—soon everything became cause for a battle.

The night of the "you're driving me crazy" scene, the tension finally broke, but the confrontation wasn't over; it just took another track. We sat on the couch, and Jeffrey told me how I constantly made him feel inadequate—financially (I freaked out when he didn't have money), in terms of his career (I criticized how he conducted his business affairs), sexually (I turned away from him). He said he increasingly felt like part of me was closed off to him, almost indifferent to him.

I was horrified when I heard these things because though I wanted to say—I do not do that—I realized I did, that when I got angry I retreated into my own safe little imaginary world where I had an escape hatch ready. *I'm financially independent from this man, and, I deluded myself, I'm emotionally independent, too. If this doesn't work, I'm outta here. Easy.*

As I sat there listening to Jeffrey, part of me felt ashamed of this behavior, while part of me felt that I had every right to be angry, every right to pull away, because when I brought up money he would explode in defensiveness, as if I were criticizing his whole being. We were locked in a stalemate—I felt I couldn't express myself without him blowing up at me. So I either pulled away, removed myself, or flew into a rage—there was no in-between, no discussion.

The more we fought, the less we had sex. Our anger made us physically as well as emotionally unattractive to each other. My husband's love handles no longer made me think of love: I can only imagine what my thighs made him think of. We had, in our anger and frustration, lost our way, lost the language we needed to communicate and to understand each other—and this scared us.

At that time, ten years ago, it didn't seem like the last gasp before the end for us, but we did feel as though we were hurtling toward a frightening brink and we needed help, someone to guide us for a while, so we could go on our married way—get novels published, write hit songs, start a family, put away for our retirement and college, buy an apartment. Though we were pushing into middle age, we were artists, and it all seemed in front of us, as if there were still time for the plot of our lives to unfold in a natural way. So, in a city with myriad therapists, we found Dr. B., and during one cold miserable January and February we trudged our way to 90th Street, to what we considered as the far reaches of the Upper East Side.

When we got to Dr. B.'s waiting room, small and windowless, I felt annoyed that we had to sit so close to each other—no place to run, no place to hide. Her office had more breathing space, walls of bookshelves and windows that overlooked Park Avenue. She sat across from us, a pretty woman with shoulder-length brown hair, steel-rimmed glasses, a strong foreign accent and sensible shoes, and I immediately started in on money problems: how Jeffrey's long-term goals of developing singers and bands and writing hit songs seemed to overlook the short-term needs of regular money coming in.

Our session quickly dissolved into Jeffrey shouting at me and me growling at him through clenched teeth. But money was not where the fifty minutes ended. As a counterbalance to my attacking him about money, Jeffrey brought up how I persisted in letting our two cats into our bedroom though he had developed bad allergies to them. I often ignored his coughing, stuffed-up nose, wheezing—as if the symptoms did not exist. He had repeatedly asked if we could shut the door and leave the cats outside, and I agreed halfheartedly. But since he usually worked late, most nights when he came home he found the cats curled up around my head on the pillows. He said this made him feel as though I didn't care about him.

And my lack of support didn't end there. He charged on. I got furious when he wanted me to cover him until a check came in. I was not a pillar of emotional strength, either. Jeffrey felt that I didn't take care of him the way he took care of me, which was true. Jeffrey was always there for me when I had a problem—long talks late at night, cheering me on in my career and my life. But if Jeffrey brought up his worries—the financial splits on a song he had co-written that was going on such-and-such an album; the singer/songwriter he was producing who had great talent but seemed, as time went on, to have a less than convincing stage presence; a meeting with a music publishing executive—I often became so anxious and worried along-side him—*you really wrote most of that song, what if this guy chokes on stage*, etc., etc.—that Jeffrey ended up comforting me.

A father in debt—I grew up listening to my parents drunkenly scream at each other about money late into the night—and a mother in denial about pain and emotion: These conflicts were nothing new. Although I'd vowed to myself that my relationship would never be like my parents', and in many ways it wasn't, in certain areas I was creating a similar mess. By the end of the first session, it was clear that money was not the only problem but one of many problems, and that below the money fights lurked issues of caring and inti-macy, areas in which I always thought we were leagues ahead of most couples. Money was the easiest thing for us to argue about.

As the sessions continued, Dr. B. supported each of us in certain grievances. When Jeffrey angrily brought up his cat allergy, Dr. B. turned to me and said, "Do you realize how serious this is?" She said the allergy could turn into asthma (which it did). All of a sudden, I saw my mother in myself, my mother who could hardly acknowledge any illness, much less provide comfort.

On the other hand, when I brought up that Jeffrey wanted us to have a child, yet he worked on spec projects rather than looked for freelance jobs—declaring the artist he was writing the songs for would surely get a record deal (at this point, Jeffrey piped in, "That is what is important to me, and if it means I have to eat pizza for two months then so be it . . .")—Dr. B. turned to Jeffrey and said, "When you have a child, Jeffrey, you have to be able to provide for a baby's basic needs, and pizza for two months doesn't sound like it qualifies."

When Dr. B. articulated each of our resentments, neither of us could deny them anymore. After one session, when we were walking out of the building, Jeffrey said, "You won that round," but the next week, I told him, "Well, you won that round." We began to see how our behavior, from the abstract to the practical, perpetuated a bad dynamic. As soon as one problem was aired, another rose to the surface. The cats on the pillows made Jeffrey feel as though the cats were more important than he was. Yet, one reason I was so attached to the cats was because he worked all the time; the cats were my companions. Jeffrey and I rarely saw each other for dinner—maybe once a week—and it was customary for him to work through the weekend. So I was convinced his work was more important than I was.

We were married, but we lived like we were still single. In the evenings or on the weekends, I wrote, read, swam, went to the movies, or ate dinner with my single girlfriends who couldn't imagine being married to someone who was never around. I had grown up in New Hampshire with a father who commuted two hours to his job south of Boston. Several nights a week, he stayed in a tiny attic apartment he rented close to his office. He spent the nights he did come home getting drunk and railing against the job he hated or arguing with my mother about money. So, on some level, I was comfortable with Jeffrey not being home at night. I rarely made demands on him about his studio addiction: I was glad he loved what he did.

During our sessions with Dr. B., we discovered how our fights about housecleaning, like our fights about the cats, were connected to issues of caring and intimacy with which we were struggling. Between my lack of vacuuming and the cat hair, Jeffrey was furious at me for not taking his allergies seriously. Yet, I was on cleaning strike because I was furious at him for not taking the need to make money seriously. And the lack of money made hiring someone to do the cleaning impossible. I thought: I work full-time, I covered this and that bill, why should I spend my free time vacuuming and cleaning the toilet? I felt Jeffrey didn't do his share, so I stopped doing mine. More energy was spent self-righteously wrangling about who was going to do what chores than actually doing them.

As I zoomed into my late thirties, the idea of having a child with a husband I couldn't rely on financially and who was never around made me panic. My distant, anxious, occasionally raging behavior made my husband feel he couldn't rely on me for emotional security. When I brought up my fears about having a child when I was the only financially stable one in the marriage, it prompted an outburst from Jeffrey.

"Your ideas of raising a child are so . . . so bourgeois!" he spit out.

Who was I with? A man who had grown up on the Upper West Side, only attended private schools, and religiously maintained a membership in a squash club, had now in a matter of seconds turned into . . . I wasn't sure what . . . a pizza-eating socialist? "If I had even one bourgeois cell in my brain, then I certainly wouldn't be married to you!" I volleyed back.

Dr. B. calmly intervened: "I'm not going to address your financial dynamic at the moment, but clearly the current state of your relationship is not an emotionally healthy environment for a child."

We both stared at her in disbelief. We could argue endlessly about our shaky finances and how they might or might not affect a child, but it was frightening to think that our relationship wouldn't provide enough emotional stability. That was our wake-up call.

There was nothing fun about the sessions. They were grueling. Each week we left Dr. B.'s office clutching our coats against the icy winds that swept down Park Avenue and wondering how we would make it through this grim part of our lives. With Dr. B.'s careful mediation, we began to clear a path through our troubles and to hear what the other person was saying. We had spent years colluding in keeping each other in our roles, each thinking that since we both had shortcomings it all balanced out. But it didn't. We had to let go of certain aspects of our relationship that we had grown uncomfortably comfortable with.

We isolated and then worked on the smaller as well as larger issues in our marriage. Household chores were divided fairly; the cats were kicked out of the bedroom for good; we bought a top-of-the-line vacuum cleaner with a special filter for allergies; Jeffrey had to figure ways to make money in the short term while working on his long-term spec projects; I had to let go of my "I'm outta here" fantasy; intimacy meant I couldn't withdraw sexually or retreat whenever I was angry; and we both had to learn how to spend downtime together.

And though our eight sessions that winter were as pricey as a Caribbean getaway, the following spring as we strolled hand in hand down a tree-lined street in our neighborhood, we both agreed our weekly sojourns to Dr. B.'s Park Avenue office had been the best thing we'd ever done for ourselves and each other and well worth the money.

In the years that followed many things in our marriage got better. The summer after our visits to Dr. B. we started renting a small cottage out of the city, and for the first time in our ten years of being together we spent weekends with each other; we actually went on picnics and bicycle trips. And that time together made us feel closer and more romantic. My husband found freelance work that brought in checks on a fairly regular basis. We decided to start a family; I got pregnant, had the baby, and after six weeks went back to work. Under much pressure, I tearfully got rid of the cats because Jeffrey's allergies had turned into full-blown asthma.

When our son was a year old, I left my magazine job for freelance writing, editing, and teaching, and got to work on a second book because my first novel hadn't sold. More money came in but more money went out to babysitting and nursery school. The year we had our second child, Jeffrey had a song that was a top forty hit: We paid all our debts from the previous year and sent our first son to private school, thinking this *is only the beginning*. My new agent seemed to think the novel I was working on, which I transformed from a very autobiographical family saga into a murder mystery (more commercial, I thought, a zippy plot line), was going to sell well. *We'll be moving from our small rented Village walk-up soon because the money will roll in now,* we thought. It didn't.

A record that Jeffrey had written and produced came out the week before 9/11 and started to climb the charts, but then disappeared into the void after that fateful day. The next artist he developed stiffed in front of a club full of eager record executives and didn't get a record deal. My book didn't sell; all the editors were unanimous in their response that the murder mystery plot didn't feel believable but the family stuff was terrific—*why doesn't she write a book about that family?*

When 9/11 came and the song that the label was betting would be a hit wasn't, Jeffrey began to come home at night. Until then I was alone with the kids for dinner and bedtime six nights a week. I've wondered if the change in Jeffrey's routine was because 9/11 made him realize that life is too short, or if it was linked to depression over the record, or if he realized that he was repeating his father's behavior of not being available to his kids at night, or if Jeffrey simply discovered how much fun it was to catch up with his children at night. It was probably all of the above. Jeffrey started coming home for dinner regularly and helping me put the two boys to bed, and then dutifully returned to his studio to work into the wee hours. And weekends had changed, too, with the two of us trying to balance a life with our children and our work.

But then, exactly a decade after our visits to Dr. B., the constant fighting returned. Jeffrey was having a bad year with project after project falling through; between book doctoring and ghostwriting, I had more work than I could handle, so I'd put the kids to bed and then work until two or three in the morning while Jeffrey came home around midnight and climbed into bed. In the middle of all this my mother who was in her mid-eighties died (my father passed away fifteen years ago). I felt I was the only one pulling in all the bread, which sadly was barely covering our expenses, but that the work treadmill I was on was making it difficult for me to grieve. The more things fell apart for Jeffrey work-wise, the more livid I became, leaving no room to support him emotionally when—as he said—he was down.

The difference now, as opposed to a decade ago, was that we had two children and we couldn't, or didn't yet, have screaming fights in front of them, but the tension in the air was palpable and no doubt they felt it. With no checks coming in from Jeffrey's work, my fury rose, and if, when we had gone to Dr. B. ten years before, I was scared by how we had lost our ability to communicate, this time round in the ring, I was petrified by our inability to pay our bills, to move from the small apartment we now shared with two growing boys, to buy a piece of property, to put anything away for the future.

I had witnessed the decline of my mother; she had been well cared for in the last years of her life because she'd sold the house we grew up in for a great profit and because she had a pension from her job as well as my father's pension. I started to worry about our lack of assets and our nonexistent retirement fund. As Jeffrey's earnings continued to decline, I felt my "I'm outta here" attitude coming back—though the reality of two kids who couldn't wait till the second their father walked through the door certainly dampened my trusty escape-hatch fantasy. We had invoked Dr. B. during fights throughout the years. *I think it's time we go back to Dr. B.! Well, I think so, too!* And it was as if just mentioning her name was enough to make us sit down and try to work things out. She was out there, the third party, the specter of the difficulties in our relationship.

But as the year drew on, our allusions to Dr. B. took on a different tone. And then we stopped bringing her up altogether. I began to wonder if, besides the fact that we didn't have the money to pay her, there was another reason for our hesitation to make the call to her—that this time we were both afraid we wouldn't fare as well as we had the first time. Our arguments about money—Jeffrey not making enough (or any for many months)—felt sadly similar to the arguments we'd had before couples' therapy, before we had children. We had both spent years sure that Jeffrey's huge success was right around the corner, and that it was just a matter of time before we moved into a two-thousand-square-foot loft, tossed out our fifteen-year-old Volvo, and got a car, at least, with airbags.

I began to see that I had as much invested in this belief system as Jeffrey, that I had shied way from doing what it took to make Big Money myself because Jeffrey and his stream of hits were undoubtedly on the way. Jeffrey was twenty-nine when I met him, had just left the life of a jazz bass player, moved from Brooklyn back to his parents' in Manhattan, and started to teach himself how to write pop music. He had never filed a tax return. Some girls might have thought twice. Jeffrey moved in with me the same week we started going out, and that year filed his first 1040.

As Jeffrey's year of little earnings seeped into the next year, he borrowed money from his elderly parents. We talked of pulling our kids from private school, but they were both thriving and so imbedded there that it was hard to consider it. By the end of the school year we owed them, as well as everybody else, a lot of money. Jeffrey and I got along okay during the summer primarily, I believe, because we didn't see that much of each other. I brought the kids and my work out to the cottage that we've rented these ten years now, and he toiled away in the city.

Then at the end of the summer, the small nest egg that I was going to save (for our future? for that down payment?) from my mother's estate came through. I waited as long as I could, hoping a check that a record label owed Jeffrey from work done some time ago might come through. And then I gave up: I paid the back rent, the school for the previous year and a half, our family's health insurance for several months, an old dentist bill of Jeffrey's, a credit card and loan he had taken out at horribly high interest rates, one of my credit card bills. I wrote check after check out of my inheritance, seething as I did it.

Do people really change? It's a question I've been asking myself. Have I made Jeffrey into a music mogul in my head? He is someone who loves to write music, who becomes obsessed with whatever song he is working on, and he is someone who always wanted kids and who loves his kids and now makes a lot of time for them, but he is not someone, even after all these years, that deals easily with the financial side of life; he doesn't like to pay bills, put away money, figure out how or what we are going to live on when we grow old. He's never felt any strong need to own a piece of property, maybe because his parents, who live in a large rent-stabilized apartment, don't. In the past, though thankfully not these last two years, he's relentlessly paid for his squash club (*I can't live without squash! It keeps me sane!*), but never thought about putting that money into an IRA or life insurance.

And sadly there have been arguments about money in front of our children, and though we try to explain to them that we love each other and are stressed and are sorry, that doesn't quiet the comment of Dr. B.'s that comes racing back to me: "But clearly the current state of your relationship is not an emotionally healthy environment for a child." When I bring up trying to do something other than write hit songs to make money—and I don't bring up bartending anymore, but suggest writing jingles or scoring—he gets that same "you've just punched me" look in his face.

I've often fantasized that each of us would be better off with someone who made a lot of money; someone who was just thrilled by Jeffrey's steel-like dedication to his art and his ability to write that perfect melody; someone who would say to me, "Why don't you concentrate on that family novel and I'll pay the bills." But I realize those people don't really exist.

An artist Jeffrey wrote six songs for recently got a record deal, but the production money upfront won't be much and isn't coming anytime soon. A band signed to a hot indie label asked him to co-write and produce half their album. And last week two major record labels wanted Jeffrey's songs for new artists, so maybe things are looking up . . . maybe those songs will be hits or even one of them will be the mega-hit we've spent years waiting for, but that's no longer good enough for me.

I like to think of the jack-o'-lantern faces Jeffrey drew as a good sign. I figure I never knew he had talent as a visual artist . . . maybe he can pull long-unexplored business skills out of the same hat. But I have no way, really, of knowing that or trying to control it. And that's what I have to remember and what is so easy to forget. In the last year, when I've been under deadline after deadline, he's taken on more and more hours of child care, of picking up and dropping off, of dishwashing and cleaning, and that is all good, all terrific. But when I least expect it, I swing back to old-fashioned notions of men, money, and success, and I relapse into resentment and anger: After editing my sixth book in four weeks and putting a batch of checks in our account, I feel furious as I walk out of the bank that no money has come from him in so long. I know I must stay away from this type of thinking, that it drains my sense of accomplishment and success.

After almost twenty years of trying to work on Jeffrey, I can only work on myself. And little by little, with two steps forward and one step back, I feel myself changing, and it feels good. My book-doctoring business has tripled in the last two years: I have clients all over the United States, some of whom fly me to where they live to work on their books. I'm getting out there in the world and making things happen in a way that I've never done before, taking on projects—ghostwriting a thriller, writing a television pilot, editing and selling an anthology—that pull in more money. Last month I bought my family a new, well, used car, but it feels like new and it has airbags.

In a funny way I feel more like myself, my real self, than I've ever felt in my life. Maybe all these decades of putting the pressure on Jeffrey to be the hitmaker haven't been good for him, or for me. If we're going to survive each other, then I have to turn that energy inward, find my inner mogul. Because maybe after all these years, just maybe, that's the way it's supposed to be.

Shifting the Midline

Elissa Minor Rust

My own marriage was not quite a decade old when my mother came to me last year to say she was thinking of leaving my father. We talked at length and concocted a plan: If things got bad enough, she'd stay with us for a weekend. (This wouldn't be hard; we lived down the street.) Maybe my dad would realize how serious their situation had become.

The five-year-old child still lurking deep inside felt heartbroken by my mother's confession, confused and lost at the thought of her parents splitting up. But the grown-up me couldn't blame her. Over the last year and a half, my father had become a complete asshole. I couldn't stand to be with him for half an hour, and my mother had to live with him. We wondered if he was going through some sort of later-midlife crisis, sans Porsche and trophy blonde. He had gone from a man who took my kids for spontaneous trips to the ice cream parlor in his VW convertible to a malcontent who yelled at them for talking too loudly and called them selfish brats when they threw tantrums.

But my mother never left him.

A week and a half after our unprecedented conversation, my dad showed up at my house on his bicycle, disoriented and groggy. He mentioned his right arm had been twitching and shaking earlier in the day. As we talked, he fell asleep mid-sentence and slurred his words—evidence that something was seriously wrong. In the next few days, we learned that he had been experiencing seizures, and we also learned the reason my father had changed so drastically: A large diffuse brain tumor, roughly the size of half a banana (why is it always fruit?) had taken over his left frontal lobe, the part of the brain that regulates personality and judgment. The tumor was mean and aggressive, like him, and deep. Tentacled into healthy brain tissue, it was hard for his doctors to tell what was tumor and what wasn't. They could treat it for a while, but the damage was irreversible, and the tumor, we were told, would soon kill him.

A year later, my mom still lives with the daily guilt of a woman who almost walked out on her husband when a foreign invader was slowly boring itself into his brain and changing, trait by trait, who he was. Instead of forging out on her own and starting a new, independent life, my mom is living a different kind of new life: as constant caregiver to a dying man, a man with the cognitive function of a ten-year-old child, a man who doesn't remotely resemble the person she said "I do" to thirty-five years ago.

———— ∞ ————

My dad's brain tumor did more than change the basic makeup of his brain, more than challenge my mom's staying power in their marriage. The tumor's tentacles made their way down the street, invisibly, into my own home, my own marriage, boring into issues we'd been happy to let lie for too long.

What happens to a marriage when you stop believing in so many of the things the marriage was based on to begin with?

When you become a caretaker for the man who used to nurture

you (talking him down from hallucinations, filling in the gaps of his lost memory, helping him take his medication and keep his balance while he walks), you start to examine things, to ask the big questions. In my case, I had been asking the big questions for years, but since my parents' "crisis," I have begun to answer them. And in answering them, I've upset the delicate balance that was my life, my marriage, my foundation. I've ripped the crisp white tablecloth from under the dishes, and in many ways, I'm still holding my breath, wondering how many of those dishes will shatter and how many will spin for a while and then come to a stop, unbroken, on the now naked table.

My husband and I met when I was thirteen and he was fourteen. He likes to tell the story about when he first laid eyes on me, though I was completely unaware of him at the time. My family had just moved to Oregon, and we were late to church, so we had to walk to the very front pew. I was wearing a red dress with tiers of eighties ruffles down the skirt and had a "rat tail" braid coming down from under my short bob, my bangs puffed and sprayed into a menacing wall above my forehead. He probably couldn't tell yet I had braces. He was in love.

Chris and I were both raised in the Mormon church, and we both have genealogy lines that include Mormon pioneers who were tarred and feathered in Missouri, who crossed the plains pushing handcarts, searching for the promised land. We both come from "good Mormon stock." We fell in love young and dated through high school. We did everything good Mormon teenagers do: We attended church on Sundays and youth group on Wednesdays, and attended daily early-morning religion classes each day before school (okay, fine, I'll admit to quitting the early-morning classes by my last year of high school, but Chris was stalwart). We didn't drink. We didn't smoke. Amazingly, given the intimacy and intensity of our relationship, we didn't have sex.

A popular song in the Mormon hymnal encourages youth, in a boisterous upbeat tempo, to be "true to the faith that our parents have cherished; true to the truth for which martyrs have perished." I cringed whenever I sang this as a teenager, because it hardly seemed fair to be forced to subscribe to something simply because my parents had, as did their parents before them. But I could hardly speak this aloud, even with my Mormon friends. I felt as if I were the only one who couldn't quite buy into it. The pressure and the guilt are tremendous—to constantly do the right thing, stay out of trouble, make your parents proud. I found myself oscillating between utter devotion and skepticism, one day faithfully convinced that I'd seen an image of God and Jesus in the church chapel with a special message for me, the next day knowing that if I dared glance behind the curtain, I'd find that the wizard with the booming voice was just a lonely, powerless man. But to Chris it was an easy balance. He could avoid the cultish fervency of Mormon youth without having it taint his devotion to the church's principles. He would sit and listen to my questions for hours and never make me feel judged or inadequate. He made it easy—wonderful, blissful—to believe in God, in the whole nine yards.

Even so, there were some things that felt so wrong, even our relationship couldn't gloss them over. When I was sixteen, I sat next to Chris at a Sunday-night regional "fireside" while the solemn Stake President in his suit and tie used an overhead projector to illustrate what, exactly, was sinful sexual behavior and what was not. He made a list: kissing, French kissing, light petting, heavy petting, etc., and then drew a thick red line under the word *kissing*. "Anything below that line," we were told, "is a sin and should be cleared up by speaking with your bishop." I was humiliated, sitting next to my teenage boyfriend, feeling guilty because we'd had our tongues in each other's mouths and had even dallied with a few brief forays of hands under clothing. The speaker concluded the evening, "Kiss your date like you would kiss your mother."

But if there were negatives about being a Mormon teenager, there were also positives. Because we were immersed in our religion daily, most—if not all—of our social activities revolved around the religion, too. There were rollicking dances every Saturday night and planned social events every Wednesday. The first night Chris and I kissed, it was after a weekly church dance. An older friend with a driver's license drove us home, and we kissed in the back of his van. There was something comforting about being part of a clan, part of a group of kids who stuck together through common belief. When so many teenagers struggle with their place in the world, their identities, it was nice to be part of the solid group that made the walk together every morning from the church to the high school across the street, holding the hand of the boy I loved.

As a Mormon youth, the course of your life is somewhat mapped out for you. If you are a boy, you'll go to a church college for a year, then serve a two-year mission at age nineteen, then come home to get married and start a family. If you are a girl, you'll attend a church college, then get married and start a family as soon as you meet the "right" person, which, in Mormon culture, is often by the age of twenty-one.

We stayed the course. I graduated from high school a year early so we were on the same track, but we headed to different colleges, mostly to prove we could. Chris went to BYU's Hawaii campus, and I went to BYU's Utah campus. That was the hardest year of my young-adult life, and I quickly learned that if I stayed at a church college, I would never stay in the church. I didn't fit in. I asked too many questions and fought the need to rebel intellectually. I balked when a lecture on deconstructionist theory turned into a scripture discussion, when I was mocked by my peers for enrolling in a controversial women's studies course, when I was required to attend a weekly prayer meeting for my dorm floor. Many students thrive at BYU; I crumbled. And Chris wasn't with me. He had always been the one to listen to my frustrations, to give credence to my fears and my questions about our religion. If he could see all the problems I saw, but let the positives of the faith outweigh the negatives, then I could, too.

When Chris left to serve a mission in New York City, I transferred to Oregon State University. We weren't allowed to speak, except on Christmas and Mother's Day (and even that was stretching the rules; he was allowed to call his family on those two holidays, but he also called me). For two years, our only communication was through letters—and he was only allowed to write one a week. For a person like me who has always fought against rules and power structure, this was torture. I would have had more access to the man I loved were he in prison.

I did crazy things to keep myself sane. Even though LDS missionaries are moved from area to area and apartment to apartment every few months, I always knew exactly where he was and did my research until I found the phone number of the apartment he was in (if this meant calling around in New York for a bit, pretending to be interested in the Mormon church and looking for missionaries in the area, I'd do it). And I would call his apartment at least once a week, at night when I hoped he and his companion would be home, just to hear his voice when he said, "Hello, this is Elder Rust." Then I'd take a deep breath and hang up the phone. I'd wonder if he could sense me on the other end of the line. Being separated from him so severely made me feel incomplete. I ached. And during those two phone calls a year, which we extended out to last sometimes six or eight hours long (definitely against the rules), we'd use the language of love as if we had invented it, as if nobody before or after us would feel as acutely our need for each other and how hard it was to be apart.

He'd say, "I think of you every time I hear a note of music."

I'd say, "Then play music all the time."

He'd say, "These two years will make us so much stronger."

I'd say, "I'm so proud of what you're doing," when what I wanted to say, but wouldn't, was, "Come home now, today, this instant."

The LDS statistics are not in the favor of the young couple separated by a mission. The girl is supposed to date other people and forget about the missionary, so as not to distract him from the Lord's work. And the boy is supposed to "lock his heart" for the very same reason. This is pretty much relationship poison. Most young women who send a boyfriend on a mission are married to someone else by the time his two years are up. Chris and I were adamant that we were not going to succumb to those statistics, that we were going to make it through. Looking back, it's clear to me that my life took the path it did because I was crazy in love, and I didn't want to lose him (can't we all say something similar about someone in our lives?). I fought the urge to leave the church for those two years, even though all the problems I had with Mormon doctrine were constantly staring me in the face. With the help of my religious leaders and my tenacious desire to stick with the religion, I was able to rationalize keeping a faith that I felt oppressed women, discriminated against homosexuals, and required blind obedience to prophets while pretending to value personal revelation.

My college experience without Chris was not filled with your average college rebellion. My rebellion came in the form of my leftist politics, a few new piercings (only on my ears), and sometimes attending only two of the three hours of services each Sunday. And I'll fess up to this: three sips of beer and two nibbles on a brownie laced with marijuana. To this day, I wish I'd at least eaten enough to get high. But I stayed the course, even referred the missionaries to teach a few nonmember friends. I tried to be everything I was raised to be. In retrospect, although it wasn't conscious (I really thought I believed in at least most of it—or, at least, I *wanted* to believe), the reason for my continuing activity in the church was fairly simple: I was terrified of losing the love of my life.

My fears were not unfounded. In the Mormon faith, interfaith marriages (even marriages when one partner is an inactive member of the church) are adamantly discouraged. The end goal, the gold standard for which every young Mormon is told to strive, is a temple marriage, and one can only get married in the temple to another active, believing, *worthy* member of the tribe. This is such a serious tenet of the faith that marriage in the temple is considered one of the necessary requisites for admission into the highest level of heaven. I had grown up seeing women in our congregation go into the crisis of their lives when their children chose to marry outside the faith, and I was taught to believe that this was the easiest way to set your life on the wrong path.

A mission does strange things to a nineteen- and twenty-year-old kid. Drop him into a life of pure religious devotion (twelve-hour days of proselytizing and scripture study), cut him off from the real world and his real-world relationships, and he becomes a bit of a fanatic. Or at least you hope he becomes a bit of a fanatic, because otherwise, well, it would be sheer hell to follow all the prescribed rules, to spend all your waking minutes tracking down potential converts. A twenty-one-year-old man, fresh off a two-year immersion of his religion, would not be likely to marry a woman who had left the faith. Period. No matter how much he loved her.

I asked my husband recently if he would have married me if I'd left the church back then instead of now. He said, "That's a completely unfair question and you know it."

It is.

I do.

Like our parents before us, Chris and I were married in the temple, two months after he was released from his mission, one week before I started graduate school in Arizona. When I was with him, it all made sense—the temple marriage, the idea that I was eternally sealed to the person I loved more than any other. Who wouldn't want that? We honeymooned in Hawaii, packed a U-Haul, and drove south to begin our new lives together. I was twenty; he was twenty-one.

In the last year, my mom and I have become well versed in the vocabulary of brain tumors, a vocabulary nobody should have to acquire outside of medical school. I can rattle off my dad's tumor type (anaplastic oligo-astrocytoma, grade III) and his daily drug cocktails (Temodar, Dilantin, Decadron) almost as mindlessly as I can sing the alphabet song with my three-year-old son. One of the terms we learned early on was the concept of "midline shift": the phenomenon when the tumor and swelling brain tissue push the affected hemisphere over into the next, and the entire brain becomes off-center and asymmetrical. A shift like this, even a subtle one, can of course have all sorts of untoward effects. It throws a person's center. My dad walks slanted forward and slightly to the left. He can't accurately track an object and tell you when it is directly in front of his face.

It's become an interesting metaphor for me, one that I find myself turning to in times of serious searching. When I look at my dad's diagnosis, I see it as a sort of barometer that told me what things in my own life were shifting the midline. Some neurologists implement a test for midline shift in patients who are cognitively unable to respond to other tests: Examine the soles of the patient's shoes over time. Wear on the toes of the shoes shows significant anterior midline shift; wear on the heels can indicate posterior shift. It's a strange notion, that you can be so sure you are in proportion to the real physical world, but your entire inner compass is off. I felt that way about my life.

It might be impossible to see someone you love lying in the intensive care unit (comatose, his head covered in white bandages, a thick tube draining fluid from his brain, a feeding tube cascading from one nostril) without seeing yourself in that same bed. My dad was fifty-four. His neurosurgeon answered honestly when my brothers and I asked: His tumor type does tend to have a slight genetic link. The questions came in fits while I took my shifts after his surgery, wondering if he would wake up: Were that me, what would I want to have done with my time? How do I want to have lived?

Would Chris have stayed?

Some of the answers were easy. Most people run toward faith and meaning in times of crisis. I guess you could say I did the opposite. I saw my dedication to the church of my youth, the church of my family, as the weighty extra that was pushing things in my life out of balance. At any given time, I could easily log ten to thirty hours a week that I was giving to the church.

And though it was the religion upon which my marriage was founded, it was a religion I could no longer say I believed in.

The hard part, the part I dreaded, the part that still haunts me, is this: How do I get my husband to believe that even though I no longer accept as ultimate truth the doctrine that initially united us, my love for him is unchanged? How do I get him to believe that even though I don't view our union in the temple as a necessary stepping stone into heaven, as a sacred link necessary for a solid, loving family, my commitment to him and to our children is stronger than ever?

How do I raise my kids in an interfaith marriage, when I have been warned my whole life that they almost always end in divorce? During the course of the last year, I've started attending Quaker meetings (polar opposite from Mormonism: anti-dogma, pro-questioning, and pro–social activism). My husband and I have spent many sleepless nights together, one or the other of us stressed to the point of crying, trying to decide how to reconcile the religion issue and what we both want for our family. There have been weeks at a time where we feel distant from one another, afraid to offend, wishing the problem would go away.

In the first weeks after my dad's diagnosis, we consulted several doctors, most of whom refused to operate. Every time I saw him, I had this horrific sense of how close I was to the hideous thing that had taken my father from me. If I could only . . . reach . . . just right there, a few inches in from his skull . . . and yank . . . and out would come the damned half-banana-sized monstrosity, snapping tentacles and all. *So close. A few more inches and I could touch it.*

The issue of religion in my marriage had felt that way for years. Hidden enough to ignore, certainly small enough to gloss over and move on.

Of course, with tumors and marital issues alike, things are more complex than yank-and-pull.

The night I told Chris I had finally decided to cease being active in the Mormon church, he was understanding and kind. We talked all night, virtually until sunrise. Sometimes we cried. He told me he wasn't surprised, that he was happy I might finally find some peace from an issue that had haunted me for so many years. Three days later, I found myself walking past an espresso cart in the local library, and instead of ordering my typical hot chocolate or steamed milk, I figured, what the hell? I wasn't going to be an active Mormon anymore. It was time to try some coffee. I ordered a chocolate s'more mocha, a drink that from the picture on the menu looked like a chocolate lover's heaven. But two sips later, the mocha was in the trash and I was looking for a drinking fountain to rinse the hideous taste from my mouth.

That night, I told Chris jokingly, "I'm going to make a terrible apostate."

He raised his brows. I told him about my severe dislike of coffee, and in an instant, a look flickered across his face, a look that sent knives through me. It said: *This is for real. She's really doing this.* It was troubled and sad and scared, and was a reaction that caught both of us, equally, off guard.

A few months later, when I decided it was time to exchange my temple-issued undergarments for regular underwear, I dressed and undressed in the dark, in the next room, and hoped Chris wouldn't notice. I was afraid of *that look*, the look he hated as much as I did. I crawled in on the far side of the bed and kept a safe distance from him throughout the night and day, knowing how ridiculous I was being, but somehow unable to stop myself. The next week, Chris presented me with a gift he'd picked up on the way home: plain, normal-person underwear from the mall. It was a gift that said: I noticed. I don't care. Be who you are.

⌘

The biggest issues are yet to come. The implications of my decision reach so much farther than whether or not I will attend services on Sunday or drink coffee. Suddenly, we have to think about our children, and how we want them raised, and what we want them taught (or not taught) in Sunday school. And if Chris and I don't agree—well, what then? If my children continue to be raised in the Mormon church, they will be taught on Sundays (and Wednesdays and early mornings when they are teenagers) that their mother is wayward, that she's jeopardizing her salvation, that she needs to be coerced back into the fold. Can I live with that? Can Chris live with that? Last month, a best friend of my daughter's had a birthday party on a Sunday. Mormons are strict about observation of the Sabbath. I wanted my daughter to be able to go; Chris didn't. I respected his decision and let him make the call. Last week, the same daughter had saved her pennies to buy a stuffed cat she'd eyed weeks earlier at the mall. The only possible time we could go as a family to make her purchase was on Sunday. Chris was okay with that. We give, we take, we compromise. But the issue simmers.

It's hard for me to come right out and admit to him that I don't want our children raised in the Mormon church, because it feels like breaking a promise. But it's the crux of the issue for me. When I was in graduate school, my church "calling" was to work with the teenage girls. I sat in on a Sunday school lesson when the teacher, a middle-aged woman with six children of her own, told the girls in the room that God makes us happy, and Satan makes us sad. She said that depression was a sin, that it was entirely the Devil's influence. And what did I do? Me, the woman who was currently taking prescription antidepressants, who was fighting my own mood disorder? I said nothing. I seethed and probably turned red and wriggled in my seat, then came home and complained to my husband about what had happened.

I think about those girls today, grown women now, who had to hear such a potentially damaging thing. And I think about my inability to speak up, to tell them that they didn't have to be happy all the time, that depression is a disease, not a sin, that life is so much more complex than just happy or sad. I should have protected them, and I didn't.

I refuse to do the same thing to my children.

What we are looking at is a drastic change in our family dynamic, one that sends ripples into our extended family as well, the way my dad's tumor tentacled into mine. Today, my in-laws are crushed. They're good people, and I've caused them pain. They don't understand my decision, and they fear for my children, who are far less likely to stay the course with a mother who teaches them to think for themselves and to reject the notion that there is only one correct interpretation of the truths of this universe. My mother-in-law, a kind, thoughtful woman, actually said she worries about my children's eternal salvation. I've put my husband in a delicate position. My younger brother, a gentle, practical-minded physicist who hasn't been active in the Mormon church since he left home at eighteen, even told me in an e-mail a few months ago: "It's definitely not worth having marriage issues, if you ask me. I mean, I still think there's much worse ways to raise a kid, y'know?" He's right, of course. There are much worse ways to raise a kid. But I've promised to be honest with my children, and with my husband, and this is the only way I know how.

In the end, my marriage will probably be saved because Chris and I are a good match, regardless of religion. In the beginning, in our youth, we would have been drawn to each other even if one of us wasn't LDS. I truly believe that. He is kind, and understanding, and the biggest surprise of all: He likes the new me better, the me who is being honest, who has connected spiritually to something real for the first time in her life. He's still unsure how he feels about the religion issue, and he's working it out for himself, with time. But in the end, going through this shift has been revealing: We've realized that the promise we made to each other was not that we would never change. Nor was it that we would be of one mind. But we *did* promise to stick it out, and to respect each other, and help each other through crises. And it turns out we do that pretty well.

I have an image in my mind, a memory of my parents, that I hold as the new gold standard of what a marriage should be. Three years before my dad got sick, before he disappeared inside himself, my parents had been in the process of reconnecting after all their children finally left home. They had time and money that they hadn't ever had, and they started enjoying a new kind of life together. My parents had never been overly romantic. I was convinced growing up they weren't really in love (maybe everyone feels that way about their parents). They had little in common: My mom was an intellectual, a book lover, who preferred quiet days and classical music. My dad preferred tinkering with electronics and cars to sitting down with a good book, was an extrovert to her introvert. But when the kids left home, and it was an empty house and just the two of them, they worked hard to find ways to connect, for things they could share together. When Dad took up biking, Mom tried her best, but lasted about a week before admitting to hating it. When Mom decided to take fly-fishing lessons, Dad politely declined. Eventually, they found something they both loved to do together: bird watching. They took a few classes out on Portland's Sauvie Island, and learned to identify the owls they heard outside their house at night by their various hoots and sounds.

For their anniversary that year, Mom asked me to keep Dad's present at my house so he would be surprised. She unloaded from her trunk a gorgeous owl box that Dad could hang from the tree outside their bedroom window, specifically designed to attract western screech owls. I set it in my garage. Two days later, Dad called from work and asked if I would mind stopping by the bird shop on my way home to pick up *his* anniversary gift to *her*. It was the same exact owl box, meant for hanging on the same exact tree. They were both giddy with excitement over the same gift, both convinced of how thrilled the other would be upon opening it.

My parents were very different people. But they had found a way to enjoy each other, something to do together, a way to connect. Essentially, they had found a reason for staying, despite everything else, despite all the baggage that invariably comes with marriage, with raising three children, with life.

I think of that moment they both discovered they'd purchased the same anniversary gift, and I wonder if it's that moment (among others like it) that helped my mom stay when she wanted to turn her back, that makes her stay now even though she is playing nurse-maid to a difficult man she barely knows, barely likes. And there's no questioning the impact her staying has had on him.

For my own marriage, I live with a hope that borders on fear. I hope my own marriage will be better off because I've chosen to be genuine, and honest, and give Chris my real self—even though it was a self I thought he wouldn't want. We're far more likely to find those moments of connection—like my parents and the owl box, or a gift of plain, boring underwear—if we are honest in who we are, and what we need. We're more likely to find reasons to stay, to keep the midline of our partnership from shifting too far from center. We'll both have to compromise, maybe, about things we believe in. Ultimately, Chris and I married each other—flesh and blood, hu-man, unique—and not a religious ideal. I hope that's enough.

It's Me or the Baby

Annie Echols

My husband collapsed in his favorite leather club chair. Tom looked gutted. Already fair, he was ashen and drained; handsome head held between his hands, he was the picture of despair. Soon enough his anger came to the rescue—his usual method of self-medication in stressful situations.

"Well," he choked, "it's me or the baby."

We already had two kids, Luke, eight years old and Eliza, four, and had decided against more children. Tom was a creative director finally making room in his life for his real art, and I was busy with my new Chelsea gallery (after years of slave labor as an assistant curator, I finally got the nerve and the capital together to open my own gallery, which, thank God, was doing pretty well). Life was getting easier again: We had a little more money, the kids were older, travel and skiing were back in our lives, summers at the beach with the kids in camp—Mom working from the deck, cell phone and laptop handy. The house was a shack, but it had magnificent views of the harbor all around; we ate dinner outside every night watching the snowy egrets forage for theirs, and the sunsets, which got standing ovations from the kids, more than once. I could squeeze in yoga classes three, sometimes even four, times a week after early-morning drop-off at school. I got myself, *slowly*, back into shape and at forty still had the nerve to wear my bikini in public. And the most important aspect, certainly from Tom's point of view, was the fact that we were starting to carve out a little time again for each other. We went out together a night or two every week. The big brother took care of the little sister Saturday mornings so we could sleep till 8 or 9.

I, too, had mixed feelings when I realized I was pregnant. That morning heading to the office, I was feeling sluggish and fat. True, I'd indulged over the holidays and packed on a good five pounds, and who wouldn't feel sluggish on a frigid gray January day wading through the slushy streets of New York? I was also a bit *late* . . . a week? Two?

I thought back a month or so ago: Tom and I, seizing time together on Saturday morning before the cartoons ended and the kids started clamoring for pancakes, simply hadn't bothered with the condoms. It had taken six months of concerted effort to get pregnant with Eliza, and it wasn't a dangerous time of the month, so what the hell. It was perhaps mere laziness on Tom's part. And mine. I'd long since grown reconciled to not having another child. The first couple of years after Eliza was born, I was always secretly hopeful when the condom broke. That morning the thought of having another baby had been long absent from my mind. I reassured myself that I'd had false alarms before, and early pregnancy felt remarkably close to premenstrual. Still, I had a sushi lunch date planned that day and decided to buy an e.p.t. (the early pregnancy test) at the drugstore on the way to work, just in case. Later that morning, in a beige institutional bathroom stall, the pink stripes appeared immediately. Lunch with the new collector was at a little French bistro, no mercury-laden raw fish on the menu for me that day.

I felt elated and overwhelmed by turns all day. The dread of breaking the news to my husband was the only constant. Maybe it was a faulty test? I bought another on the way home that night. As I hopped on the subway line going home, the local had seats aplenty when the express was the usual standing-room only crush. I calculated I must be seven weeks pregnant, still in the tired stage. I took the local train so I could sit and hoped that "slow train" was not going to be the metaphor for my career after the third child.

I thought of our summer plans. I was hoping to go to surfing camp with my son, and we'd mapped out a family trip to Greece in July, but it was too near the due date now, we'd have to cancel. As the train rumbled downtown, I tried to convince myself of the practicalities of ending this pregnancy, but I found the idea devastating. The two children we had were already my favorite people on the planet. I thought about how much Luke and Eliza enriched our lives, how much they brought to us every day. And I'd wanted another child. For years I'd stifled my jealousy when friends made that brave move of having a third child, but after the exhausting yearlong battle convincing Tom to try for a second child, I wasn't sure that our marriage could survive another fight or another child.

Our bitter discussion that first night continued, after the second e.p.t. of the day confirmed the pregnancy.

"You always wanted a third child," Tom accused me. "You always light up when you're near a baby," he said with disgust.

I felt a flash of hatred for my husband, and sorrow. Why did the prospect of a third child feel like a punishment to him when the two we had brought us such joy?

"I don't like being a parent," he continued. "Getting up at dawn every day to take them to school. I love them, but I don't like any of the work," he confessed.

"Do you want to know what I hear when you say that?" I responded, in a fury. "I hear I don't want to be a grown-up." I knew he loved his kids, and actually seemed to enjoy some aspects of being a parent, but not many of the demands. I continued, "For God's sake. Didn't you ever have a pet growing up?"

"You know I did."

"Well, you had to take care of Augie Doggie, right? You couldn't just enjoy cuddling and playing with him. Or did your mother do that for you, too?" By now I was wondering if maybe he should move back with his mother and let *her* cook him his favorite dinners and pick up his damn socks. "You need to appreciate what you have in your life, our children before you are pearls before swine," I choked out the old, apt cliché and stalked out of the room.

Could I spend my life with such an ungrateful and bitter man? I hated him. He was poison. I couldn't believe my own thoughts. This was the man I had actually thought of as *noble* in our early years together. And now divorcing him seemed like the only answer.

I came back a few minutes later carrying the measuring tape and carefully took measurement of the alcove in our foyer. The foyer, a modernist cube, could be turned into its own little room, I thought, and I could put in a Murphy bed. I wondered how much a customized Murphy bed cost? Tom could move out and the kids could have the bedrooms. Could I do that to my children? I felt like I'd be sending them out into the world wounded. Then I started to think that if Tom and I did stay together, our loft might actually be too small for a family of five. We might have to move to a suburb with good public schools, because we certainly couldn't afford more space in the city and private schools for three kids. The suburbs might be bearable but not with a miserable man blaming me for being there. My husband didn't even like uptown Manhattan, because it felt too suburban to him. I could see him now pale, sullen, and bloated, commuting to the city to some job he hated. If he didn't make it in the next couple years with his art, he'd promised to go back to advertising for the paycheck. A divorce was starting to seem like the less painful option than life with him in the suburbs.

Week Seven

I was thirty-six when I had Eliza, and now at forty I was not eager to deal with the mess, the sleep deprivation, the bulgy body, and leaky breasts again, but one glimpse of that beating heart on the sonogram screen at a mere seven weeks into the pregnancy and those concerns evaporated. That glimpse of new life felt like a miracle, no less miraculous this time though bittersweet; I hadn't invited Tom along because he'd been so negative I didn't want him there to ruin the experience.

"Will your husband be meeting you here?" asked the nurse.

"Oh, he can't. He's in London on business," I lied.

I immediately thought of the first time I'd seen Luke and Eliza in utero—with their nervous but happy father by my side.

While Tom is a loving father, he's hardly cut out for family life, at least the early messy stage: A glass of spilled milk is not just a mess to clean up, it's a metaphor for the disaster that is his domestic life. Fifteen years ago when Tom told me he suspected he'd have a midlife crisis and want to join a monastery in his middle years, I had dismissed that charmingly idiosyncratic idea, but I should have listened to him. The twenty-one-year-old also told me about the dream house he planned to build, which defied certain aspects of reality. One plan was to convert a firehouse in a tony Manhattan neighborhood into a (twenty-thousand-square-foot) residence for us—this when he'd gotten his first job in advertising and I was a gallerista. Together our salaries didn't crack six figures and neither of us were trust-fund babies.

Later that week after the first sonogram, Tom gazed out the window across the street. "I know you tease me about wishing I were one of the guys across the street, but there's a grain of truth in that."

The guys across the street were two gay men, whose windows we could peek into from our apartment. They lived in an elegant, modern, pristine home; honey lighting aglow, one man reading the paper in the living room, glass of wine in hand, the other preparing complicated meals in the kitchen, table beautifully set every night with gleaming glass and fresh flowers. The glamorous and serene lifestyle, not the men (both of whom were a bit plump and homely), seduced both of us. I wanted to be one of the guys across the street sometimes, too. Their home looked like a sanctuary; I'd gaze over, stepping on Legos and sticky places on the floor where the nanny missed mopping up that spilled milk, and try to guess what music they were listening to, piano concertos? Jazz solos? My night was juggling the demands of two kids in those precious few hours after work with them: puzzles with the four-year-old and Scrabble with the eight-year-old, homework, proper toothbrushing techniques endlessly reinforced, bedtime stories.

Tom's sense that I was neglecting him, he was "last on my list," was the major fault line in our marriage. Two years ago, after stockpiling enough money to cover his share of our expenses for several years, he quit his very demanding job as an advertising creative director. He found a cheap studio and got to work on his installations the very month I launched my own business. Prior to quitting, for all the years of our marriage and even before, Tom worked very long hours; I was delighted when he didn't have to cancel weekend plans with the kids and me. Now he was alone struggling with his art ten hours a day. He would be hungry for my company *every* night at the same moment I wanted to put my time and energy into my new business, not my ten-year-old marriage. We'd wrestle the kids to bed by 8:30 or 9, and there he'd be, ready for his evening of adult attention, conversation, sex.

He once jealously noted, "The kids don't even know how hard you're working, they don't notice anything different." It was true. Even as I brought a new business to life—found office space, partners, an architect, kept clients happy, wooed new business—I still arranged my days with the kids' schedules in mind, made sure I spent time with them and was available for field trips and the like. When I immersed myself in my work at night, on "his time," he suspected they, not he, might be number one on my "list." He was right.

Unlike Ayelet Waldman, who proudly states that her passion for her husband comes before her kids, I was madly in love with my children, and it had eclipsed some of the passion I'd had for my husband in the early years. It felt like a temporary eclipse, but I was perhaps more diligent about making sure I met my kids' every need than meeting his. They came first. Wouldn't Tom understand that we were responsible for forming the people our children grow into? Wouldn't he understand that the business I was building was for the whole family? Wasn't my husband a grown-up?

Love wasn't the problem, but the care and feeding of the relationship was. What I forgot was this: Wives in so many marriages, certainly my own, were the center of their husband's emotional lives. As my husband and I struggled over our decision about this third child, I had close friends with whom to discuss it, not to mention my mother. My husband had only me, the enemy.

Week Eight

Tom told me he sometimes wished we could run away and be together again, just the two of us. "I miss my *girlfriend*," he said. One way I tried to keep my husband happy was sex, of course. He has a strong sex drive (according to data collected comparing notes with my friends). "Thank God I didn't know you in high school," I joked. What's twenty minutes or so a day for a happy husband? He knew what I was up to, of course. That became one of our favorite jokes: "It's time to walk the dog so he doesn't shit on the rug." Not terribly romantic, but it worked—until I got pregnant. He couldn't even look at me after that, much less touch me.

"My sexy wife is a baby-making machine," he railed. "Who knows if I'll still find you sexy after this third kid? Your body's gotten a little worse with each kid, you never got your pre-Luke body back . . ."

"Well, I got back to within five pounds . . ."

"Well, your breasts aren't the same after all that nursing . . ."

"No, that's true, they're not." Asshole, I thought, struggling not to say it aloud.

"The worst part is, I won't have you back for myself until you're *sixty* and this baby leaves for college," he mourned.

Week Nine

The laments continued for days.

Tom said, "I know I sound like a Neanderthal, but you're choosing this baby over me."

"You're choosing this baby over the two wonderful kids you have."

The threats continued.

"I'm moving out, it will be the four of you, not the four of us anymore."

"You're bringing the family down, there'll be no time, no money, for the two great kids we have."

"Private school? Forget it."

Et cetera, et cetera. The campaign continued; friends called us up to go skiing, and Tom declined the invitation.

"That sort of activity is gone from our lives." (Subtext: if we keep the baby we are on an austerity budget for the rest of our lives and we will be poverty stricken in our old age.)

"The only *trip* we're making is to the corner ATM to get money for more fucking diapers," Tom hissed.

Week Ten

I thought about Tom and his role as father; his parents thought he was father of the year because they once saw him change a diaper. He did genuinely enjoy our kids and went on long bike rides with them, played chess happily with Luke for hours, came up with imaginary games with our daughter Eliza that got her laughing like nothing else, bought Eliza her first portfolio and helped her organize her drawings in categories: ballet, princess, My Little Pony, happily read her favorite bedtime stories, over and over and over. He taught Luke to whittle and shared all sorts of information with our son, an aspiring survivalist (after reading *My Side of the Mountain*, Luke was determined to survive in the mountains equipped with nothing but a Swiss Army knife, sleeping bag, maybe some candy bars). Tom gave him very useful information on building a shelter, starting a campfire, setting animal traps, and other tricks of survival he'd learned from his Eagle Scout days. Tom still played computer games himself for fun; obviously the two boys had that in common. Tom would practice baseball with Luke. He liked spending time with the two kids.

But Tom had problems tolerating "kid world" and didn't much like hanging out with the kids' friends (or our friends' kids, either). I think he went to a birthday party with Luke once, and it took him a full day to recover his equilibrium. I'd ask Tom, "Who should we have over for dinner on Saturday?" His answer: "Someone without kids." This put a crimp in our ability to socialize as a family, a practical and affordable option for parents in Manhattan who otherwise have to pay a babysitter $75 before they even walk into the restaurant. He'd last about fifteen minutes in the park on Saturdays, growing visibly more antsy by the minute. During those frenetic family barbecues, I could pretty much tune out the swirl of kids and concentrate on grown-up conversation—and still keep an eye out so no one fell in the pool. But Tom would watch them like a hawk—constantly monitoring the kids for dangerous or inappropriate behavior, or too many cookies before the burgers were off the grill. Of course, when my daughter toddled over covered in chocolate from head to toe (who suspected one frosted cupcake could cover so much acreage?) leaving chocolate handprints on my white linen blouse, it didn't ruin my night as it would have certainly ruined Tom's.

I took care of the mechanics of the children's lives: doctors' appointments, all the paperwork having to do with their activities (gymnastics, ballet, soccer, baseball, fencing, chess, and the scheduling), everything related to school (permission slips, medical forms, field trips, emergency contact forms, etc.). And I took care of the day-to-day stuff: getting them ready for school in the morning, making breakfast, our coffee, packing up the kids' lunches, picking out their clothes—or at least vetoing their selection when necessary. Tom eased into his day (the newspaper in the bathroom—a male rite?), though he'd be there to snap at the kids to hurry up if he felt that was needed. The purchase and wrapping of the birthday presents, Christmas presents for family and teachers, supplying pocket money for the school book fair and cupcakes *and* pocket money for the bake sales were Mom's responsibility.

We shared the financial costs of raising the children and yes, we'd have to sacrifice the summer beach house rental and a coveted Ted Muehling bracelet for me on my next birthday, but the idea of trading in the life of my child for these material things tasted like ash in my mouth. I was aware of the hard facts of the financial pressure a third kid would add; the extra five years paying for full-time babysitting *alone* would rack up a cost of nearly $150,000. Not to mention the extra nursery school tuition, braces, camp, or the move to a bigger apartment in the next year or two in a super-heated real estate market. But my business was growing. How would I feel ten years from now running a very successful business and fully able to comfortably support a third child if I chose not to have him? I know myself, and I'd feel his absence like a phantom limb. Our parents had us when they were young and poor (as they never tired of telling us).

As the fighting relentlessly continued, I thought maybe I could handle life as a single mother. Tom might be happier divorced, visiting the kids during the week and caring for them every other weekend and living a peaceful life of monklike solitude. The question now was: Did I want to be a single mother of two children or three children? After three weekends with Tom away and working freelance gigs (*"Now* we really need the money, *how* could he turn anything down?"), I worried that being a single mother of three would sink me.

Week Eleven

Still standing in my coat ready to leave for the office but instead trapped in the same relentless argument we'd been having for hours, for the seventh morning in a row, exhausted and defeated, I told Tom what he wanted to hear.

"I will end this pregnancy," I sobbed, walking over to the phone and dialing my midwife. "But you are getting yourself a shrink. Tom, you better find the joyful person I married, or I won't want to stick around with you until the kids are out of elementary school, much less college."

Tom, pulling the phone out of my hand, said, "But you'll hate me forever."

I said, "I hate you right now. Who knows if it will be forever?"

He hung up the phone, and I sank into his embrace. "I'm going to try. I love you, and I'll love this child," he said.

Week Twelve

The battery of prenatal tests showed good results; we had a healthy baby growing. Appointment with the couples' therapist booked, I let Tom escape for a week and borrow a friend's studio in the woods to work on his art without us. He came back happier and calmer, and missing the kids and me.

I said, "What can I do to make you happier about this third child?"

Thinking to myself that regular weeks away to work on his art would be the answer. Tom grinned. "Well, " he whispered, "maybe some *special attention* from you *every day* would make me feel better."

Three Weeks Post-Delivery

These past months have been the most trying of our marriage, and we're both still bloody and bruised, but we are all smitten with the new baby. A big, healthy, beautiful girl. My husband drops the kids off at school the second day, and true to form, he's still not remotely interested in chatting with other parents, and leaves the schoolyard as fast as he can. When he hurries in the front door and asks breathlessly, "Is Sparkles awake?" he's disappointed to find she's still sleeping. He walks over to Natalie's bassinet and gazes down at his perfect daughter, marveling, "How did *we* get *her?*"

My Fair Student

Kim Barnes

He's out there, I know he is. And I know just what he's doing.

He's settled into the small study he built himself, fifty yards distant from the house. There's music—some torch song turned low—in the background. He's changed from his mud boots into his slippers, pulled on his lucky denim shirt, positioned his chair just so. The fire crackles in the woodstove. He looks out over the sweeping vista that stretches before him: undulate hills and, in the distance, the steep rise of the Blue Mountains. He takes a deep breath, lowers his eyes to the blank page, and begins.

I imagine him as I sit at my own desk tucked into the corner of our bedroom, where I've been re-relegated since our eighteen-year-old daughter's temporary return home. During her first journey toward independence, I had the run of her bedroom, which I turned into my office. Her interim stay here may be brief or extended: for however long her transition takes, I'm back where I started, no room of my own.

I hear the churn of the washer, the hum of the dryer, the clatter of another load of denim, and I think about Bob in the calm of his study, imagining another poem into existence. This morning, in addition to sorting through the first of many loads of laundry, I've made appointments for both Bob and myself with the optometrist, paid the week's bills, called our mortgage company with a question concerning interest rates, spoken with two different organizers who would like to have me for a reading, and coached our daughter through a job interview. I've planned what we'll have for dinner, answered e-mail, and called my mother.

In the past, I've said that it's easier having my office inside so that I can keep the household wheels turning even as I write: A few more paragraphs, and I'll hear the dryer buzz, run downstairs to transfer clothes from washer to dryer, dryer to bed. I might stop to gather the food wrappers and empty soda cans littering our sixteen-year-old son's room, make a quick sweep of the kitchen for dirty dishes before resuming my place at my computer, before trying to recall that last good sentence and just where my creative train of thought was headed before being derailed by duty. This is efficiency, I think. Or lunacy.

I remind myself of the many responsibilities that my husband shoulders: He most often does the dishes and vacuums; once a year, he tackles the taxes in a twelve-hour frenzy of flying receipts and sweaty estimations that makes me shudder. Though we work in different environments and tackle very different chores, most everything else in our lives is done in tandem. We teach at the same university, in the same writing program. We fix dinner together, drink wine together (we both relish an earthy Rioja), sleep together, and rise once again into the presence of each other's company. Whenever we can, we give joint public readings, and we travel like twins: identical roller bags, Dell laptops, and matching cell phones. We have much, much in common, and it is this characteristic of marital bliss that some (not all) of my women friends, both married and single, envy: It must be wonderful, they say, to share so much. I nod, say that yes, it's true, I'm very lucky. And I am. Yet there are times when the intertwined nature of our lives combined with the competition we engage in for creative time and space makes me wonder if I've given up too much, if I have lost track of that independent firebrand I once was—if I have become not only my husband's life partner but his lifelong protégé as well. I wonder if, given the way in which Bob and I first came together, I am forever positioned just a little lower on the totem pole. Because, you see, in the beginning, we were not peers but were enmeshed in one of the most defined hierarchical relationships of all: Professor Robert Wrigley was my teacher, and I was his star student.

But before I tell you the story of the life we have come to share, let me tell you how it was we came to share it. It is a love story, after all, one whose ending, though not uncomplicated, continues to be a happy one.

Once upon a time, there was a boy named Bob. Raised in an Illinois working-class family, Bob married his high school sweetheart and worked through two degrees, the second taken at the University of Montana. His thesis, a book of poems published by a small press, was enough to land him a teaching position at a small state college in Idaho. His star rose steadily from that western horizon—a National Endowment for the Arts grant, another book of poems, rave reviews. He and his wife had a son. His entry-level appointment became a tenured position. Everything was going as planned . . . and then he met me.

I was the girl whose history at the age of twenty-two read like a bawdy mix of genre novels: the Western, the romance, and those sixties cautionary tales that always delighted me with their covert store of knowledge (think *Go Ask Alice*). The daughter of a logger, I was raised in the small camps and mill towns of northern Idaho,

and my family adhered to the strict dictates of Pentecostal funda-
mentalism. In the heyday of miniskirts, fishnet stockings, and blue
eye shadow, I shuffled to school wearing long hems, knee socks, and
no hint of lipstick. The list of sins seemed endless: no drinking, no
smoking, no swearing, no dancing, no bowling, no playing cards, no
going to movies, no mixed swimming. What I *could* do was go to my
classes, return home, and then attend church service, prayer meeting, youth group, choir practice.

It's probably not surprising that by my second year of junior high,
I had rejected the church and my father's draconian restrictions and
opted instead for the dope-smoking, rock-and-roll-infused '70s lifestyle that my parents had always feared. My grades dropped from
As to Fs. My school hours were spent in the girls' bathroom, the
principal's office, and detention. I ran away from home at fourteen,
was forced back, and, after a few years of relative calm during which
I returned to my life as a church-going, straight-and-narrow honors
student, I had a final confrontation with my father. I left home the
night of high school graduation and never returned.

With the little money I earned as a drugstore clerk, I rented a
studio apartment in town, only a few miles from my parents' house,
though I seldom saw them. The next two years were a hot haze of
psychedelic music, neon cocktails (Screaming Orgasms and Flam-
ing Gorilla Tits), and Virginia Slims menthols. My boyfriend was
a 250-pound football player who drank himself into tearful stupors
each night while listening to the soulful complaints of Janis Ian.
After a close girlfriend dropped him at my apartment one morning,
he crawled into bed reeking of her perfume and made his mournful
confession. In the wake of our breakup, I found other men who were
less gentle and much less interested in "going steady." These were
men who, like me, had been raised in the rural West, and their incli-
nations were reflected in their upbringing: sex, beer, country music,
and millwork, not necessarily in that order. Some were jealous, some

were violent, and some were indifferent, but none sparked the kind of interest that made me long to hang on. It was a lark, I thought, this flitting from one man to another, except on those nights when the phone didn't ring and the loneliness crashed down on me like a tidal wave, swamping me in desperation so intense I could hardly breathe. I still believed that there was a man out there meant just for me, and I read myself to sleep each night with Harlequin tales of flirty but fateful love affairs whispering their dreamy promise.

And maybe that's why David's sudden and intense wooing won me over. David was a Vietnam vet many years my senior who courted me with roses and expensive dinners at the only steakhouse in town. He'd been around; he knew some things. He could talk about hunting and sports like the man I wanted him to be, but he was also intelligent and relatively literate. We talked about books we'd read (Carlos Castaneda's *A Separate Reality*, *Jonathan Livingston Seagull*, *The Godfather*), and movies we wanted to see (*Saturday Night Fever*, *Up in Smoke*, and *The Godfather I* and *II*, again). When, by the fourth date, he hadn't tried even to kiss me, I was convinced this was my knight in shining armor—or at least my soldier in faded fatigues.

David's exaggerated abstinence proved to be something other than courtly behavior, however, and by the time I realized his intent, it was nearly too late. His romantic demeanor was a façade, his courtship the methodical seduction of a predator. What he sought from me was what he had sought from other young women: complete physical and mental control. It would be years before I recognized in David the perverse extension of my father's dominating demand that I subjugate myself to his patriarchal authority.

By the end of that year with David, I had lost all the trappings of my hard-won independence: my job, my apartment, my car. I relied upon David for everything, including my food, my bed, and my shelter. When he made his final demand—that I prostitute myself to other men while he watched—I refused. What followed was a scene of humiliation and violence that left me ashamed and aching. Because I believed I could not turn to my family for help, I fled to the house of my friend Cindy, who took me in.

That promising and naïve young woman I had once been . . . well, she was someone I no longer recognized. I wasn't yet twenty-one, and my life lay in shambles. I had been brutalized, emotionally and physically, and had brutalized myself in ways that make me tremble to remember. The shame that I felt over my misjudgments and failures was an emotion I could not purge: I had no one but myself to blame. Cynical and callused, I was determined to close myself off to further pain and to reclaim some semblance of my hard-won independence: I would expect nothing; I would never again give myself over to anyone.

With my former dreams of an Ivy League education in ruins behind me, I filled out the one-page application to Lewiston's single institution of higher learning: Lewis-Clark State, once a teachers' college and now a small four-year school. Cindy was already a nursing student there, and when I received my financial aid, I paid her fifty dollars for a month's room-and-board, then used three hundred dollars to buy a rusty Dodge Coronet. The remainder I put into a sock, which I pushed to the farthest corner of my lingerie drawer. I spent it quickly—on cigarettes, liquor, and gas to get me to the bars where I could find more of both. (I think of the sticker that one suitor had slapped on the dashboard of his MG: ASS, GAS, OR GRASS—NOBODY RIDES FREE.)

Instead of pursuing a degree in English as I'd planned in high school, I settled on pre-med. I'd always had an interest in medicine, and now seemed the time to jettison romanticism in favor of a more practical career. I pictured myself ten years into the future, dressed in a white coat, successful, respected, and in control. Biology, chemistry, and basic core classes filled my schedule. I took notes next to newly divorced mothers with four kids at home, loggers disabled by falling trees, eighteen-year-old boys whose naïve flirtations made me smirk. I smoked and drank gin until I no longer cared what had happened in the past or might yet happen in the future. I spent all my grant money in the first month of the semester before finding a job as a cocktail waitress at Lewiston's only disco, believing it was an ideal setup: I could go to classes and study, then work from three until closing. I'd make wages and tips besides. I'd have all the free drinks I could hold.

And that's what I remember about the winter of 1979: rising just in time to pull on my jeans and flannel shirt; sleeping through lectures on DNA and molecular biology; racing home to curl my hair, put on makeup, and pull on my black leotard, polyester skirt, and four-inch heels. Serving vodka tonics and dry martinis, smoking between, drinking the mistakes the bartender made. Dodging the caresses of businessmen who told me I looked like Farrah Fawcett (only the hair) and had a voice like Lauren Bacall (only when I had strep throat, which was often). Sitting at the counter after closing, laughing and counting tips, woozy from exhaustion and watered-down whiskey. Going home, reading myself to sleep, waking too late to make my first class of the day. By the end of fall semester, I was on academic probation. Determined to keep my financial aid, I focused on liberal arts courses, which I had always enjoyed and been good at.

It was around this time that a girlfriend and I were walking down the hallway between classes. Through the small pane of glass in one of the doors, I saw a man gesticulating in front of the blackboard. A man I had never seen before, and I would remember if I had: thick dark hair reaching nearly to his shoulders; large brown eyes and olive complexion; a mustache. Like a composite of the Beatles in their *Sergeant Pepper* days, I thought. I stopped, backed up, took another look.

"Who's that?" I asked my friend.

She peered through the window. "Oh," she said. "That's Mr. Wrigley. He's a poet. I hear he's kind of weird."

Weird. From the Anglo-Saxon *wyrd*—those ancient people's word for fate.

Was it fate, then, that Professor Wrigley taught the only section of Honors Introduction to Literature the next semester? When he handed out the syllabus and I saw that *The Adventures of Huckleberry Finn* was on the reading list, I was confounded. *Huck Finn?* I had read the book in junior high and could not imagine what greater meaning could be brought to the story of Huck and Jim rafting down the Mississippi. When I petitioned the department chairman to test out of the class, he urged patience. "Wrigley's one of the best," he said. "Give him two weeks, and then, if you still want out, I'll let you take the test."

I sat in the front row, first as a show of mock seriousness, and then because it was the only place I wanted to be. Mr. Wrigley was passionate, articulate, radical, and hilarious. ("Like George Carlin," my friend said, "but a lot better looking.") The day after John Lennon died, he came into class grieving, then spent the hour in a free-ranging monologue about music and memory and politics. I'd seldom seen a man with tears in his eyes, and certainly not over the death of someone not his kin.

He surprised me. He entertained me. And there was this: He reminded me of something I had forgotten. Throughout my girlhood, I'd been an avid reader. In those logging camps miles from any town, we didn't have television or even radio, but we had books. Some came with the set of encyclopedias my mother had bought from the traveling salesman; others came via the children's book club my mother subscribed to through the mail. I read them all: not only *Huckleberry Finn*, but also *Swiss Family Robinson*, *Black Beauty*, *Le Morte d'Arthur*, *Little Women*. Mr. Wrigley rekindled memories of my first intimate relationship: my love affair with stories. He taught me to love deeper, to comprehend music and meaning. He loved these things so dearly and wanted us, his students, to love them so dearly that he would lose himself in fits of impassioned recital. He marched back and forth across the room, throwing his arms as though conducting an orchestra. One time, the blackboard eraser flew from his hand and sailed out the open window. He often pounded his fists against the podium, pleading with us to see how beautiful, how mournful, how reaffirming were the poems of Keats, the dramas of Shakespeare, the stories of Chekhov. I was enthralled, not by Mr. Wrigley—not yet—but by his passion. And by the poems and stories themselves. I felt some extinguished part of myself, some ember, fan back to life. And with that quickening came fear. If I had learned anything in my two decades, it was that emotions were not to be trusted. That caring leads to vulnerability, and vulnerability to pain. I did not mean to feel anything for a long, long time.

This was not an easy charade to maintain in the face of the fact that I'd recently become engaged. Don was a first-generation Italian American from New Jersey, in Idaho temporarily while working on a lucrative engineering project. I'd moved my disco dresses into his closet, my shampoo into his shower. He spent thirty minutes each night on the phone with his mother, vainly attempting to convince her of my virtue. No, I wasn't Catholic. Yes, he had met me at a bar, but . . . and here his end of the conversation would degenerate into repetitive bleating: "But, Ma! Listen! Ma!"

Our plans: Don would return to New Jersey at Thanksgiving, break the news of our engagement to his family, then send for me. I agreed to these arrangements even though I didn't love Don. I didn't even pretend to myself that I did. He represented one thing to me: escape. Escape from my past, my disappointments. He was my one-way ticket out of town. I didn't expect it to last, and in that I felt no disappointment.

I remember that *The Thorn Birds* miniseries was broadcast that fall. The evening of the final episode, I called Mr. Wrigley to tell him that I had wrenched my back and wouldn't be in class—an easy lie, and how could I miss those last delicious moments of Richard Chamberlain striding so manfully in his cassock?

I thought that what I heard in Mr. Wrigley's voice was simple disapproval. It would be some time before I learned the truth: that it was not consternation but disappointment that caused him to hesitate in his reply. He would miss me in class, he said, and I nodded without answering. I wasn't listening to his words but gazing at the TV, afraid that I might miss something.

The next week, I waved as Don pulled away in his Camaro, leaving me with a set of sheets he no longer needed and a runty tomcat we had adopted named Devo. I moved my dresses back into my own closet and tried to focus on my studies. In literature class, I watched as Mr. Wrigley paced back and forth in front of the classroom. "*Nada,*" he said. "Nihilism is the belief that nothing matters, that existence is senseless, that there is no objective ground for moral truth."

I listened intently, forgetting once again to take notes. We were reading Hemingway's "The Capital of the World," and I was stunned into rapt attention, both by the author's articulation of my own sensibilities and by my teacher's zealous recapturing of the story.

Later that day, when I stopped by Mr. Wrigley's office for a conference, I told him that I empathized with Hemingway, that nihilism made sense to me.

"Why are you here then?" he asked.

I shrugged my shoulders, looked out the window. "I want to be a doctor," I said.

He swiveled in his chair, jotted a few notes across the poem I had brought in for our conference. Professor Wrigley also taught creative writing, a class I was taking as an elective.

"Have you thought about majoring in English?" He leaned back and folded his hands together. He wore jeans and a flannel shirt, just as I did. He seemed too young to be teaching college. When he smiled, his cheeks dimpled.

"Before," I said. "When I was in high school, I wanted to be an English teacher."

"What happened?"

I thought back to that young woman, walking down the aisle at graduation, her hopes for scholarships and degrees. I thought of the year I had spent with David. What part of the story could I tell him that would make sense?

"Nothing happened," I said.

"Where will you go to medical school?"

"I'm moving to New Jersey."

He raised his eyebrows. From class discussion and the bits of writing I'd produced, he knew about my visceral connection to the wilderness in which I'd been raised. Until Don, who knew how to formulate the angle of a dam face but couldn't pitch a tent to save his life, my previous boyfriends had been something akin to mountain men, much like my father. I felt my greatest pleasure and sense of safety along the banks of a free-flowing river with a rod in my hand, or deep in the dense growth of forests, scouting for grouse.

"In New Jersey," he said, "they hunt deer with shotguns. Bullets carry too far. Too many people."

"Don didn't tell me that."

"Who's Don?" He leaned his head to the side, smiled pleasantly.

"My fiancé."

"And you love him enough to move to *New Jersey?*" Mr. Wrigley widened his eyes in mock astonishment.

"I didn't say anything about love." It was true. What Don offered me was a direction, a respectable man to marry who didn't beat me or sleep around or spend his nights at the bar: I'd always been made to understand it was the most any woman should expect. And who knew? Maybe I'd convert to Catholicism (who'd care if I meant it?), become a part of Don's clan, get pregnant, and have a clutch of dark-eyed babies to confirm in white lace.

Mr. Wrigley turned suddenly serious. "You shouldn't marry him if you don't love him."

I looked out the window at the students huddling in their jackets, books held tight against their chests. "Like I said, I don't believe it really matters."

"You're too young to feel that way."

"Am I?" I saw a flicker of regret pass across his face. "Some things aren't worth believing in," I said, and reached for my poem, but he caught its edge.

"What does this mean, this image of bones washed up on a beach, 'startling in their whiteness'?"

"I don't know," I said. "I just like the way the words sound."

"Well," he said, folding the paper neatly and placing it in my hands. "That's a start."

And it was.

Why, I ask myself, did he choose me? Because I was the sole Honors Student in his class of forty? Because I was the only one to raise her hand when he asked who had seen *Last Tango in Paris?* Or did he understand that there were places we might take each other, things he might teach me and I him, that would satisfy our hunger to know the world in new and startling ways?

Here's a scene that Bob remembers: I've come to his office for another conference about my poems. We talk at length because he's interested in the story of my life: my wilderness upbringing, my knowledge of the outdoors, my love for the mountains and rivers of the West. I don't yet realize how he envies my Western identity, how the very things I take as given are gifts to him, raised along the flat floodplains of the Missouri. I know how to split wood, fire a rifle, track a deer. If all his life he has longed to light out for the territories, I represent the very person who might share his raft.

As I ready to leave his office, I stretch out my arms to shrug on my denim jacket, and my blouse gapes slightly, just enough for Mr. Wrigley to catch a glimpse of my bra and *a dainty pink rose, right there, nestled between your breasts.* He doesn't tell me this then, of course. He's my teacher, after all. He's a married man, has a four-year-old son, whom he adores. That rose, well, for a time, anyway, it's just a rose.

And here is a scene that I remember: It's dark, the late hours after our evening workshop. The dozen student writers in the class have adjourned to O'Brien's Lounge. I like to be in the company of these people, who talk about things that seem to matter: literature and music, politics in a way that makes sense to me, travel and religion and ecology. I feel my world beginning to open, and I am hungry, hungry, hungry, as though all my life I have been living on nothing more than bread and water. Mr. Wrigley is there, laughing over his scotch. I know that he is handsome, intelligent, talented, and fun. I know that, when we leave the bar, he will drive home to his wife and son. I do not fantasize about him. I do not entertain ideas of some illicit romance. These things never enter my mind. I'm focused on my move to New Jersey, my wedding dress, my ring, what will happen next.

We all say good night and leave the bar, and I'm stepping from the sidewalk into the parking lot when Mr. Wrigley pulls up in front of me, leans across the seat of his yellow four-wheel-drive pickup, and rolls down the passenger side window.

"Kim," he says.

"Yes?"

He waits a heartbeat, holds my eyes with his intense gaze. "I'll see you," he says. And he drives away.

Just like that, I know. The look on his face that, even in the dark, holds the smudge of lust and longing. Damn him to hell. I know.

I take a shower that night and wash away the mark I don't realize is there. He'll tell me about it later, as will others at the table who witnessed the act: How, at the bar, he had taken his pen and scribbled a line across my thumbnail. How I never noticed, never stopped talking. How he etched his intent upon my body, and I did not feel a thing.

⚮

It was my roommate and best friend Cindy I turned to for advice. Intimidatingly beautiful—sassy short hair, green eyes, tall and lean as a fashion model—Cindy was also smart, practical, and her mother was French. She'd know what to do.

We met for drinks at Lewiston's only upscale lounge, a place called Jonathan's Oyster Bar. Seafood was flown in fresh each day, but we preferred the drinks made by Fast Eddie, who favored us with doubles on the house. Cindy lit a Virginia Slim as I laid out the problem.

"It's Mr. Wrigley," I said. "He wants . . . well, I know what he wants." I rolled my eyes, motioned to Eddie for another round.

"Is he cute?"

"Cindy, he's married."

She shrugged her shoulders. "That doesn't necessarily have to mean anything." She cradled her right elbow in the palm of her left hand and blew a jet stream of smoke.

"Besides, there's Don."

"He hasn't called you since he left Lewiston."

I stirred my vodka tonic. It was true. Over a week, and still no word. I told myself that he was simply waiting until he'd had a few days to prepare his family. That he was tight with his money and his time and didn't want to waste either on a phone call until he had something meaningful to say.

"I'm afraid I'll lose my A in class."

"You think he'd do that?"

"I don't know," I said. "I don't know this guy at all."

Cindy raised her eyebrows.

"Yeah," I said. "He's cute. He's a poet. He's kind of weird."

Maybe because I seemed more vulnerable in the days after Don left for New Jersey, or maybe because he had simply decided to do so, Professor Wrigley began calling me at home.

Would I meet him for a drink, just to talk?

"Do it," Cindy said. "What can it hurt?"

And so I agreed, telling myself that this meeting would allow me to set things straight. I accepted his offer of a ride, and, as we careened toward Main Street, I was aware of a pair of women's dress shoes left on the floorboard, which I nudged beneath the seat. We parked in front of Bojack's: liquor, billiards, and darts upstairs, steak and spaghetti down. I knew my way around the bar and led us to a table against the wall.

It was the first time I'd studied Mr. Wrigley up close, and I liked what I saw. He was tall and handsome, with the kind of dreamy eyes that pull down at the corners and what I recognized for the first time was a *sensitive* mouth. He seemed jumpy, distracted by the group of young mill workers who shot pool behind us, their sport loud and foul. I was in my element, or at least an element that was familiar to me: blue-collar, backwoods, redneck Idaho, where I knew the rules and how to play the game.

I ordered schnapps, watched him pick the label from his beer and wad each shred into a tiny ball, which he piled into a little pyramid. He wore a button-down shirt, corduroys, a black-and-red plaid wool jacket. He looked more like a Midwestern college boy than he did a college professor. When he ran his hand through his hair, it fell perfectly into place. More like fur, I thought, long and alive, the color of melted chocolate.

I waited him out, smoking in the silence although he had told me he disapproved of people who smoked. When he did speak, his voice was deeper than in class, less pitched.

"First, you should call me Bob."

"Okay."

"Do you know why I asked you here?"

"No," I answered. "I don't." I wanted to hear him say it.

He took a deep breath, then settled back against his chair. He seemed suddenly tired, beset by sadness.

"I'm not sure I do either," he said.

I felt a stir of emotion for him then. He was a poet after all, given to bouts of unrequited love and Petrarchan angst—words he himself had taught me.

Then he leaned toward me again. "What if this were a come-on?"

My heart sank. A *come-on*? Nothing romantic here, only lust common as dirt.

"Is it?" I asked.

He covered his face with his hands and answered from beneath his fingers. "I don't know."

He fell back in his chair as though overwhelmed with exhaustion, so unlike the professor who tirelessly paced the classroom, sure of his vision and authority. He looked less threatening than he did vulnerable. Still, there was the ring, the gold band with its thin line of diamonds.

"You're married," I said. It was an easy way out for both of us.

"I am," he said, "in a way."

He began talking, a disjunctive monologue on marrying too early and staying too long. All this I'd heard before, from other maudlin s.o.b.'s at the bars, who left their regrets in five-dollar bills. I was disappointed. I had hoped he would keep the swashbuckling bravado going. I did not want to witness his lapse into a married man's pathos.

"I'm engaged," I interrupted, "and I don't mess around." I pulled my wallet from my purse, an empty gesture, since it didn't hold a dime.

"But I'm not really . . ." He shook his head at me and reached for his billfold. "I mean . . ." He looked around the bar, at the waitress waiting to clean our table. "Shit," he said, and his shoulders dropped. "I don't know what I mean."

He lowered his eyes, aware, I was sure, of the weakened position he found himself in. Where, a few minutes before, he had seemed a lothario, he now appeared as nothing more than a bastard. A whining husband whose wife—oh please!—did not understand him, who did not want to leave his family but who needed something more. *Someone* more. Someone like me.

"Why don't you just take me back to school," I said.

When we stepped back into the late sun, I felt disoriented, a little dizzy, like a sailor just back from the sea. Mr. Wrigley drove the streets like a teenager, fast into the intersections, quick around the corners, and I braced myself against the dash, his wife's shoes clattering beneath me. He dropped me at my car, then peeled off in a burn of rubber. I shook my head, started the Dodge, and drove back home, thankful to have made such an easy escape.

If I thought our talk had dissuaded Mr. Wrigley, I was wrong. Instead of snuffing his amorous intent, our meeting seemed to feed the fire of his interest. His calls increased to three and four times a day. He would not, he assured me, allow *any* of this to affect my grade, but wouldn't I consider just an evening's dalliance? Dinner out, perhaps, or dinner in?

When I reminded him of my impending marriage to Don, he simply stated what he knew: "You don't love him."

"It doesn't matter," I replied. "I'm not going to sleep with you."

Oh, but he insisted. He parked outside of my house for hours (we would now call this stalking), called from the phone booth down the street. Would I see him that evening? No. Tomorrow? No. Over the weekend? No, no, no.

The phone rang again, only this time it was not Bob but his wife. She wasn't calling to harass me, she said, but to encourage me: It was a midlife crisis, an infatuation; wouldn't I consider just *sleeping* with him? Help him get it—*me*—out of his system. Maybe then he would remember what *really* mattered: not a fling with a schoolgirl eight years his younger but his marriage of nearly ten years, his child.

I was stunned, and even as I told her why I couldn't honor such a request—my own engagement, the moral argument against adultery that I could hardly believe I was making—I felt a pang of empathy. This woman loved Bob in a way I might never understand. She could give up a night or two, allow him a spate of infidelity, if it meant keeping him in her life for the long run.

Between conversations with Bob and a host of friends who phoned with their varied opinions about the non-affair, I waited for

Don's call. I'd given him time to drive across the continent and had thrown in several bonus days for car trouble and sightseeing. I'd adjusted for the time it would take for him to be greeted by his family, to unload his car, to make the transition from the life of a single, independent man to a thirty-year-old son once again living under his parents' roof.

Finally, after two weeks had passed, I dialed the New Jersey number he had given me, to be used only for emergencies. His mother answered, and I listened as she cupped the receiver in her palm, muffling the sound of her voice. When Don answered, he seemed curt and irritated.

"Don," I said. "It's Kim."

"Yeah." Recognition. Acknowledgment. Nothing more.

"You haven't called."

"No."

I sat down and looked out the window, at the poplars bare of leaves, grown rampant and brittle in the backyard.

"Were you going to?" I asked.

"No."

It was that easy.

As I hung up the receiver, the phone rang in my hand.

"Kim. It's Bob."

Yes, I said. Yes.

We met at the Airport Lounge because I liked the dark room overlooking the short runway that dropped off into the mouth of the canyon. I could watch the lights flicker away and not have to think about the lover who had left me or meet the intense gaze of the man who sat on the other side of the table. Bob drew my hand to his mouth, kissed each fingertip. He was shivering, out of longing, he said. Out of need. I shivered as well, but what I felt was a chilling numbness. I was determined not to give in, to keep myself safe from what I believed could only breed pain. I knew how to enact passion, how to pretend desire. I told myself that if I threw everything at him that first and only night, what his wife believed might prove true: He would go home sated, forgo anything more. And it was the *more* that frightened me: What if he really loved me? Even more terrifying, what if I were falling in love with him? There are times when I long for that night back. I want to recast myself as a healthy young woman who still believes in passion, if only for that moment. I want her to believe that she is opening herself not to pain but to possibility. But there she remains, her jaw set against emotion of any kind, knowing, as she does, that to feel is to become vulnerable and to become vulnerable is to invite loss and despair.

When Bob recalls that night, he remembers scraping the ice from the windshield of my Dodge. He remembers the bureau mirror in my bedroom, the taste of my skin. He remembers anticipation and delight. What I remember is pulling him through the door, pushing him to the couch, straddling his lap. A sense of urgency that came not from desire for connection but from a desire to *disconnect*. I wanted to burn the night down, turn it to ashes. I wanted a pyre on which to destroy any part of me that might still harbor a foolish belief in love.

The next morning, over cinnamon toast and black tea, I related for Cindy the details in bitten statements of cold fact, as though I were reporting a crime: Mr. Wrigley, in the bedroom, with Rachmaninoff on the radio.

"Two birds," I told her. "Don is dead and gone as far as I'm concerned. Bob got what he wanted. To hell with them both."

Cindy studied me through the gray haze of the day's first cigarette. "Bet it's not over."

"With Don?"

"With Bob."

"It's over." I gathered my book bag, checked to make sure I had the packet of poems for workshop. "I'll see you at the disco."

But it wasn't over, of course. Though I had sworn to myself I would not see Bob again, he convinced me otherwise. He courted me with flowers, wrote me poems, hung banners professing his love across my bedroom wall. What did it matter, I asked myself, if I slept with him or not? It was all *nada*. It meant nothing.

Even as we met at the park, in cars, under bridges, on the back roads that led out of town, I convinced myself that I was still secure in my cynicism. At first, it was easy to keep him at a distance, even as I spent hours cradled in his arms, listening to the deep resonance of his voice reciting Keats, Roethke, Plath. The fact that his wife waited for him with patience born of desperation was a strange comfort. When it came time to show him the door, she'd be at hers, waiting to take him back.

And then, one morning, *I* found *myself* waiting. Sitting at the kitchen table, holding my coffee cup, listening for his call.

The decision was easy, I told myself. Things were getting complicated. It had already gone on too long. Time to bail.

"Are you crazy?" Cindy asked, when I told her I was breaking it off. "He's romantic, sensitive, handsome. He's got a good job. He's strong, *and* he leaves flowers on your pillow. He can talk to you about *books*, for god sakes. Don't be a fool."

"Cindy, he's *married*!"

"So was the Duchess of Windsor."

"This is not a fairy tale."

Cindy tilted her head back, exhaled a smoky breath. "Just don't believe it can't happen."

What I believed was that he would never leave his wife and son. I wasn't even sure I wanted him to. Why, then, did I remain in the wings through that awful spring while Bob lived out his dual life on the stage: husband, father, and teacher by day, adulterer by night? His wife's one requirement was that he be home before his son woke for school, and so we parted at sunrise, like Shakespeare's lovers, he whispered, and I laughed. "We're just cheaters," I said. "Don't romanticize this."

In response, he wrote aubades decrying dawn. He took pieces of my clothing so that he could breathe my scent when we were apart. When I called him crazy, he nodded. Yes, I made him that way. He was an intense man, he said, and he was intent upon making me love him.

At his urging, I changed my major to English, and as a kind of celebratory purging, Bob helped me clear my shelves of Danielle Steel, Kathleen E. Woodiwiss, and *The Thorn Birds*. We headed for the used bookstore, where we exchanged my library for Philip Roth, E. L. Doctorow, and Zora Neale Hurston. We spent hours together doing nothing but reading, making love, then reading some more.

And then all hell broke loose.

After several months of allowing him to have his cheesecake and eat it too, his wife demanded that he make a choice, which he did, but it was a choice that shifted by the hour. He could not leave his son; he could not live without me. All our lives became unhinged, and we flapped and shrieked like doors straining against a gale-force wind. Bob and his wife threatened each other. When Bob came to class morose and smelling of scotch, the college administration made its own threats. When I saw the damage being done to their son, I said I would no longer be a part of such a ruinous entanglement. I decided that, if I truly loved him, I would make it easy and walk away. And, though I had not meant it as such, that was the final ultimatum. Bob separated from his wife, moved into his own apartment, and began custody arrangements.

We were both dead broke, and so we filled our hours playing strip Scrabble. With him, I learned words I never dreamed existed. I listened for the first time to Vivaldi, Arcangelo Corelli, Zoot Sims, Barber's "Adagio for Strings." When I told him my fear of nightmares, he lit a candle by our bedside and swore to keep it burning, and another after it, and another if need be, watching over me in my sleep, guardian of my dreams. When I couldn't sleep, he told me stories—bits and pieces of his young life spent in Illinois, his graduate work in Montana, his new life in Idaho, where he came to stay because the mountains and trees caused his soul to sing. I would wake in the early light to find him watching me, seeing for an instant who I might be before I covered my eyes.

After two years of what my mother referred to as "living in sin," Bob and I began planning our wedding. I would attend graduate school in the fall—a move that motivated Bob to one of his least elegant utterances as a poet: "Guess I'd better put a ring on your finger before you get away."

I know now how fearful he was, how he was fighting a particular kind of trepidation. I was twenty-five, and a great deal had changed since we first met: Although I still sometimes said, "I've *went* to that restaurant before" instead of "I've *gone*" and insisted on the rural version of the past tense of to *drag*—*I drug myself out of bed*—I could hold my own in respectable conversation. It would be my first time away from Bob's tutelage, and he wasn't sure he trusted the instruction of those other men who might be my teachers.

Instead of being fitted for tux and gown, Bob and I spent our prenuptial weekend hiking the western Montana mountains. In the two years we had been together, Bob and I had shared our love of the land, camping, backpacking, fishing, whitewater rafting. It was a pleasure to be in the company of a man who not only knew how to pitch a whip-tight tent but could, after the last light had left the sky, pull my head to his shoulder and whisper the words his own teacher and mentor, Richard Hugo, wrote for his wife Ripley:

. . . Believe you and I sing tiny
and wise and could if we had to eat stone and go on.

Our five-minute ceremony took place in the Missoula County Courthouse. Bob's best man was fellow poet and bronco-riding cowboy Paul Zarzyski, who wore his new boots for the occasion. It was Ripley Hugo who stood up for me. After decades of living lost and lonely, Richard Hugo had found his lifelong love in Ripley. Eight years later, while being treated for leukemia, he died suddenly. Only a few months since Dick's death, and Ripley was still mourning, and will always be. But she believed in the promises Bob and I made before the judge. Such a short time they'd had together, she said, but worth it. She hugged us with tears in her eyes but didn't stay for champagne, which we popped in the cab of Paul's aging Ford pickup and drank with the rain coming down hard around us, the air inside sweet with alfalfa.

⸎

It is most often women who, upon hearing my story of courtship and love, say it sounds like something straight out of a storybook. Yet, no marriage is a fairy tale. That "ever after" is sometimes happy, sometimes sad, and sometimes so devastating that you doubt your ability to eat *anything* and go on.

Bob and I have quarreled (if that is what you call those awful fits of accusation and extended periods of sullen silence). We've been to counseling. We've had moments when we believed we might truly despise each other. Mostly, we soon forget what fueled our discontent. Was it *my* critical appraisal of his driving skills? Was it *his* failure to plan dinner when he knew I had a deadline looming? Yes to these and other seemingly trivial complaints that pile up on one another until the back of the marriage sags and threatens to break.

Any partnership involves a perpetual negotiation of who does what when: It is the thing that keeps the couples' counselors in business. But my and Bob's situation raises the stakes: because Bob is not only my husband but my mentor as well, I often find it difficult to demand my own space, to commandeer equal time, to put my needs on par with his.

This was never truer than those years when our children were young. Because we both crave connection to the land, our homes most often have been rural and separated from nearby towns. (I think of the words of my friend, Judy Blunt, who raised her family on a remote Montana ranch: "Before you have children, it's called solitude; after they're born, it's called isolation.") Because Bob was and will always be the senior writer with the most years in the saddle, it seemed only fair that he be given the office in whatever house we were occupying. While Bob sequestered himself behind a closed door, I scribbled lines while standing at the kitchen counter, a nursing baby cradled in one arm.

It was Bob who sent out my first poems without telling me. When they were picked up by first one journal and then another, he mocked my surprise. "Keep at it," he said, and I did: at the picnic table while my daughter and son played on the swing set; at the dining table while they napped.

Although I started my writing life composing poetry, I quickly shifted genres. I believe that I find my truest voice in narrative, but I sometimes wonder if my decision wasn't also driven by the fact that there were too many cooks in that small stanzaic kitchen. My shift to prose contributed to another problem: Whereas, before, I had been able to draft an entire poem while the children slept, I now needed greater blocks of time to produce short stories and essays. By this point, Bob and I each held positions at the college at which we'd met. How could we both find time not only to care for our children and household but time to write as well?

As it turned out, we couldn't. Our minimal salaries didn't allow for day care, and although I could have insisted that we split child care duties, I wasn't prepared, emotionally or mentally, to argue against Bob's superior dedication to his art—he must *write or die,* he said, a position I found both maudlin and impractical. Whether out of failure to recognize my own worth as a writer or out of fear that Bob might once again grow restless if I didn't give him all that he wanted, I could not bring myself to make my own demands: I needed not only time but space as well. I needed a room, with a lock on the door. I needed someone to whom I could give the children while I gave myself over to the muse.

I realize now how the codes of conduct I inherited from my family remain deeply entrenched: The men work, the women labor; the men create, the women tend. Whatever inroads I had made toward self-liberation in the face of gender expectation were lost when I weighed the needs of my husband and children against my own.

Bob seemed blithely unaffected by my dilemma. Or at least he seemed willing to ignore it as long as I was willing to provide the solution. This was my decision as much as it was his, of course—a decision informed not only by gender but by pecking order. I was, after all, the apprentice, the novitiate, the one to whom the less ethereal tasks should fall. While he wrote, I nursed, laundered, and watched endless hours of *Sesame Street.* When our son and daughter grew restless and threatened to disrupt the tranquil silence that Bob required to compose his poems, I loaded them into the car and drove to the closest playground, twenty miles away. In bad weather, I spent hours at the nearest McDonald's thirty miles north, sipping coffee while watching my children play in a cage filled with brightly colored balls. I cruised the streets of small towns until their small heads nodded in their safety seats, then parked and crawled into the back with them. While they napped, I multitasked, clipping their nails, listening to National Public Radio, and jotting notes onto old receipts and the torn-out pages of coloring books—an image, a phrase that I meant to remember and someday use.

And then, just when I thought I might break, our daughter entered first grade, our son preschool. I hoarded those few precious hours like gold, writing as fast as I could—first short stories, and then personal essays, and then a memoir that received national attention and won several prizes. Bob's own work continued to gain increasing recognition. When he received news of his Guggenheim Fellowship in the mail, he ran down our steep gravel driveway at breakneck speed, yelling at the top of his lungs until he skidded and tumbled into an ecstatic heap. I was there to pick him up, urge enough restraint to keep his bones intact. When I received the phone call telling me I was a Pulitzer finalist, it was Bob who insisted that I howl through my disbelief. We remind each other to celebrate the fat times when and for as long as we can because we both have learned that the lean times are long and hungry indeed. I sometimes think that marriage is just this way: periods of extraordinary closeness and intimacy, followed by times when we feel so distant that we look at each other as strangers and wonder what drew us together in the first place.

———— ∞ ————

People often ask what it's like to have two writers in the house, and I tell them that, for the most part, it's grand. We are each other's first reader, cheerleader, and most kind and demanding critic. We inspire each other; we steal from each other. Sometimes, we can't remember who first wrote what. Is that image of burning the dead horse his or mine? (Mine.) Is the descriptive phrase "nighthawks stitching the darkness down" mine or his? (His.) We barter back and forth, pulling coins from the same purse, robbing Peter to pay Paul and then borrowing from Paul to repay Peter. It's rare that we feel a need to assert singular ownership over something that flows between us like blood.

But there have been times when the best of times for our work has been the worst of times for our marriage. Because the promotion of my books involved extended publicity tours, Bob had no choice but to shoulder not only his share of the child rearing responsibilities, but mine as well. I would call from New York or Chicago or LA, and he would be bereft and desperate. He couldn't sleep without me. The kids were driving him crazy. They all missed me terribly. Other times, I would call to hear Sam Cooke playing in the background. They were fine, Bob said. Making spaghetti for dinner. Dancing around the kitchen. Having a good time, even without me.

Sometimes, I was relieved. Sometimes, I missed them all so badly I thought I might die. Sometimes, I couldn't fathom the emotion that Bob brought to our separation. Was it fear I heard in his voice, or resentment? Was he jealous of the attention my work was getting, or was he jealous of the admirers I might encounter? I'm not sure he himself understood what simmered inside of him and boiled over into fits of frustration and rage. Perhaps he felt some part of me being stolen away; perhaps he feared that what had first attracted him to me might attract another. More than anything, he said, he simply needed me in an impossible and all-consuming way.

When I ask him about this now—those nights when he and the children visited me on the road and his longing became a kind of angry desperation—he shakes his head. "I still get a little crazy when I'm away from you," he says. "Just like in the beginning."

Time itself has brought us to a deeper awareness not only of each other but of ourselves as well. Just a few hours ago, Bob read to me from an article addressed to men in *Esquire*—"Ten Things You Don't Know About Women"—and quoted the female author: "*You say: 'I'm intense.' We hear, 'I'm a psycho.'*"

When I lifted my eyebrows in bemused agreement, Bob grinned

sheepishly, and I was reminded of that twenty-nine-year-old man I first met, his cheeks dimpling. I felt my heart beat a little faster. I like him better this way, able to see outside of himself, able to laugh at what he'd once believed to be morbidly defining. This is the part I might have missed if I had chosen to turn away in the beginning—or yesterday.

This June, we will have been together for twenty-five years. Bob's son from his previous marriage is now a man whose presence in our lives is a gift. Bob's first wife has found her own truest love, and I feel blessed to know her and her husband. There are so many ways in which my life seems miraculous to me, and I remind myself that the rooms I must share contain the lives of those people I choose to love.

I picture Bob in his study. He has aged in that way handsome men do: silvering at the temples, his face taking on more character, his mouth still sensitive but also set with a calm and confidence born of years. I'm not the only woman who finds him attractive, and I realize that he is presented with bright, young minds and rosebud bras every day. I have never known him to stray, and, just as I still wonder why he picked me so many years ago, I sometimes wonder now why it is he chooses to stay with me, even as those other rosebuds are gathering, eager to hear what he might have to teach them.

I think my reaction to infidelity might be different than his first wife's response. I'm nearly two decades older than she was then, secure in the parts of my life that will endure even if the marriage doesn't. Still, when I allow myself to imagine what that pain might feel like, that betrayal, I sense the old familiar hardening begin. How easy would it be for me once again to grow cold? To shroud myself against loss and disappointment? It seems to me its own miracle that any of us can believe in love, that we have the faith to rise each morning into doubt, knowing, as we do, how quickly love can be taken away—by death, by an inexplicable sea change of affection. "Believe," Hugo said, and I try. Each day is a reaffirmation, a renewal of my vows to go on.

For Bob, there is the Pygmalion complex—the fear of the older professor who takes the rough but promising pupil under his wing until that day when she departs his tutelage, no longer in need of his instruction. But we're *both* older now, and Bob has come to feel less threatened by my time away from him, perhaps comforted by what the cycle of our lives has taught him: like the tides, I always return.

That girl he first met, her body now moving a bit less languidly toward the end of half a century, her hair gone from a layered mane of auburn to cropped salt-and-pepper—she's still his student in some ways, still surprised to learn what he can teach her of language. And there are times when she still reminds him of that feral girl she once was, the one with the sharpshooter's medals on her wall and fishing rods in her closet.

He still writes me poems. He brings me flowers for no reason. We make love along the banks of rivers, the flickering fire and stars allowing our bodies some semblance of youthful grace. He teases, turns my own rural phrasings against me: "You cleaned up real nice," he says. And I remind him that he's come a long way from that Illinois neophyte who first came West with a ten-pound tackle box full of bass plugs, which he hauled miles into a high mountain lake populated with nothing but trout. We fish the current together now with little more than wisps of thread and feather on the ends of our lines, light as night's last kiss.

Maybe, as a mother and wife, I give too much and don't take enough. Maybe I still can't claim the right of my gender to be both artist and muse. Maybe, for whatever reason, some part of me doesn't believe that I deserve a room of my own. Maybe, no matter how far my writing takes me, I will always believe myself the student and

Bob the master. All these observations and arguments are ones that I recognize. Yet here I am. In this chair. In this corner. In this marriage. With this man who, no matter the number of years or books or awards, will always be my first and most important teacher.

"Mr. Wrigley," I sometimes call to him when I have a question about diction or the name of an author. "Can I bother you?"

"Why, of course, Ms. Barnes," he replies. He moves to stand behind me, kisses the back of my neck, whispers the answer in my ear, and I feel a twinge of excitement. Anticipation. The beginning of something that just might be real.

Divorce, Foretold

Laura Fraser

My ex-husband proposed to me on a smooth sandstone ledge in Arches National Park, next to a towering hoodoo rock that resembled an open-mouthed woman laughing—or maybe screaming. On that bright day, I saw her as a totem of joy, not pain, and so I said yes to J. and felt blessed by the rock's powerful presence.

That evening, at dusk, as we walked along a dirt road near a ranch in Utah's La Sal Mountains, J. spoke about his fears. We'd had conversations about the terrors of relationships before, and one of the things I loved about him was that he was not only willing to examine his dark side, but trusted me to see it, too. He'd told me one reason he cherished me was that for the first time in his life, he felt truly seen.

On that walk he confessed that his worst fear was that he might leave me, or, if we had a child, abandon us both. I listened calmly, figuring his worries were a holdover from his childhood, when his mother abandoned him at the age of nine. She'd taken off to another continent to pursue an academic fellowship, in competition with her more famous husband, and left them both behind. I was confident that J.'s anxieties about getting married were natural—all men have them—and that by bringing them to light, they would disappear.

"So what are *you* afraid of?" J. asked me.

My fears? I had a brilliant, funny, successful man in my life, who surprised me with irises, took me rafting down red-rock canyons, and sent me beautiful cards for no occasion, saying I was the first person to make him feel truly alive.

I took his hand and squeezed it with conviction. "Nothing."

Just then I heard a distinctive, paper-dry rattle. My heart slid down to my boots. Two feet away, a diamondback rattlesnake, thick as a fire hose, was coiled up, flicking its tongue, ready to strike.

I'm so phobic I can't touch a photo of a snake in a magazine. I screamed, leaped, and shot ahead on the trail. When J. caught up with me, I was still trembling.

"You shouldn't have startled it," he admonished me, crossing his arms. "You should've just taken a quiet step away."

Two years later, when I was stretched out on the floor, pain swelling throughout my body, barely able to breathe, I thought about that damned snake. Being bitten by real fangs would've been a lot easier than what I was going through. I'd been struck, venomously, and left to suffer with no antidote but time. Two weeks earlier, I'd walked in on my husband with another woman, and that day, he'd walked away forever.

It only seemed like it happened without warning. Up until the moment I found my husband with another woman, I believed we were happy newlyweds, and J. was undergoing a period of unusual stress at work. He was a criminal defense trial attorney, so I understood why he might come home uncommunicative at times, in front of the television, silently consuming the wild mushroom risotto I'd prepared. That was temporary: My faith rested with my memories of his meeting me, flashing his brilliant smile, complimenting me on the column I wrote, sending me flowers and a book of sensual essays the next day. I held onto snapshots of our vacations together in the wilderness, taking hikes that were as long, varied, and surprising as our conversations. I thought about our cozy, animated dinners, talking about authors we both loved—Paul Auster, Robertson Davies, John Irving, Vladimir Nabokov—knowing we shared not only an appreciation of good writing, but a worldview of quirkiness, mental play, and against-all-odds morality. All the times we'd talked so long there was nothing left to do but kiss were more than enough insurance against a few tired and cranky evenings.

But that belief in our happiness, along with my trust in my judgment and men in general, collapsed without warning. Or had there been signs that I'd ignored?

When J. started coming home late, I trusted it was due to his job. When he mentioned his high school girlfriend had called, out of the blue, and they'd gone to yoga and dinner together, I thought it was nice he was renewing an old acquaintance. That evening when I'd come home earlier than expected, it took a while for the scene in the dining room—candles, flowers, and a hastily departed meal—to sink in. Even when I climbed the stairs to our bedroom, with its recently mussed covers, and went out to the porch, where J. and his high school girlfriend were cozily entwined in sleeping bags, polishing off a bottle of wine and watching the moon, I didn't want to believe my eyes.

"Hello," I said to the woman, wanting everything to be normal, offering her my shaking hand. "I'm Laura. J.'s *wife*."

She was out the door before I even had a chance to decide whether she was prettier than me. I turned to my husband, outraged, and he answered me with a look of disdain. When I threw one of their dinner plates across the room, he gave a slight, satisfied smile.

"See?" he said. "*That's* the problem. *You're* always so angry."

Suddenly, everything I trusted—our secure marriage, honest communication, and deep understanding of each other—turned false. How could I not have seen it coming?

During the months after he left me, I sifted through the ruins of our relationship to uncover clues to why our marriage had crumbled. I first asked the marriage counselor we saw briefly in the weeks after I walked in on J. and his old girlfriend. People make mistakes, and I was prepared to forgive him and work it out. He agreed to see a therapist, but his emotions were so sealed, his responses so walled off, that I had to resort to tears and screaming to try to get some reaction, some remnant of feeling out of him. He never lost his cool, and by comparison, I seemed like a maniac.

After J. left for good, the therapist agreed to debrief me alone.

"You never had a chance," she told me, sighing. "At first, I thought if he could really be heard, you could work things out. But by the second session, I realized he was out of the marriage before he walked in the door." He'd gone to counseling just to say he'd tried. "You got on a train that was headed for a wreck, and there was no way you could've known," she said.

There was a lot of comfort, initially, in thinking that there was nothing I could've done to stop that wreck, but as time passed, I became more and more uneasy about my ability to make good choices about the men in my life.

Like most women who married late, I'd had enough experience in relationships to spot the obvious red flags. After just one date, I ditched the art director who told me about the temporary restraining order his ex-wife had against him. Ditto for the chef who, on his third bottle of red, told me how he lost his last job when he couldn't drive to work after getting a DUI. When I encountered men who split the check to the penny, made mysterious excuses for canceling dates, or left in the morning before coffee, I knew enough to run in the other direction. But for three years before we married, J. was all I dreamed of: witty, well-read, well-off, attentive, polite to strangers, and engaging to my friends. He wasn't perfect, but everyone has flaws, and every marriage involves compromise. So what if he wouldn't eat cheese, didn't like to have dinner parties, thought my work was a bit trivial, and spent too much time trading Grateful Dead tapes with strangers?

I trusted my husband, but in retrospect, I have to say I wasn't thinking clearly. Otherwise, I might have noticed a few signs—not only from the universe, but also from my friends and family.

That snake for instance. If the rattler itself wasn't enough of a warning, what about J.'s reaction when I was shaking with fear? Did I really need a lecture right then, or wouldn't a man I wanted to marry have held me tight until I stopped trembling?

There were other portents. The wedding itself was full of signs, both hopeful and disastrous. We married outdoors, in a redwood grove on a clear warm day. When I walked into the circle of friends with my parents, J. was nowhere to be found; finally, one of his pals in the back pushed him up front. Our friends read poetry, we made vows we'd written together, our minister playfully waved a magic wand over our heads—"Shazam!"—and everyone told us it was the most beautiful ceremony they'd ever seen. But when J.'s famous philosopher father gave his toast, not only didn't anyone understand a word of his obscure speech—something about Mammon?—J. told me later that a friend's Native American wife in the back row had to shield her face from the "evil wind." Not to be outdone, J.'s professor mother gave an even longer toast, invoking a pantheon of obscure Greek thinkers, aimed not at us, but at impressing her philosopher friends (and enemies).

When at last it was time for the first dance, J. and I waltzed under the trees. At the second dance, when my father came for his turn, the DJ put on a raucous punk-rock song by the Clash. My father, disappointed, shrugged, smiled, and took his seat.

After the wedding, and a late-night party that dwindled to friends laughing in a hot tub, we finally got to bed. J. got up immediately and started vomiting, presumably from too much to drink. By morning, it turned out that a third of the people at the wedding had become violently ill with food poisoning. We were halfway to our honeymoon cottage on the northern California coast when I told J. to pull over, and got sick by the side of the road. It was three days into our honeymoon before we could even stomach poached eggs.

When the formal wedding photos were developed, everyone in both families was smiling, except for J., who was scowling (I blamed myself for hiring an ex-boyfriend to shoot the wedding). When I took the disposable cameras from the reception to be developed, every single one of them came back blank.

I kept my humor; it would all make for a great story to tell later on, to our kids and grandchildren, a story about funny mishaps in a long and lasting marriage.

It's one thing to miss the intuitive and mystical signs, but surely there must have been more practical signs that J. wouldn't make a good partner. When, a few weeks after we split, I saw my own therapist— whom I'd quit seeing when I married, thinking my life was perfect now—she was also baffled, and even hard on herself.

"What did we miss?" she asked.

To her, it had seemed, finally, like a perfect match, and she couldn't believe what had happened. She mused it over in retrospect. There was J.'s bizarre relationship with his mother. Since she'd left J. and his father for a year when J. was nine, he never really separated from her, and so they had an awkward relationship of guilt, resentment, and attachment. She wanted J. to forgive her for abandoning him and to be close to her only child. She knew no privacy boundaries in our house and treated me like particularly dim competition.

J.'s mother had indeed been at the root of the few serious moments of tension that occurred between J. and I—moments I simply thought would pass as she came to accept me. When my first book came out, complete with readings, reviews, and television appearances, I invited J.'s mother to New York for the party, and she managed to turn all the attention to herself, creating scene after scene over perceived slights. That put so much strain on J. that the morning I returned to the hotel after being on the *Today* show, eager to call my family, he wearily told me to keep it down, he was watching the game.

I called my mom whispering from the bathroom phone to tell her about the Green Room, the limousine, and Matt Lauer. I was so upset at the way my exciting literary debut was dampened that when a producer from NPR's *Fresh Air* called an hour later to try me out for the show, I was nearly incoherent, and of course, never made it on the show. I vented by yelling at room service for not bringing me tea after ordering it an hour earlier. J. looked up from the TV and shot me a disapproving look for being out of control, too emotional.

"You can't blame him for his narcissistic mother," I told my therapist.

I suppose if I'd been smarter, if I'd had a Ph.D. in psychology, I could've predicted that J. would be resentful of my success because his mother had abandoned him for her career.

My therapist nodded. "All in all, you couldn't have seen it coming. You were just dealt a really bad hand."

My therapist, of course, had only heard my version of events. I suppose she was as taken with him as I was. But when I asked my good friends who knew J., some of them had clearly seen that it wouldn't work out. That was surprising, since they'd been supportive when we married. I guess I was so in love that they knew they couldn't express any reservations without risking our friendship. But after J. left, it all came spilling out.

My close friend Cristina recalled when J. surprised me with a thirty-fifth birthday party, then stormed upstairs at 11 p.m. that Saturday night, angry people were making so much noise. I love to entertain, but J. never wanted to have dinner parties, actively disliked my college friends (he'd decided against an elite college like mine out of rebellion against his uber-academic parents, and perhaps regretted that decision), and mostly kept his own solitary friends to himself. A plain dresser, for a Deadhead, he ridiculed my red shoes and sassy outfits, criticized my weight, and only complimented me when I was wearing navy blue or polo shirts (his academic Princetonian upbringing coming out).

"It's like the real you went underground," Cristina said. Marriage is about compromise, all right, but she thought I'd compromised myself out of existence. Now *there's* something to fear.

My oldest sister, who is generous to everyone, revealed that she never liked J., either. He was completely disinterested in her life, never asked her anything about her kids or work, and treated my entire Colorado family like a bunch of hicks.

My friend Larry liked J. well enough, until just before the wedding, when I told Larry I'd hired a jazz band, and he asked me if I was going to sing. I love to sing: I sang at my friend Leonora's wedding, I sing after too many bottles of red wine with friends, and I've sung in bars and cafés.

"J. would be mortified if I sang at the wedding," I told Larry.

"That's when I knew he was the wrong guy for you," he told me later.

Another friend recalled the issue of our—well, J.'s—house. When we met, J. owned a house. Before our marriage, we went house hunting and found one we both loved, which, with his large trust fund, he could well afford. We were going to put in an offer, when, after a conversation with his mother and lawyer, he said the finances were too complicated—his mother owned half his house; they'd have to sell another one they owned. We'd buy a bigger house later, when we had kids. I trusted him enough that I didn't consider that under California law, if we divorced, I'd have no stake in his house, except for the actual money I paid him as my share of the mortgage (the value of J.'s house doubled during the dot-com boom, but I went back to renting an apartment with a roommate, forever priced out of the San Francisco market).

That wasn't a sign, my friend said. "That was stupid."

It may seem that the signs were everywhere, that I was a fool to get married. But I was thirty-four and ready to be married—like most of my friends—and to have children. After years of insecurity as a freelance writer, living on the margins, I wanted the support of a partner. J.'s excitement at finding someone he initially thought was as unpretentiously smart as he was fed my ego. J. told me he loved me, and he was adept at hiding his ambivalence. When, after he left, I finally asked him why he married me, he said, "I married you with my fingers crossed." I wondered which way he meant that—as children do, meaning, "I don't really mean it," or, "with any luck this will work out." I didn't have the heart to ask.

I may not believe in superstitions and omens, but crossed fingers are a sign I could have read. I wouldn't have married J. if I'd known that to him marriage was a means of hedging his bets, so he wouldn't lose me if he decided he really wanted to keep me. Our understandings of what marriage meant came from two completely different cultures. I meant it for life; I grew up with parents who are devoted best friends and have now been together more than fifty-five years. J.'s divorced mother lives in bitterness, and his remarried father, abstraction. J. thought so little of our commitment that when he left a year and a half later, he didn't take any responsibility for our breakup.

"It just didn't work out," he said, refusing to be generous, wanting to pay me only moving costs, when it would have been so easy for him, with his millions, to help me with a down payment on a small house I could afford. His stinginess and his sharklike behavior at mediation were sure signs that we weren't going to remain friends, as he hoped; they were signs that I was lucky to have him out of my life.

It was difficult, afterward, to develop new relationships. I preferred to take men lightly, knowing that they wouldn't work out in the end, but feeling hurt just the same. I dated men with many of J.'s traits—intelligence, charm, humor, professional accomplishments, literary acumen, wealth. It took me far too long to realize that those weren't the signs of a good partner, but generally speaking, of narcissism.

Lately, I've been dating someone who is quite different, a bright spirit, and more down to earth. We are taking it slowly, offering no promises, just enjoying each other when we see each other. But I am noticing signs: My friend Cristina immediately liked him, as did my old college pals. We're good at completely different things—he's a scientist—but he thinks it's wonderful when he finds out I can do something he can't do, like speak foreign languages or make risotto. He admires the exuberant way I dress, but likes me better naked. I feel like myself with him.

There are warning signs, too, I suppose: He doesn't read books, watches a lot of sports on TV, and told me his mother will hate me. It may or may not work out. But if it doesn't, I'll know at least I'm getting closer, and that, too, is a good sign. And I'll always appreciate that when we hike, he tells me to sing loudly, not only to scare away the rattlesnakes, but because he likes to hear me sing.

The Marriage Coma

Betsy Israel

The time: Tuesday, any Tuesday, 10 p.m.

The place: Our New York City living room.

The dramatis personae in so-called action: My husband, an entertainment lawyer, home after twelve hours of Very Difficult People, rests briefly in the Eames chair, once a proud modernist icon, now a leather collage of prehistoric snacks, art projects, light-saber attacks, c. 1991–2005. I watch him from the couch, a formerly vivid, now indiscernibly colored Duncan Phyfe, our son, nine, perched on my legs as he updates me on his current research—tonight, the aesthetic evolution of skateboards; D-Day if you "were Axis"; forensic pathology as applied to mummies. Our daughter, fourteen, glares at her geek brother in disgust, then, peeling a clementine, blasts her iTunes. For tonight's impromptu gathering, she's scrolled down to the "classical" section, an assemblage of songs popular when I was precisely her age.

And then, the denouement, we stay that way, our soundtrack a strange brew of "Layla," "Rocket Man," CNN, and my son, who wants me to know that embalmers pulled the mummy's brain out through its nose. As the play list descends into sad-lost-girl Cat

Stevens—at about the time my not-so-young legs go slightly numb—
I call out to my husband with happy news: after he checks in with
LA and I put out the garbage, once he's tuned our son's violin and
I've done Latin vocab with our daughter, hey, we can at last—our
very favorite thing—go to sleep!

At our wedding—narrow NYC town house, snow outside, guests inside huddled as if on a Belle Epoque elevator—the chaplain seemed
to lose his way amid my handwritten vows. One pause stretched on
so long I heard familiar muffled snorting from my sisters, an ancient
childhood signal indicating, "We are about to snort really loud, then
crack up and then possibly fall over." At last the poor guy abandoned
my personal hieroglyphs, my arrows and inserts, and oddly impro-
vised: "Forever, forever, for-*ever*—so glorious a concept and yet . . ."
—long pause, loud warning snorts—". . . it is, forever, seriously, well
. . . It is a *very long time.*"

After, there was amused debate: A truth so basic it seemed mo-
ronic? Strange tautological stand-up comedy? Oh, who cared! We
were married at last and everyone who was not laughing or crying was applauding. Forever and forever, even "a very long time,"
seemed less glorious or serious a notion than it did just irrelevant. It
was 1989 and it was time to cut the carrot cake.

During our first few years of marriage, many of our peers began to
break apart at an alarming rate. As known duos unraveled all around
us, our own union came somewhat prematurely to represent the gold
standard of commitment. We'd been an official, if unusual, couple
five whole years before we'd wed. We'd never broken up even briefly
nor had affairs—a charmed record made more remarkable given that
throughout this time we'd been stubbornly, and a bit self-righteously,
bi-coastal.

When we met, I was an editor in New York City; he was a film lawyer and songwriter out in LA. Manhattan was the ancestral homeland, meaning he didn't want to go there all that often. And I hated to fly, meaning I didn't want to go anywhere at all. We'd come to life once a month, like a couple out of *Brigadoon:* dancing around, having sex on every available surface, then traveling for dispiriting hours en route back to our respective time zones. Even after I quit working to write a book, even after he'd made a desk for me in his pristine all-white place at the beach, even after we got married—I routinely left LA for The City, climbing aboard doomed aircraft, to see my family, my editors, and once, famously, my dentist.

A number of my girlfriends found this arrangement—the fact that I'd kept my New York apartment *and* that I hadn't changed my name—somewhat threatening. How could my husband stand for it, meaning how could there be so nice a guy? All the men they knew made them angry or physically ill. That is to say, few of my single gal pals felt very happy for us. Once, in a Chinese restaurant, a newly divorced friend smashed a fortune cookie, then, after reading the paper slip, shoved it with her red-lacquered nails into my noodles.

What I dug out: "Marriage, it has four rings: Engagement ring, Wedding ring, Suffe-ring, Divor-ce-ring."

Friends had applauded at our wedding because if anyone deserved to be married, it was us. We'd survived not just the uncertainties of bi-coastal love, but also the nasty reactions of many key people we knew—a persistent Greek (actually, Jewish) chorus that had hounded us, commenting on the improbabilities since our first New York date in '85.

The Jealous: "Okay, look, he's thirty-six. Not that I'm not saying he has issues. I'm not saying anything. I'm just saying there is road-kill. The kind where you can't tell what the animal was."

The Concerned: "What about babies? Unlike you, babies *need to live in one time zone.* I mean don't you want babies? I mean, you're thirty! I mean . . ."

. . . *The Family:* His family, anyway, the ones who en masse looked at me and saw a mere half-Jew wearing a mere half a skirt possessing the merest of proper good-girl credentials. They'd have agreed, I think, with our . . .

. . . *Most Severely Jealous* friend, the one from the Chinese restaurant, who called us, and I paraphrase: "too-cool hipster yuppies in love with this quirky faux-bohemian concept of themselves."

That was at least partly true. We happily, wildly adored not only each other but the *Concept of Us* as if we had established a unique romantic trademark: an LA duo in matching sunglasses and near identical cars who, when in New York, threw "Hi, we're back!" parties in our mysteriously secure rent-stabilized places. Having three apartments when most friends had barely one—that was obnoxious. More obnoxious, we wrote screenplays while flying between apartments one and three. We both, it turned out, played the flute, a coincidence that transcended obnoxiousness and entered the realm of toxic cuteness.

But our self-love, our commitment to the Concept of Us, was not, as some claimed, overly precious, faux, or even particularly cool. Despite a shared worldview best described as sardonic, we saw ourselves anachronistically as meant-to-be. Very early on I'd told my mother that I planned to marry Him, and she had sighed.

"Why," I asked. "Why must you be negative?"

"Because," she replied, "you haven't *even met him yet.*"

And he, I believed, had without knowing it waited years for me. In a piece I wrote after we'd met, I observed that if you took all his exes, '68–'88, and lined them up, you'd have an evolutionary time line of small, pale, dark-haired, thin-wristed women ending in me— the prettiest and, as he'd put it, "the most unlikely," the least conventional, meaning in our evolving lexicon, The Absolute One.

As uncharacteristically corny as it was, we *knew*. Or at least we pretty desperately hoped. For us both, this union was not a means to show off. It was a chance to establish something neither of us had ever had: profound unquestionable connection to another person.

After a teen life we'll delicately call "disturbed," I'd spent my twenties crawling into and awkwardly out of damaged liaisons, pausing only for outbursts of severely unrequited crushes analyzed so furiously my pen tore angry gashes in the paper. (It's scary to think what I'd have done if we'd had e-mail.) By the time I met Him, I was convinced I'd never find someone who'd honestly "get" me and then, knowing what he knew, still want to marry me. (Which raised that twisted but essential question: if such a man actually accepted me, how could I want him knowing his questionable taste?)

Some eight years earlier, and about thirty minutes north of me on Long Island, my husband had emerged from his own teen life comparably dazed. The product of a distracted, unhappy family, he'd moved cautiously into the world in his words "disconnected . . . some emotional dimension missing." After settling as far from home as he could—Yale, Africa, China, Guam, Tokyo, then stopping back in New York for law school, before LA—he allied himself with women who seemed to share his inner skittishness. With few exceptions, they were cool, distanced, and emotionally unavailable, key qualities he'd intuit in five minutes flat. Intimacy was not central to what my editors would have called his "overall conceptual framework."

About a year and a half after our meeting, he came home one LA night and found me in his favorite chair wearing a T-shirt plus his underwear. I'd assembled his flute, which I liked better than my own, and was flipping through a journal he'd written in French West Africa. He forced himself to go on talking or at least saying words—

movie, tennis racket, restaurant—but all color visibly had drained from his face. He had invited me to LA into his life, offered half a closet and a shelf on which our books were touching. Yet still it seemed I had invaded.

But this time there was nothing he could do—any more than I could reject him because he was "nice" and accepted me without my formerly prerequisite psychodrama. It's hard to describe the alchemical eruption that makes some other person suddenly flat-out irrationally yours. I'd try to describe our need to enfold each other within one life, but adjectives and nouns seem to collect in clichéd piles and then just sit there. And that need prevailed despite his annoying outbursts of minimalist precision. (Every object in the fridge was lined up in neat vertical rows, like an all-food marching band.) And it remained despite my own annoying tendency to Object Trails, the papers, scarves, socks, barrettes I left behind me wherever I went. ("Are you afraid you won't find your way back to the patio?") I tried, on his behalf, to drink beer, a beverage I associated solely with high school puking. For me, he ate vegetarian. Out there on our balcony—the surf and some howling Venice psychos as ambient sound—he'd loyally choked down lentil-kale loaf as I secretly dumped his lager into a cactus.

After we married, we bought a small place in New York and purchased our first real mutual object, the Duncan Phyfe. Together we directed its massive rehabilitation, then debated what could and could not touch it. Any food, clothes, shoes, my bag, in which pens exploded—all of this was prohibited. He was "mixed" on the pillows I'd kept out for years but opposed openly to my apartment mascot: a Raggedy Ann I called the Doll of Dorian Gray (mine since birth, she was bruised, torn, and actually filthy).

The mere idea of dolls, even the most benign sock monkeys, seemed to unnerve him. For he correctly sensed that, nine months married, I was stockpiling precious objects for a fantasized family.

My latest fixation was a holiday gift basket someone had given him, a towering construct of pink, red, and purple straw; gold Mardi Gras beads; lifelike stuffed finches and many Christmas-colored bows. He knew I wanted kids and he knew that as a half-Jew I'd been raised with alien Other holidays. But to call this gaudy mess the "Easter Basket of Our Unborn Children"? To get worked up over stale yellow chicks and little bonnets (*"bonnets? What bonnets?"*)—well, he really just didn't want to hear it. Ever. Still, when we moved back to New York—his new job, my new pregnancy—the basket came with us on the plane.

Secretly, I thought, he was amused and, more than that, touched and actually happy. He'd used the words *family, kids,* and *relatives* with mock tongs for so long, he did not seem to think these words might ever apply to him. At his first real birthday party—or at least the first with balloons—I gave him thirty-five gifts, one for each year, among them a one-armed cactus named Hamilton and a moose-shaped oven mitt from our beloved Rose Café in seedy Venice. I think even he recognized that these would be totemic objects, like the Vegas Easter Basket and the Doll of Dorian Gray, symbols for our kids of their prehistory.

Of course, our life, pre-kids, had complications. That is an understatement. We fought with an intensity accessible only to highly opinionated writers and lawyers, one of whom (me) rarely left the house. I overreacted to anything he said about my work. My cooking. My clothes. I overreacted when his movie friends would not talk to me. Everybody, including Him, said this was standard—these film guys did not, as I feared, find me boring, a short, too-literary New Yorker who wrote books they did not want to look at. They liked me, they really liked me! They just liked people who wrote scripts more. Half kidding, he'd add, "But what was that ruffly shirt thing you had on?"

There is one picture of me, taken mid-LA battle: I am stomping down a desolate desert road wearing inappropriate shoes. My husband drives behind me, alternately snapping shots of me through the windshield and shrieking, "Get back in the car!! Get in the fucking car now!!"

But every time we fought we missed each other, missed "us," and so most fights lasted only an hour. And by the next day these fights had become little theater pieces we'd re-enact, quoting the most outrageous parts to each other at the Rose Café or Caffe Dante back in the Village. My defiant march through Joshua Tree National Park was memorialized and hung on the fridge. Friends were invited to contribute captions.

There's another picture of me in LA. It was summer, 1997, and we'd come out from New York to spend two months in a '50s-era glass house overlooking the ocean. Every day he'd go to work and I'd stay home with our kids, writing and doing the job of our local nanny who spoke no English, had no experience with peanut butter, and feared all bugs. The day of the photo, the kids, aged five and one, watched a friend load the camera, then, before she was ready, stripped off their clothes. Since birth they'd been committed nudists, and the pictures that day capture them prancing around two sprinklers twirling and fracturing the light. On the print, clumps of rainbow and starburst sun hang like lanterns. My daughter, in a faux Scottish accent, declared it "proof of faeries." I declared it proof of Motherhood. In the background, in a black sleeveless dress, I can be seen, lying facedown on the grass, perhaps napping, perhaps just sick of trying to determine where their underpants had landed.

Looking at this photo, I thought back to my angry girlfriend and her silly warning of a fortune cookie. Hopeful marriage did not necessarily descend into "suffe-ring or divor-ce-ring." More often, one underwent a gradual *Surrende-ring* to be replaced by eventual, inescapable *Slumbe-ring*.

That summer, passed out on the lawn and in other places, I first experienced what I've come to call the Marriage Coma: a slow, logy malaise that seeps into any long-shared or wedded life, like anesthesia. Over the years, I'd hone my understanding of the phenomenon and even devise a reliable Coma Equation: *The point at which your combined ages, added to the number of years you've been married, exceeds ninety-three.* (Note: if you need to work this out on a calculator but can't find it, and so spend ten minutes in search of paper, a pen, well, chances are good that you've already qualified.)

The mutual stupor of the Marriage Coma sounds well beyond numbing—an all-natural tonic for sleeping soundly through sex— but it is, in fact, an essential piece of the blueprint, the master plan, for long-term marriage. I think of my parents—wed fifty years plus— and their World War II–era marital glossary. As they'd explain (at length), *slumbe-ring* is merely a warm-up, a dress rehearsal, for the key concepts of the long haul: *endu-ring,* to be joined in hard times by its pompous British cousin, *perseve-ring.*

Many just pull the plug. Others remain comatose, stuck, watching reruns of *Full House* with the kids, unable to contemplate dinner or to recall whether anyone present ate lunch or breakfast. Still, there are those who push straight on through the stagnant Sundays, the conversations containing ten small words ("Where is the remote? Um, are you sitting on it?"). Then, having for years sat out the marriage coma—the very real sense that all of life has crawled its way over and come to a stop on the couch—they may turn to each other and start to laugh. Pushing themselves up, perhaps losing balance, possibly falling into each other, they might actually go for a walk.

Looking back, attempting to excavate a full-out marriage coma, it's tricky to pinpoint the onset, that precise moment the eyes metaphorically began to close. But for us, I believe, it started there that summer in LA, the first of many spent in our glass house overlooking the ocean—just us, two rude cats, oblivious movie people, and by then our two spectacular, *all-singing! all-dancing!* sleepless babies.

If we had secretly idolized Us as a concept, that was a mere emotional warm-up for our kids. Yes, yes, many parents feel this way, but we adored them so outrageously, idealized them so profoundly, constantly, exclusively, other kinds of love seemed suddenly secondary. As one semi-repulsed friend observed, after being interrupted by yet another verbal miracle, "You behave as if they are tiny babbling gods." We brought them everywhere (welcomed or not) and talked about them incessantly like two psychotherapists analyzing their most complex and captivating patients. Again, I guess most parents have similar conversations but usually at night, once the kids are asleep. Our kids, outside of the car, did not sleep. Even in the dark, they talked, fought, attempted to read, performed in costume. To induce sleep, I had to firmly grasp each of their pinky fingers, sitting or squatting there until they dropped off or I fell over. Then, soon after, they'd come in to see how we were, meaning that most nights we all slept in the same room, a camping arrangement my husband called "immigrant family."

While the marriage coma, that most extreme state of bored familiarity and annoyance, evolves over time, there are certain guaranteed ways to speed it up. One is to provide a backdrop of cranky sleeplessness that extends for up to or over a year and thus eliminates sex. The other is to add a seemingly unsolvable problem.

My coma saga, as it evolved, was pure marital scripture.

That first summer in the glass house, I'd sold another book—a survey, going back 150 years and exploring how the prevailing media portrayed single women. This was something I'd written about in the past, but the book I was to write now was huge and historical and nothing at all like my other published books, a fact that was both thrilling and prone to induce bouts of insecurity bordering on hysteria. I spent the remaining summer deep in planning. I found a new assistant who, awaiting me in New York, began collecting ancient magazines and essays. I had long talks with the children, who immediately began writing their own books. And I devised schemes for getting more non-immigrant sleep.

Back in New York, everything worked out brilliantly for one week.

After that, I'd start to work, to read, to research, at least to organize my color-coded folders, and after ten minutes—twenty on a good day—I would stop, too distracted to connect and assess any thoughts outside the realm of my tiny life. And those thoughts concerning my tiny life were catastrophic. Did this nanny really comprehend the variables of crossing avenues? Did my husband really know how to use the nebulizer? Even if I left home, went out to an office, I'd work ten minutes, then spend another ten visualizing one child lying inert after a taxi crash.

Even if I'd seen my children two hours before, I missed them terribly, almost physically. I missed the hundreds of demanding or pleading notes beneath my door. (*"Momi we in hal. We wat. Opin dor and you wil se us!!!!"*) We'd had nannies (plus Daddy on call) without incident, and now there was preschool, but something else—and something I couldn't quite explain—was in my way. No matter how long I worked, I produced nothing but notes. I couldn't concentrate, and for the first time in what was by now a long career, I felt mentally paralyzed. I told no one of my sudden disability—not my sisters, who had their own life worries, and especially not my friends. (The few I'd told suggested that anyone with such a career *and* two fabulous children and *that husband* should immediately cease having problems.) My therapist of fourteen years had recently died ("from me droning," I joked morosely). On some days I wondered, to paraphrase Joan Didion, whether I'd suffered a small stroke but didn't know it.

Here I was at just That Moment, the one every working mother I knew had craved: the harmonic convergence of a well-developed career and an established family—in short, the sum total of every fantasy I had written and directed on all those endless New York–LA flights. And here I was blowing it, too proud, embarrassed, and terrified to admit as much, to say out loud that I might no longer be that person, you know, the immensely productive one in the sunglasses. The woman who would not, like others she'd observed, mentally decompose once she'd had children.

And the one person I most needed to confide in was my husband, the man I most counted on, and the one who was also counting on me to fully function. But I was terrified he'd reach the same conclusion I had: I was dysfunctional and an economic threat to my family. He knew that I was having trouble and he tried to help. For months he had offered to read and to edit, as always, to suggest a viable "way in." But the discussions always went the same way: I'd say there was nothing to read. He'd say that was impossible. And no matter how he'd say it, I'd accuse him of screaming at me. Here he was—always busy, intellectually engaged, and successful. How could *he* understand? To which he'd respond, But that's you, too! What are you doing?

At his suggestion (a very calmly, carefully stated proposal), I started on Prozac, which helped with my concentration but effectively neutered me, leaving neither of us much choice at night but to roll over and sleep. Or at least he would. I'd stay up until 3 or 4 a.m. watching Turner Classic Movies. I didn't care what the movie was, as long as it was from the 1940s or '50s. In this way, I communed with stand-ins for my parents: *please William Holden, please Barbara Stanwyck, what should I do?*

The only person with an answer was the one who'd taken to sitting across from me, pretending to watch the BBC news, or sorting the mail, often tossing me a bill I hadn't paid. At the two-year mark in my project, he made a career decision of his own (in part perhaps to offset the entrenched sludge of mine) to move into private law practice after years at film companies. But when he told me that it was final, I seemed surprised, as if I just hadn't heard that much about it. He looked at me, his mouth open, head shaking as he asked again, "What are you doing? Where have you been? Just where have you been? How we going to get through this?"

I might have said, honestly, *I don't know. Too many years, non-stop kids—and kids attached to me as if by suction cups! Plus all that traveling to LA with the forty-five shipped boxes every June. And then it's June again! But of course I'll get it done! I mean, I'm ME.* But instead I started crying. He'd worked so hard and been so good to us. (I actually said this.) I wasn't sure the Concept of Us could incorporate my epic failure. And then he spoke as if from deep within one of my black-and-white parental movies.

"Hey, come on! It's . . . me. It's Us, remember."

The book came out after four years, and a dosing of Tough Love from my husband and others with whom I still believe he held secret phone conferences. There were good reviews, lots of press. I traveled all over talking about it, while at home my kids sold copies, at self-determined discounts. My husband became more indispensable than my publicist, assessing where and what I should do and Googling me five times a day, checking Amazon, "just to see." We began after many years to relax. But so many exhausting years later—long years he'd been working hard to support us all—relaxing often led straight into sleeping. And in the living room. If a marriage coma passes through an acute stage, usually a collision or catastrophe that acts as catalyst, it then morphs into what I'll describe as an unending landscape of lethargy. And that lethargy (ambient sound: "Where is the remote? Uh, are you sitting on it?") is in some ways a means to hide from harsher truths. In our case massive time wasted, the monies not earned, the anger, frustration, and the realization that in the midst of this we'd gotten older.

When we met, when I first joined Us, I was twenty-six. At the time, I thought I was quite the grown-up professional (with red lingerie underneath). Of course, as it turns out, I was only twenty-six, meaning that I've now spent nearly twenty years in this relationship, which is a huge relief. Whatever's happened, we're a matched pair, residing deep within the comfort zone of our own language—a repertoire crammed with jokes, apocrypha, lines from Preston Sturges films, unrepeatable obscene remember-when's, and the incomparable ability to expertly mimic each other's family members.

And that's why, finally, I believe that the marriage coma is in fact a muted accomplishment: It means that despite all your anger, your evasions, and temptations, you *stuck it out*—did everything you could to make a life very different from the one you had before. And to make it work. After so many years inside of that life, after ten thousand dinners and movies and trips, whole generations of friends, illnesses, deaths, fights, stand-offs, family battles, plus in our case two children and five apartments we moved between in seven years while he changed jobs and I freaked by myself in a room and made myself get onto planes . . . Well, understandably anyone would be tired.

But, tired, annoyed, exasperated, we still love each other. Perhaps more important, we still *like* each other so very much. If wild sex has taken a sabbatical, or rather, if the devoted tabletop sex of 1986 is not stage-able with kids and sensitive spines, sex, if in more traditional places, is still an activity with the relevance and importance of eating.

And though this next topic is a less popular one, we both know that we're moving into middle life. In four years, our daughter will be in college and our baby boy in eighth grade. In less time than it took to write that stupid book, both kids will be taller than me and we'll be living a very different story. The one element that won't change in our lives is the Concept of Us. Maintaining that— actually looking at each other, no sarcastic faces, actually hearing and responding—requires discipline. No falling asleep or mentally planning the next day while he/she is speaking. No making fun when he can't once again find his wallet (the subject of a short story by our son, age five: "The Very Curious Wallet and Where It Goes Tuesday"). He needn't comment again on the alleged neurological failing that causes house keys automatically to drop from my hand.

It's true as all the happy self-help marriage books say: You really do have to have a sense of humor. Because you *were* sitting on the remote the whole time!

And of course—and especially if you're Us—the marriage coma can in its own sick way be kind of funny. For example, when one partner, after dozing for several hours, tries to get up, but drops off the couch with all the drama of cliff fall. At last, when the other one stops laughing:

"What was that?"

"I got up."

"Yeah, and I almost had to call 911 . . ."

". . . So, we're old? I have a bald spot. I won't say a word about your breasts."

We are lying on separate slabs of furniture, arms and legs hanging limp over the sides. "Oh, so soon we'll be shopping for one of those remote control beds?"

"What beds?"

"You know, the adjustable beds that '50s movie stars advertise on TV."

"Actually, I think now they're using movie stars from the '60s and '70s."

"Oh my God, you're right—yes! I saw the bionic woman on the bed! You know, sometimes those beds look really good."

"The children would make fun of it. It would be worse than Magic Feet." (Another story.)

"No, they'd love it! It could be like, you know, adjustable immigrant family."

"Honey, they're too big."

There's a long pause: "Honey, do you really still feel like it's Us?"

"Yes, honey," he says. "Yes. It's just Us with Epstein-Barr disease," which is so sick, so Us, I have to laugh—a snort—which reminds me of our wedding years ago and how, though indecipherable, it was absolutely on the mark. As it turns out, *forever and forever* is a very long time. So long it is entirely possible to sleep through the more impossible parts. Or, looking at it differently, to hibernate in anticipation of the next phase.

What you need, of course, is the ability to snap awake and to start again with that important task, for us the essential work of marriage: refining and updating our connection while committing all over again, forever and forever, to the expanded, amended, Concept of Us.

"Come on, honey," he says. "It's time for bed."

Though I'm quite comfortable where I'm sprawled, I sit up. Sounding like our teenaged daughter, I say, "Yay!"

Tracking Love

Zelda Lockhart

When I was seventeen, my future husband, T., strutted onto an almost empty city bus and spotted me, like a hawk spotting a mouse in a field. "Is someone sitting here?" he asked, standing six foot four inches, lanky like the men in my family, and stroking the beginnings of a beard.

I responded with the words of a Lockhart woman, "Do you see anyone?" adding under my breath, "Fool!"

I had prayed for God to send me a boy so my mother would be happy with me. My face twisted with attitude, I moved my backpack out of the seat, deciding not to look a gift horse in the mouth.

T. lived on the southside of St. Louis, and I lived on the westside, but we managed to get together every Saturday night. After high school graduation, T. went to boot camp and was then stationed in Norfolk, Virginia. I went to college in bum fuck Missouri until I ran out of money and had to return home to live and work.

One Sunday morning, my only day off as I worked two jobs, my father said I had to cook in the kitchen at his tavern or get out of his house. My mother turned to finish cooking breakfast. I said no to him for the first time in my life, and he chased me to my room, but

I barricaded the door with my bed, my dresser, and managed to hold against the kicking until he exhausted himself.

I didn't get hurt that time, but took out a road atlas and measured the mileage of red lines: Norfolk, Virginia, one thousand miles. No one in my family had ever been on an airplane, and a thousand miles would be too far for my father to drive. So, I spent my college money on a plane ticket. My four older siblings had made both effective and ineffective escapes of their own. I never cried when they left and did not know how to cry over the loss of three younger siblings—sacrifices for my escape.

For two years, T. and I paid low rent and lived at the low tide end of the beach, along with prostitutes, drunken sailors, and drug addicts. We worked and paid bills, went to the Laundromat on Saturday, had sex all day, out of boredom, on Sunday. Saltwater air and abrasive sand beneath our feet scrubbed away the toxins of our abusive childhoods.

In June, it was my twentieth birthday, and in two months, my older sister was going to throw me a huge wedding. I knew I wanted a bigger life but hadn't decided marriage was what I was looking for. My parents' long, tumultuous marriage was no role model. I really just wanted to have a baby, but didn't have the language for parenting solo. That night, I told T. that for my birthday, I wanted to make love without condoms.

The whites of my big brown eyes were all that was visible beneath the wedding veil. I was pregnant, but hadn't told anyone. I stood at the altar, grappling with last-minute thoughts of aborting the marriage and the baby, of aborting the marriage and keeping the baby. My sister cleared her throat for the third time, and I returned to my body to say, "I do." We had said our vows, making promises to the universe I couldn't keep.

———◁※▷———

In the moments after my son's birth, I looked in his one open eye and got a glimpse of the night sky, the Little Dipper turned on its side, Polaris, his iris. Then I slept deep, confident that I had found the beginnings of whatever I had been seeking.

For those first months, I was complete with caring for my baby, and with excelling in my undergrad work. I enjoyed the comfortable distance from T., who was away on double-header six-month naval tours, and rediscovered a part of myself that I had buried at seventeen years old. I desired women. It was everything I could do to uphold my vows. "Forsaking all others," I awaited his return so I could consult with him about ravaging some flirty woman, like my physics lab partner who was forty years old, and giving me glimpses of her cleavage. Glimpses, winks, and touches that set a girl who was never fit for running on a daily jogging regimen to dispel the sexual energy.

By the time he returned, I was on my third or fourth crush. Something had to be done. I went from feeling like I just needed to experiment and could contain myself until the time came, to feeling like I was caught in a straitjacket and just wanted out.

At the start of the conversation, T. didn't think anything of my issue. It just reminded him of the night I told him to fuck me like my French teacher, a woman with bright red lips. Those moments had been the highlight of our sex life. So, the news of my new label, "lesbian," initially brought the response, "Great!"

Eventually, he graduated to anger, then physical force.

He punched the ceramic teddy bear light switch that I made for the nursery in my third trimester. He twisted my arm behind my back and whispered in my ear with his nighttime voice, "No one's going anywhere."

Our son stood in his crib and watched us, and I knew the second T. left the house, I would walk away from reenacting my childhood in front of my son.

After I moved out, T. and I remained friends. His curiosity brought him to my apartment, not in hopes of having sex with me, but in hopes of tagging along to a gay bar for the cheap thrill of watching women together. This all ended when he saw two of his ship buddies grinding cocks on the dance floor.

One Thursday night, T.'s girlfriend called and said I should pick up my son before his dad's visitation week was over. She didn't explain further, but I knew I wouldn't sleep with my mind dwelling on the strangeness of her phone call. I got to T.'s Virginia Beach apartment at midnight. He and my son were watching TV. His girlfriend was gone, and I questioned T., but when he answered he was incomprehensible, like an innocent, sleepy little boy. The stare in his eyes, the beer bottles on the table. I realized that alcoholism had been there all along. We had been like siblings, both with wholesome ideas about how we would raise our children—unlike how our parents raised us—but I didn't recognize him that night.

I brought my son home, and the two of us curled up in a perfect "c." That night, I had horrible nightmares of punching my father in the face over and over. I awoke nauseous and late for work. I hustled my son to the shower for a quick washup, and uncovered his back— red belt marks, crisscrossed, x'ing out T.'s promise to never hit our child. I nearly passed out before my adult voice struggled to the fore of the voices in my head, and said, "Take him to the hospital."

For a year and a half, I fought the Virginia court system that qualified "child abuse" with photos that will forever mark that night in my son's life. The system established a file with Child Protective Services listing T. as an abuser, but they issued no punishment, juxtaposing terms in their letter, stating that my child was at "moderate risk." Our judge insisted that it was in the best interest of my child to immediately reunite him with his father. The Guardian at Lightem, whose role was to stand in for the best interest of my child, agreed.

I had to work three jobs in order to pay a lawyer and make the case that my son deserved to be protected by the courts, who had a responsibility to at least monitor T. through therapy, before throwing my baby back in the arms of his assailant. The judge said he would hold me in contempt of court if I continued to challenge his ruling, which was weekly visitation. I was an adult victim of childhood abuse, and when I had spoken in the past, no one helped. My mother beat me for speaking out.

I told the judge I had nothing but my life with which to protect my son's life, and that if he would punish my child and me for asking to be protected by the system, then he was cooperating with my son's abuser. My lawyer was not pleased with my speech, and showed the judge that she was not about to ruin her relationship with the court on my account. She closed her folder and sat down.

The judge made furious strokes with his pen before he told me and my lawyer to get out of his courtroom. I stood proud with my knees shaking in the clerk's office while I waited for a copy of his ruling, which ordered mediation that I would pay for—six sessions, after which T. would be allowed to visit with my child.

T. would attend mediation, skip three or four sessions, and attend another. There was no petitioning the judge to override the process. After six months, T. accomplished the six sessions necessary to have his first visit. For two hours I sat in the car, watching them interact in the park—words muted. My son wore red and could be spotted like a cardinal against the backdrop of green grass and maple trees. I weighed and assessed their movements—tall and short stick figures. I pushed away images of T. lashing him with his good leather belt.

The next day, T. did not show for the last mediation session, but left a message saying he wouldn't be questioned before spending time with his own child, and that my lawyer should contact him when our son turned eighteen. He moved, leaving no forwarding address. Seventeen years have passed since that day.

Guilt consumed me. I was up late nights with memories, dreams, and reflections of how I could have stopped the beating, of how I could have kept father and son together. I walked right to the physical and emotional edge while I overcompensated as the model mom. On an average day, I threw newspapers while my son slept in the backseat, took both of us to my university, where he attended the day care, and I worked toward eighteen credit hours with an A average. I edited the school's literary journal, worked in the language lab, and read to his day care class during my lunchtime. I took him on nature walks, to the park, and the library, like a good mom, and on Saturday nights, I got a sitter and joined my new age musician friends in obliterating the stresses of the week with a minimum of five mai tais. The reality of abuse, of how much it all reminded me of my childhood, led me to a raw duality of overly responsible and reckless behavior.

I felt as though I were unraveling, and each week, Saturday could not come soon enough. My good grades, my good parenting, everything stood the risk of slipping away from me. The rent was due, the electric bill was unpaid, and when I woke up hungover one Sunday morning, embarrassed to throw up in front of my two-year-old, I decided to take my friend up on her suggestion that I visit her slightly odd mother, who lived in the Kentucky mountains. I packed my car the next morning, and ran. As I crossed the Blue Ridge Mountains, as my son and I curved around the mountain face, I felt small, among green nappy trees, but I felt free—the way I felt when the plane left Midwest soil when I was eighteen.

That night, when I drove up and down the unlit roads of narrow Appalachian mountain paths, with my toddler asleep in the car, my bravado gave way to fear. My headlights seemed the only sign of life, and soon I began to feel as though I had done the most foolish and irresponsible thing in my life, until I came upon an open meadow, lit only by the stars in a moonless sky.

There, I lived off the grid with my son and my friend's sixty-four-year-old mother in a house that had no phone or amenities. My son learned how to pee off the porch and how to conduct the orchestra of lightning storms with his two-year-old hands. My friend's mother taught me to trust the dark and not to be afraid to walk in it—to find lost objects by being still and remembering where the lost thing is rather than stirring around in circles looking for something that sits still. She said she was not teaching me anything, but helping me to remember.

Somewhere between scrubbing my butt in the creek and befriending a bald eagle, I felt free like my little girl self who loved to watch raindrops roll off a Midwest milkweed. Beside the pleasant memories lay dormant truths, half-remembered nightmares that began to emerge. Suddenly, the mountain woman seemed untrustworthy to me, so I orchestrated an escape.

I argued that I needed to go find my mate in life. "How can I find love on the side of a mountain?" My backsliding and doubt disappointed my teacher. In my emotional state of fight or flight, I could not distinguish between words of wisdom and curses.

"One day," she assured, "you will live out in nature, tracking animals, looking for antler rubbings on tree bark, gathering herbs by their scent or by a sighting in a dream—*alone* with no mate."

With twenty-two-year-old attitude, I laughed at the absurdity of this, especially that "no mate" part. Was she not aware of my sex appeal? And, be damned if I would turn out to be some lonely old wilderness woman like her. Being angry made it easier to take what she had taught me for the last seven months and throw it into a gorge, then drive down from that mountain.

I returned to Norfolk, Virginia, feeling strong, no longer lost, but free. I earned the last three months of my degree. But my guard was down, and trauma that had been long buried in my psyche surfaced in flashbacks—memories threatened to consume me. One time it was at Uncle Buck's house, where my father fished near a river. The grass was tall and the covers on Uncle Buck's bed were sandy and full of earth, where my father violated my body. On the way home the world outside the car was dark, and my father told me a snake was inside the car, ready to strike if I talked.

But the Appalachian woman's assurance that to walk through darkness is to learn the placement of things in the light became something to believe in. I found a therapist who reminded me of the mountain woman, and I worked on healing in the same way that I worked on getting good grades. As a stage of my healing, I told my family of my memories and was labeled ill. They banished me, called me a traitor and a crazy woman. My oldest brother was the exception. He was my gay ally, the same brother who defended me against schoolyard bullies when I was a little girl and took many of my father's belt lashings to spare me.

At the end of that year, he was diagnosed with AIDS.

Though I lived in Virginia, I cared for my brother in New York, making twenty-four-hour car trips, because I developed a fear that if I slept in New York, I would die there. I watched him become more the disease than my big brother, and I realized the vast space around my body. I grabbed for the comfort of a new partner.

On our first date, I convinced myself, "She knows, she knows," having never acknowledged my attraction. I sat by her side on the sofa that I had proudly fetched from someone's trash on my way to the university job I hated—the job that helped me seek the graduate degree I loved from the people I hated. We tapped our bare feet nervously ignoring the movie, because we both knew it well enough to giggle when the funny parts emerge from the dullness of the script.

From where we sat, I looked beyond the light of the TV screen and saw the spirit of a little girl step out from the mirror. The woman kept tapping her foot and nervously rubbing her index finger and thumb together. Beth did not see what I saw, and kept rubbing. I wondered if I would venture to kiss this thick Italian woman with conservative white feminist values. I wondered what she would think when she found out that I see light in the form of those who have not moved on to the next life. Or, that I hear their spirits surge through the electric workings of my house. Or, that smoke detectors go off when I ignore the spirits, or that candle flames threaten to leap from their holders if I am upset enough.

"May I hold you close?" I asked.

She stayed the night and never went home again.

By the next fall, we co-parented my son who was six years old. By the glare of the sun and pale of moonlight, we did the dance of committed living.

One day, my brother called with the sound of death in his voice, and I drove through torrential rain to spend the last night of his life, awake, listening with my flashlight perched on the edge of his bed. He passed away, December 16, 1992.

Beth allowed me to cling to her at the funeral, where I watched my family display emotion, but my tears would only come when she and I were alone. That night I sobbed into her elbow, assuring myself that I would never be able to be alone with my old family without her and my son.

That night I dreamed about my brother's burial, which was to take place the next morning. In the dream, he was alive, and only I could hear him crying as they shoveled earth, making a sound like fingers drumming, bored, on a wooden surface. I awoke to the rustlings of Beth packing her suitcase. "I'm driving to Pittsburgh, to be with my family for Christmas." She was stern and challenged me to have words. I was raw, without an ego, and I groveled for her to be with me at the burial, not to take the car and leave me stranded in the Midwest, a thousand miles from the cleansing salt of the ocean. But she pulled away from the curb, before my son could wake.

I knew Beth was not the woman for me, but with my brother gone, my son's uncle gone, I was emotionally desperate and didn't see the contradiction of her saying that she loved me, and leaving me stranded, with a child, among my strange family with no way home.

After a week of dwelling unwanted in the homes of family members, I gained the motivation to get myself to the airport and get home, where I disappeared into the loveless rhythm of my relationship with Beth and the writing of my master's thesis. The pain escaped in slow, time-released bouts of mourning, and Beth and I lived together for four years.

We taught at separate colleges. I busied myself with my son's education, birthday parties, library visits, bill paying, and teaching night courses. On top of it all, I started a legal action fund for lesbian moms. Beth went for a less strenuous avoidance tactic. She went out of the country for any conference the university would allow her to attend—the more remote, it seemed, the better. That summer I turned thirty, Beth turned thirty-six, and we celebrated on separate continents.

One day, Beth's student, who had gone to Vietnam with her, called in a fit of confession about the length and depth of their love affair. I tucked the pain away until after Beth had moved out. I added cleaning houses to my already full teaching schedule to cover my now exorbitant rent in the historic district. As I sat on the kitchen floor one afternoon—with the smell of her body still in the place where the sun heated up the carpet, her hair still in the drain of the bathtub—I told myself to get up, fetch the money from the demeaning cleaning job. I struggled to hold on to my self-esteem, cursing myself for not recognizing Beth's affairs. I reviewed every scenario of her avoidance and remembered how I lay on my bed and prayed on a bright star for Beth to be mine. How could I so desperately have wanted someone who was so bad for me? I made myself get to my feet with the mantra, "move, move," and went to work.

I walked to the cleaning jobs in order to keep my heart and lungs working through the sluggishness. There was often a woman out walking her dog, and she always giggled deep and guttural when we crossed paths. One day, she said she recognized me from my poetry reading and invited me to join her support group for women artists. At first, I fit in with the manic-obsessive artists whose focus on being forlorn kept them from creating anything, but the more my heaviness lifted, the less I needed the group. When I stopped showing up, the woman with the dog left me a note: "At the risk of sounding forward, I adore you. Love, Augusta."

Where Beth could turn a walk on the beach into a political analysis of oil rigs and economic seaport development, Augusta turned a walk on the beach into a dance at the line where the shore brought life and death together. In those days, I cried tears of joy and ambiguity. In one breath, I said, "I'm not ready," but in the next breath, I said, "I want to give you a Zelda kiss," and laid my full lips on hers.

I wanted to do what I had never done, date, but Augusta wanted commitment. I took my dilemma to a number of feminist self-help books that said, "Get comfortable with your own company." So I pushed her away. But it was hurricane season, and Norfolk, Virginia, was in the path of Hurricane Fran. She was promising a direct hit for the Chesapeake Bay. I simply could not bear to evacuate. I turned on the Weather Channel for my panicking son, opened the patio doors, and let the breeze in. Coming up the sidewalk was Augusta and her timid pit bull. She walked in that wind with the boldness her pooch lacked.

"Can I sleep in your bed with you?" she asked.

I answered with the sexual energy of the hurricane swirling in the pit of my tummy. We made clumsy love on my office futon, and for the next month, she brought me flowers, having no idea that I despised the practice of cultivating something for the purpose of cutting it off. She wrote me poems. She did sweeping, insanely romantic things—short Greek woman with a body like a loaf of bread dancing beneath my bedroom window on a city street. I fell in love with her passion—half of me screaming, "Run," the other half screaming, "Fly." Late that fall, she accompanied me to NYC, the city of my brother's death, and the city of her birth. The smell of good espresso replaced the smell of my brother's antiseptic hospital room. She said she was in love with me, and before saying it back, I had a short, internal conversation about learning to love her and not needing the superficial, physical attraction.

We gave each other pet names, "Shmoolie and Shmoolie," and my son skipped along in the sometimes tumultuous, sometimes Mardi Gras nature of our lives. I followed her dominant passionate energy, and she followed my logical overprotective energy.

We moved to central New York State so I could live in a writer's community near New York City and she could be near her family. Augusta was passionate about everything she pursued. She loved deeply, had enemies she hated to the bone, and was as prone to flamboyant temper tantrums as she was to spending money she didn't really have and buying me the moon. Our hot and cold temperaments sent us into fits and starts of love. We were either deep into the romance or sitting with our backs turned from each other. I found myself becoming primarily responsible for keeping some balance. "Just pay off the credit card," was my refrain. She hand-painted Greek tiles, and often got distracted, forgetting to fill a tile order, and would then need my help painting tiles overnight, though the next morning I had to take my son to school, go to work, and have something left to get my own writing done.

While grocery shopping one day, I picked out the two flavors of seltzer water that Augusta and my son liked, and asked myself a question, "What do you want?" The fact that I couldn't answer helped me realize I was lost. Art, music, nature, dancing, and meditation—somewhere between her and Beth, I had snubbed myself out. I sat down to write in my journal and read back in time. I realized those pages were the only place where I had continued to tell the truth. An entry from Augusta and my dating days: "I think I am over what we are doing. I seem to have started falling away from a deep *like* and into a nonromantic place with her. Although I can't and won't tell her this, I have never been physically attracted to her. And I would have to be talking myself into something in order to fantasize that our similar respect and hunger for life is enough to make me fall in love."

With these revelations, I became less and less tolerant of throwing myself wholeheartedly into her Greek tile business, which consumed half of my savings, and she became less and less tolerant of my new need for artistic solitude exactly when I needed it. We separated for a painful year of dating other women.

By the following summer, I had saved enough for a down payment on my first house. I was thirty-three and proud to have lived to be older than my brother. My sense of self resurfaced. My son and I traveled to D.C., and to my birthplace in Mississippi, then to Virginia, where we met Augusta for an afternoon at the beach, an afternoon of addictive nostalgia that brought us back to the passion of three years prior. We found a babysitter, and that night made love in white shirts on the dark beach. I felt guilty the next day when all I wanted was to carry on with the solo journey I had finally started;

I received a note from her, "At the risk of seeming forward, I adore you."

"Run," I heard in my heart.

When we got back to New York, she was the first person to show up to help me move into my new house. "Shmoolie," she said, calling me and pleading with me in one breath.

Two months later, she insisted on moving in. I told her I had moved on, but I did not slam my foot down, and she said that resistance was part of my personality and part of our relationship. I emotionally retreated in order to question myself, asking, *Is the idea of love a myth of childhood?* She wrote me notes that made sense to my heart, "Think about what you have to gain, not what you have to lose."

We got back together and fought our way through the next year. "Shmoolie, I want us to have a baby." When she brought this up, I managed to always change the subject, because I wanted the same but couldn't imagine doing such a thing until we got our acts together. My friends shook their heads each time she threw a tantrum. I journaled daily in an attempt to identify myself in the context of the relationship again. That summer, Augusta wanted to get married.

My family refused to come, and that was no shock. For them, marrying a woman was absolute proof of my insanity. Friends came from far and wide with a look on their faces, as if side bets had been taken. The friends who had known me the longest came up with acceptable excuses for not attending at all. Augusta's family came with bells on. They supplied ninety percent of the wedding gifts, and I thought how ungrateful it would be for me to assume that I was losing *me* as opposed to gaining a new family. I wore white lace, she wore blue lace, and my son and my godchildren gave us away. A huge white tent at the bottom of Ithaca's West Hill, caterer, white chairs, florist, candles, bartenders. My nest egg was spent. We headed up the road to a Northampton honeymoon. As we traveled through the reminiscent valleys of two mountain ranges, I ached so deep that I felt my spine merge with my belly.

When we arrived, Augusta drew a bath with candles in our spacious bed and breakfast suite. From the bathroom, she talked to me in fits of laughter while she scented the water and swirled in bath salts. I lay on my back, on unfamiliar sheets crying uncontrollably. The room smelled so much like saltwater.

Neither of us knew what to say about the release of tears that represented some repressed longings. I cried in my sleep, through breakfast, and all the way home from our eclipsed honeymoon. I couldn't get the sun to come out again. Colors disappeared; my job became like my childhood room, a place for escape. I disappeared into my writing and the directorship of a community not-for-profit. When I wasn't working, I was writing or volunteering at my son's middle school. Augusta was my best friend, she was my wife, but I couldn't bear to be in our reality for more than the eight required hours of sleep. Coffee kept me away from tears, and I noticed her drinking more wine with dinner than usual. By our second anniversary, we were so far away from where we had vowed to be.

It was New Year's Eve, new millennium, and Kuumba, Creativity Day of Kwanzaa. At our party, one friend painted our hands with henna; one friend read our tarot cards. Two readings showed me standing alone with a weapon in my hand and a wolf by my side. Augusta called for a third reading, and my friend refused, and I refused. We ended the evening with Augusta having a bit too much wine and me with too much caffeine. "I hate the new you," she proclaimed, sloppy snot and tears, and I didn't say it aloud, but thought the same thing of her.

A month later, as the cloud cover grew thicker, and the blanket of snow layered its way up the tree trunks, I chose life over death and asked her to leave. Augusta and I tried to hash out the "why and how come" of our relationship in therapy, but it became an extension of tolerated abuse. She drank and cursed me in my sleep for a month, and one day when I came home from work, she was leaving and said she hated me and would never talk to me again.

Every day, I went to work early to think and to cry behind closed doors. I wanted family, and to have lost it again made me feel as though my insides were being eaten away. To kill the pain, I had an insane secret affair with my friend the tarot card reader. When that drama grew cold, I resolved to be romantically still until I could recognize someone who didn't bear some emotional resemblance to my family from childhood. I went to see the therapist alone, and she asked me what my tears represented. It took me three weeks to answer, "The possibility of a larger family, lost."

That summer, I turned thirty-five. I was a single, lesbian mom. I didn't have the marriage, but I wanted the baby. I set out to find a partner who was up to the task. I interviewed a battery of beautiful women of various shapes and sizes, who all endured painstakingly awkward dating. The sweetness of a tongue, the moistness of an open hand—none of it mattered if she harbored any habits that made child rearing impossible. I stumbled on every pot-smoking, alcoholic, bulimic, nicotine-dependent lesbian in Ithaca.

I even considered a male, bisexual friend as potential donor, but one evening, before the two of us settled into a movie and a bowl of popcorn, I walked to the bottom of the stairs and yelled up for my thirteen-year-old son to complete his chores and put the dishes away before going to bed. My bi friend said, "That was ghetto," and added that in his white, Milwaukee upbringing, his mother would not use the atmosphere of the house as her personal microphone.

Child rearing with a prude? He was immediately zapped from the possibility of mate.

I remember the day I decided to traverse the lines of nature's prescription of love, and get my baby, fifteen years after my first. All I needed was a sperm, an egg, and, "voilà!" baby.

In the reflection of my computer screen, I stared at my thirty-five-year-old face and began the online search through the sperm bank data for the proper count of swimmers, one destined to become my child's other half. For my thirty-sixth birthday, I inseminated. My birthday party was at the bottom of Ithaca's West Hill—night sky, so many dancing feet, DJ, speakers jacked up on platforms, my sexy black dress, and big grin.

———————

My baby girl is four years old now, and it seems that every lover, every fortune and misfortune has been by design to lead me to this yellow house where I live in Hillsborough, North Carolina, just outside the woods, where the pond sinks and rises with the vernal and autumnal equinox, where I dream of red spiked flowers to cure an aching back.

I am bound to home by the seasons and their dance of chores and treats, the way the body follows hunger, the way circling vultures are drawn to their magnetic hovering to find death so that they may live another day. The red in my brown skin recedes as the red in the leaves burst forward, and I walk this space without a mate, but with my daughter's hand to hold.

My son comes home for Thanksgiving, and we are family. When we drive him back up the mountain to the small university town, he chronicles the internships and ski trips that will keep him away for six months. I am admittedly lonely and promise myself that the next time I am presented with the phenomenon of falling in love, I will try to rest my wings and commit to its unpredictable alchemy.

As I walk in meditation across this gentle place of land, like a Choctaw hunter familiar with trees and weeds, I find a cure for a lonesome heart in the sweet red honey of the bergamot flower— a little something to keep me from falling into the wrong arms as summer disappears. The tannic acid in the leaves pits red and orange against a blue sky, turning to the metal flat cold of winter. My heart is safe here. I am being still, so that my son can come home from college, and my daughter has wide-open space to grow, and I have time to rest.

I stack wood in the shed and feel disoriented, like a senile woman, because I can't distinguish the moment from the first stacking of wood last fall, or the fall before that. My growing children and my slowly emptying egg sack are the only things that mark time. I clean my closet and my daughter's closet, bag the things too small for next summer, and unpack the bag of last winter's stored clothes, and we are new again as the old forgotten clothes come back and kiss our skin. I decide to store the summer clothes in my closet, but the crib, stroller, potty chair, snugly, walker, mobile, and countless bags of baby clothes make shadows that block the ceiling light.

I'm saving clothes for my next baby, which I insist I will have though I am forty, but refuse to have until I am with "the" woman who is my true love. I daydream of making love with someone in my too-small bed next to the closet that spills open with treasures, and I think to myself, Lover, where will I keep her? I stare into the closet with the familiar seasonal disorientation, remembering both wedding days, remembering my commitment to Augusta, because commitment temporarily filled some forever gaping space.

At night, I watch two bucks in the full moon back away from each other and charge like silver ghosts, clashing antlers. It is not mating season by my almanac, and I wonder why they are doing what they are doing. The sound is like bamboo on bamboo, and I think it must hurt and am sure that at dawn I'll find dew-moistened antlers on the green.

The does stand in a warm pack, rubbing noses, rubbing hind-quarters, the bucks still charging, lost in the ritual of mating. I crawl, sleepy, away from the window and to my bed where I drop off and dream all night about cheating on my ex-husband with my ex-wife. In the dream, we are discovered, and I wake in shock, feeling guilty and exposed.

In the morning, I feel exhausted and disturbed by the depth of my emptiness. I find myself missing both exes, going back in old journals to remember why it didn't work. All morning I think constructive thoughts—Split the wood; Collect kindling—in order to resist, as my loneliness pulls me toward obsessive thoughts of self-pity.

I take myself to the land. There are no antlers, but warm spots on the earth where the bucks tore away passionately at each other while the does nuzzled together, watching. I let my daughter's ability to laugh and my ability to make her laugh carry me. I use the sensation of raking leaves on a cold, drizzly November afternoon to keep me so that I do not succumb to believing in the curse of the sixty-four-year-old mountain woman, who promised me I would live out in nature, alone, with no mate. I now know there is harmony in being with the love of my children, and my love of nature. I spend the day trying to simply know this, without obsessing on finding a husband or wife. I remember the Appalachian woman's words, "Remember where the lost thing is rather than stirring around in circles looking for some-thing that sits still, not lost." In every action of my day I ask myself, "What do you want Zelda?" so that I do not fall into performing my old trick of pulling elaborate cloth over the plain cloth of lovers I am not attracted to.

My daughter fetches the moldy wicker basket, and we go back out into the damp to collect black walnuts from the tree with the yellowest leaves. We are both methodical, only picking up the ones where the wood is slightly cracked revealing the fruit. We are quiet and deliberate in our task. I stop to notice her intention, the way she examines each one. It is chilly, and her breath escapes in little clouds. I look down at her muck boots and mine. She is content in the rain. I follow her to the mint leaves, which she picks and stares at long before eating the whole handful.

"That's good," she comments as if talking to someone else closer to her size. She kicks the water on the grass and asks if we can have a picnic, and I dare not chuckle and call up the fierce tantrum that always brews inside her.

It is past dusk and we do not want to go inside. I pup our tent near the bamboo, beneath the fairy ring of old maple trees. We make a bonfire, fetch grillable food from the house. After we eat, before we retire to a sound outdoor sleep, I drum, and she dances around the fire, singing.

The sky clears, and the moon is full that night. While my daughter sleeps soundly, her heartbeat comforted by the earth beneath her body, I climb out of the tent to greet the rising moon. The Little Dipper is just above the branches of the maple where a few remaining leaves dangle and wave. The constellation offers its hooked ladle. Polaris craves my attention, sets me to fix my lips in a wish, but nothing comes out.

In my bare feet, moon bathed over a bed of wet fall leaves, I walk the triangle of open space—woods, creek, house, and then crawl back into the tent where my daughter's breath makes warmth.

To Dream

Martha McPhee

I married the same man twice in four months, and over the span of eighteen months we went on seven honeymoons. We traveled to New Hampshire to watch the leaves change; we skied in Lake Louise; we sipped tea in a medina in Morocco and trekked on camel through the Sahara at sunrise; we spent Easter in Seville, watching a bullfight; we toured London's museums; we strolled the streets of Amsterdam's red light district; we watched kites illuminated by candles sail in the night sky above the Ganges like so many stars. We had no money (he was a poet and I was a novelist), but we were dreamers and patched the trips together in one way and another.

Our first wedding was a fast one at City Hall—planned at the last minute as a way to distract ourselves from the fact that Mark, my husband, had been diagnosed with a rare form of T-cell lymphoma with a bad prognosis. The second wedding, a much more lavish affair at St. John the Divine on New Year's Eve, was the correction. Two months after being diagnosed with cancer, we learned it had been a misdiagnosis. He did not have cancer at all. At our second wedding, we had a sixteen-piece big band orchestra, a splendid caterer we could not afford, plenty of wine and champagne, 150 guests, and we all danced until the wee hours. My sister, Laura, made the wedding cake. Outside, it snowed—a graceful, gentle storm that covered the city in white.

After learning Mark did not have cancer, we sat together at our dining table, a piece of paper between us. On it we wrote everywhere we wanted to go in the next year or so and then drew a diagram with dates, fitting each trip into a spot. Together, we came up with ways to afford the adventures: a writer's colony (Spain—we tacked on Morocco), a book tour for foreign editions of my first novel (London and Amsterdam), a visit to a sister (India). For Lake Louise, we told them we were on our honeymoon and they heavily discounted the honeymoon suite for us. New Hampshire, our first honeymoon, only required a car. A friend of ours loaned us her house. As it turned out, we arrived late in the night, settled in, and began munching on leftovers from the fridge only to discover we were in the wrong house. The owner returned home and politely asked us what we were doing there. The six honeymoons that followed New Hampshire were also corrections.

In retrospect it was a magical eighteen months. At the time, however, I worried. First, I worried that Mark would die, then when I couldn't worry about that anymore I worried about how we were going to afford all that we were spending on the wedding and the trips. Somewhere in the midst of all this we had an enormous fight. I do not remember what it was about (probably my worry), but I remember how it ended.

Mark said, "When I married you I thought I was about to die."

(I am certain that I deserved that.)

"So divorce me," I shot back, throwing those three words out there easily. They hit the air and shattered all around us.

Suddenly I was a thirty-two-year-old married woman. I was, even if I had not registered this before, a grown-up, in charge of my life. I was married. I was married. And thus, with the spray of those words, *so divorce me,* the concrete action implicit in them, I was shocked by the fact that since I was married I could now get divorced. Divorce, the potential of that act, was a viable choice I could make. I had thought much about getting married over the years, but not about divorcing. Mark stood in front of me, surprised, too, by the power of my words. Mark's words were awful, hurtful yes, but they didn't offer us an option for a way out. He wasn't going to die. My words held the solution, and the notion fairly stunned us.

I was not unfamiliar with divorce. My parents began their separation when I was five years old. When I started writing in my early twenties, divorce was a theme I explored, turning my childhood into fodder for two novels that explored the ramifications of divorce. Indeed my parents (and sisters) are a little tired of me delving into this subject. So to protect them (finally), suffice it to say here, in this essay, I learned that divorce is a suffering I would not wish on anyone and to boot is just no good for children. My parents were not fated to remain together, and as a grown-up now I can see the reasons clearly. At the time, I could not understand and felt simply the longing of something that could not be—the ugliness of want, when the desire is legitimate, but satisfying it is impossible. I longed throughout my childhood, and into my young adult years even, for my parents to fall in love all over again as if somehow that would make me whole. Of course, that did not happen. As a small girl, I became withdrawn. I did not care about school. I skipped it whenever I could and stayed with my mother. When in school I was distracted, worrying about the chaos at home.

Details of the divorce included a vocabulary that was entirely new to me: custody, alimony, child support, visitation rights, lover, affair, adultery. My three older sisters and I would lie in bed together late into the night and throw these words into the darkness, where they'd hang suspended for a while until one of the older girls would translate the words one at a time. During the day we played a game called Normal Day, a variation on House, in which we had the chance to use those words. We were paired off with various movie stars—Steve McQueen, Robert Redford, Paul Newman, O. J. Simpson, even. We married and divorced, took on lovers, charged mightily on the credit cards of the loves who spurned us. Normal Day.

With our parents, our love ricocheted between them like pinballs. We were afraid to settle our love too long on either parent, afraid we'd hurt the other. At this time, early 1970s, divorce was not common. My parents did not have the vocabulary to talk about what was happening to their marriage. In our town, our parents were essentially the first to split up. As it turned out, many other couples followed suit, but not yet, and thus the divorce instilled a certain terror, and people wanted to stay away from us as if divorce were contagious.

How, with this experience, could I see anything good coming from divorce? Indeed, though I definitely believe now that my parents made the correct choice for them, the decision has haunted them ever since. "Not a day goes by where I don't think about it," they have both said on one occasion or another.

⤜⤏⤞

So here I was, recently married, using divorce as a threat. That was not the only time. Over the years (Mark and I have been married for close to ten and now have two young children), I have used the threat more than a few times, and each time I am still amazed by how frightening the idea of divorce is. I believe I throw divorce out there, between us, as a reminder to myself of how much I don't want it. At forty-one, however, the theme of divorce is in the air. Friends are starting to divorce; parents of my children's friends at school are divorcing; friends who aren't yet divorced speak of it all the time. These are the ones I listen to the most, their complaints, as a way to compare, to test the waters of my own marriage. These friends are tired of their husbands, wish they would pull more weight, have more ambition, earn more money, help out more with the management of the children. I hear these friends long for something wistful, something new, an affair. Here we are, fast approaching or recently past the seven-year-itch mark. We're sick of our spouses and they of us. We've created bad habits, avoided fixing them, and find ourselves wondering mightily how in the world we'll last the rest of a lifetime with this person?

Two close friends are turning this conversation into fodder for a screenplay they are writing entitled *Losing Dick* about three married women who are scheming to ditch their husbands. (Dick, by the way, is one of the husbands.) The screenplay is hilarious, a comedy that dramatizes everything I'm hearing on the subject of, and desire for, divorce. One of the couples, for example, a pair of artists, is too poor to get divorced. Divorce becomes yet another luxury that only the wealthy can afford.

We all know the fact that fifty percent of American marriages end in divorce. In a culture that breathes and breeds divorce, how is a long marriage sustained? What are the tricks? How do marriages survive? This is what I am interested in, because I decidedly do not want to get divorced. Sure I have the fantasy, and I'm certain my husband does, too, of a clean slate and someone new. But I know the wreckage divorce leaves in its wake. I could not stand to live that pain. I do not want to feel that all over again. I do not want my children to feel that. And the complaints I have about my husband aren't tragic enough to warrant divorce. Perhaps another correction for me is my marriage; my marriage corrects the marriage of my parents. I get to live out and finish what they could not. But I also understand I am in love and they were not.

Often I wonder who I would have been had my parents stayed together? Would I have been a confident and self-possessed girl? Would I have grown up to expect and demand everything, to deserve? Would the model of their love have showered me with a sense of belonging to something large and beautiful? I see my daughter and son. I watch them with a careful eye. From a young age it has been clear to me how Mark and I and our love is one thing for them: everything. In some ways watching my daughter is like watching the girl I always wanted to be. How could I wreck her world?

In reflecting on my marriage here, it has occurred to me that the connective tissue, that which binds my husband and me together through the struggles and disappointments, is our capacity to dream. Mark and I dreamed from the beginning when we mapped out the seven honeymoons we could not afford. We continue to dream, many dreams. They lie in front of us, mirage-like. In Maine, where we go in the summer, from our bed late at night we can see the ferry that runs from Portland to Nova Scotia. In the dark it is all ablaze, a crystal ship. We laugh at it, our ship, just within our reach, glittering before us before it inevitably disappears. But no matter. We keep dreaming. The dreams involve our children, of course, our careers, our hobbies, our desires for adventure. They proliferate in our imaginations. For every thousand we have, we seem to realize one and that suffices. It seems to me that as long as we are able to share dreams we will remain together.

But ultimately I am not so earnest or naïve. In fact, speaking of dreams, in the past few nights, after days of pondering this essay, I have had a couple of vivid dreams. In one, I am flirting with Baryshnikov (clearly a *Sex and the City* inspired dream), and in another with a famous writer I am too embarrassed to name. In both dreams we are just about to kiss, when I realize I am being tested and that I am failing. I am flooded with that wonderful sensation of the new, all its implicit mystery. I am being tested and I am failing and then I wake up. My unconscious, of course, is reminding me that as much as we wish for something and make proclamations of our hopes, we will never know what tomorrow will make of us.

In Morocco, on one of our honeymoons, I became drawn to the word *Inshallah*, the simplicity and beauty of it and to how often it was uttered by everyone. *I am going to have some tea. Inshallah. I'll see you in a little while. Inshallah. I am traveling to America tomorrow. Inshallah.* It means, If God wills it. I love the word because in English there is no one word, let alone expression, that so completely surrenders to fate. I remember this, I recall it often: Mark and I are trying to buy a rug from a rug merchant—actually, I am trying to buy the rug. Mark is watching me. We are in a small room deep inside the medina in Fez. Rugs surround us. We are offered tea and are sipping it from thin, hand-painted glasses that are hot to the touch. I barter hard, and the merchant, a wizened old man with bright eyes, says, "Madame, you are trying to buy a camel for the price of a rooster." I ponder the man, the fez that he wears. I want the rug. I want him to sell it to me for the price of a rooster. Mark breaks into a prism of beautiful laughter. He is laughing at me, my tenacious character, at the man who understands me, at the fact that I am trying to buy a rug we can't afford whether it is the price of a camel or a rooster, at my desire to pursue anyway that which I should not be pursuing. He pulls out his wallet and hands the man the amount he wants. I see all that cash pass hands. We need that cash. But the rug is not really what he is buying. He's indulging the dream. I thought then and I think now: I love this man. I never want to divorce this man. *Inshallah.*

ABOUT THE EDITORS

ANDREA CHAPIN has been an editor at art, movie, theater, and literary magazines, including *The Paris Review, Conjunctions, Translation,* and *The New Theater Review.* She has lived and worked in Mexico and Spain and acted professionally in Germany in a thirty-six-city tour of Edward Albee's *Seascape.* Her fiction has appeared in literary journals, and her articles and essays have appeared in magazines such as *Self, Redbook, More,* and *Martha Stewart Living,* as well as in several anthologies, including *The Day My Father Died* and *Kiss Tomorrow Hello: Notes from the Midlife Underground by Twenty-Five Women Over Forty.* She is a writer and an editor and teaches writing at New York University. She lives in New York City with her husband and two children.

SALLY WOFFORD-GIRAND is a literary agent and founder of Brick House Literary Agents. She worked on Wall Street before seeking refuge in book publishing. She is a member of the international rights committee of the AAR and a board member of Ledig House, an international writers' colony in New York State. She lives in New York City with her husband and three children.

ABOUT THE CONTRIBUTORS

KIM BARNES was a finalist for the 1997 Pulitzer Prize for her memoir *In the Wilderness: Coming of Age in Unknown Country*, which was also honored with the PEN/Jerard Fund Award for an emerging woman writer of nonfiction and a Pacific Northwest Booksellers Award. *Hungry for the World*, her second memoir, was published in 2000, and her first novel *Finding Caruso* was published in 2003. She is the co-editor of the anthology *Kiss Tomorrow Hello: Notes from the Midlife Underground by Twenty-Five Women Over Forty* and the co-editor of *Circle of Women: An Anthology of Contemporary Western Women Writers*. Barnes's poems, stories, and essays have appeared in numerous journals and anthologies, including *Shenandoah, Manoa, The Georgia Review*, and the *Pushcart Prize: Best of the Small Presses* anthology. She teaches creative writing at the University of Idaho and lives with her husband, the poet Robert Wrigley, and their children on Moscow Mountain.

A. R. BAUMANN is a fifth-generation Texan, who modeled in London and Italy before pursuing an acting career in New York City and Los Angeles. Baumann has written the screenplays for two short films: *What's Next*, which she directed and was a finalist in the short film category at the Houston International Film Festival, and *Lorean*, which won second place at the Mobil Awards and was screened at the Museum of Modern Art in New York City. She lives in Malibu with her husband and three children.

DEBRA MAGPIE EARLING, the author of the novel *Perma Red*, has won many awards for her writing, including the American Book Award, the Mountains and Plains Association Booksellers Award, and the Spur Award, and an NEA. Earling is a member of the Confederated Salish and Kootenai Tribes of the Flathead Indian Reservation. She dropped out of high school at fifteen, married at seventeen, and moved to the reservation, where by eighteen she became the first Court Advocate / Public Defender in the Flathead tribal court system. She is currently an associate professor in the English department at the University of Montana.

ANNIE ECHOLS is a pen name.

LAURA FRASER is the author of the much-acclaimed memoir *An Italian Affair*. She has written for *Salon.com*, *Vogue*, *More*, *Mother Jones*, *O, the Oprah Magazine*, *Self*, *San Francisco Examiner*, *Gourmet*, and *Health*, among other publications. She has taught magazine writing at the Graduate School of Journalism at the University of California at Berkeley. She lives in San Francisco.

NICOLE LEA HELGET, the author of the memoir *The Summer of Ordinary Ways*, has a forthcoming novel. She is the winner of the 2004 Speakeasy Prize for Prose and the 2005 Tamarack Award for Fiction. She teaches writing at Minnesota State University at Mankato and lives in Mankato with fellow writer Nate LeBoutillier and her four children.

ANN HOOD is the author of seven novels, including *Somewhere Off the Coast of Maine* and, most recently, *The Knitting Circle*; a memoir, *Do Not Go Gentle: My Search for Miracles in a Cynical Time*; and a collection of short stories, *An Ornithologist's Guide to Life*. Her essays and stories have appeared in many publications, including the *New York Times*, *Tin House*, *The Paris Review*, *Traveler*, *Good Housekeeping*, *More*, and *Ladies' Home Journal*. She has twice won a Pushcart

Prize as well as an American Spiritual Writing Award, and the Paul Bowles Prize for Short Fiction.

BETSY ISRAEL is the author of four books including *Grown-Up Fast* and *Bachelor Girl* and has written many screenplays for feature and cable films and documentaries. She has contributed to the *New York Times Magazine*, *GQ*, the *New York Times* Styles section, *Vogue*, *Real Simple*, *Elle*, *Rolling Stone*, *Talk*, *People*, *Mademoiselle*, among others, and was a columnist for *Glamour*, *New York Woman*, and *Mirabella*. She's currently finishing the first in a series of young adult mysteries.

DANIELA KUPER is the author of the critically acclaimed first novel *Hunger and Thirst*, which author Joyce Carol Oates called, "One of the most vividly imagined and moving works I've read in recent years." The book was one of three in the country that made the finals for the Harold U. Ribalow award in fiction with a Jewish theme. Kuper has been widely published in literary journals, magazines, and anthologies and was nominated for a Pushcart Prize. She divides her time between Boulder, Colorado, and Brooksville, Maine, and is working on her second novel, *Holy Ghost*, inspired by the essay in this book.

ANNE LANDSMAN is the author of the *The Devil's Chimney*, a critically acclaimed first novel nominated for four awards: the Pen/Hemingway Award, the Janet Heidinger Kafka Prize, QPB's New Voices, and South Africa's M-Net Book Prize. Foreign editions of the book have been published in the U.K., Germany, the Netherlands, Norway, Denmark, and South Africa. Landsman was commissioned to write the screenplay adaptation for *The Devil's Chimney*. Her work has appeared in the *Washington Post*, *The American Poetry Review*, *Bomb*, *The Believer*, and *Poets and Writers*.

LESLIE LEHR's novel 66 *Laps* won a gold medal from the Pirate's

Alley Faulkner Society. Her nonfiction books include the parenting books *Welcome to Club Mom, Club Grandma,* and *Wendy Bellissimo: Nesting,* a celebrity design book. Her essay "I Hate Everybody" was published in the anthology *The Mommy Wars.* Her screenplay credits include *Heartless* and *Ashes to Ashes,* and she is working on a mom blog on CitizenHunter.com. She lives in Southern California.

ZELDA LOCKHART is the author of the novel *Fifth Born,* which was a 2002 Barnes & Noble Discovery selection and won a finalist award for debut fiction from the Zora Neale Hurston/Richard Wright Legacy Foundation. As well as a master's in English from Old Dominion University, Ms. Lockhart holds a certificate in writing, directing, and editing film from the New York Film Academy. Her other works of fiction, poetry, and essays have been anthologized and appear in journals and magazines. Lockhart is also the author of *The Evolution,* a serial novella, currently appearing in the archives of USAToday.com's Open Book series. Her most recent novel, *Cold Running Creek,* will be published in 2007. Zelda is currently working on her third novel and facilitating a variety of workshops that empower adults and children to self-define through writing. She lives in Hillsborough, North Carolina, with her two children.

JOYCE MAYNARD is a former *New York Times* "Hers" columnist, contributor to NPR's "All Things Considered," frequent contributor to *O, More, Redbook,* and other national magazines. She is the author of the best-selling memoir *At Home in the World* as well as five novels, including *To Die For* and *The Usual Rules,* named one of the ten best books for young readers, 2003, by the American Library Association. Her latest book, *Internal Combustion: The Story of a Marriage and a Murder in the Motor City,* will be published in fall 2006.

PATRICIA McCORMICK is the author of several young adult novels, *Cut, My Brother's Keeper,* and *Sold* (which was nominated for a 2006 National Book Award). She is happily reunited with her real husband and lives in New York with a teenaged son who will be mortified when he reads this essay.

TERRY McMILLAN is the author of six books, including the best sellers *Waiting to Exhale* and *How Stella Got Her Groove Back*, which were both adapted to films. McMillan, who was born and raised in Port Huron, Michigan, got her degree from Berkeley and attended graduate school in film at Columbia University before embarking on a writing career. She is also the editor of *Breaking Ice: An Anthology of African American Fiction* and lives in Northern California.

MARTHA McPHEE received her MFA from Columbia University. She is the author of the novels *Bright Angel Time*, a *New York Times* Notable Book in 1997; *Gorgeous Lies*, nominated in 2002 for a National Book Award; and *L'America*, published in spring 2006. She is the recipient of fellowships from the National Endowment for the Arts and the John Simon Guggenheim Memorial Foundation. She teaches at Hofstra University and lives in New York City with her children and husband, the poet and writer Mark Svenvold.

LEE MONTGOMERY's work has appeared in *Story*, *Iowa Review*, and *Denver Quarterly*, among other publications. She is the editorial director of Tin House Books and executive editor of *Tin House* magazine. Her memoir, *The Things Between Us*, was published by the Free Press in August 2006.

ALICE RANDALL was born in Detroit. Shortly after graduating from Harvard in 1981, she moved to Nashville to become a country songwriter. The only African American woman ever to write a number one country song, she has had more than twenty songs recorded, including two top ten records and a top forty. Randall is the author of two highly praised novels, *The Wind Done Gone*, which was a *New York Times* best seller in 2001, and *Pushkin and the Queen of Spades*. She is also a screenwriter and has worked on adaptations of *Their Eyes Were Watching God*, *Parting the Waters*, and *Brer Rabbit*. She was awarded the Free Spirit Award in 2001 and the Literature Award of Excellence by the Memphis Black Writers Conference in 2002, and she was a finalist for the NAACP Image Award in 2002. She lives in Nashville, Tennessee, and teaches at Vanderbilt University.

PAMELA BOL RIESS is a writer and executive search consultant. Her nonfiction has appeared in the *New York Times*, *Details*, *Mademoiselle*, and *Glamour*. Her short story "Glorious Gloria" was published in *Girls: An Anthology*. She lives in New York City with her husband and their four-year-old daughter.

ISABEL ROSE is a summa cum laude graduate of Yale and received her M.F.A. in fiction from Bennington College. The *J.A.P. Chronicles*, published in 2005, is her first novel. She has also co-written several screenplays and co-wrote and starred in the movie *Anything But Love*. Rose also regularly entertains on the NYC club circuit with her nine-piece band. She is currently working on her second novel.

ELISSA MINOR RUST's stories have appeared in *Baltimore Review*, *The Ledge*, *Crab Creek Review*, *Carve Magazine*, *Honolulu Magazine*, *Peregrine*, and *The Beacon Street Review*, among others. Her short story collection, *The Prisoner Pear: Stories from the Lake*, was published in December 2005 by Ohio University Press / Swallow Press. She is the recipient of the Peregrine Prize for Fiction, the National Society of Arts and Letters Cam Cavanaugh Literature Award, a Honolulu Magazine Fiction Award, the Swarthout Fiction Award, and the Leslie Bradshaw Fiction Fellowship from Oregon Literary Arts. She lives in Portland, Oregon, with her husband and two children.